50 GREATEST RED WINGS

Bob Duff

50 GREATEST RED WINGS

BIBLIOASIS
WINDSOR, ONTARIO

FIRST EDITION

Library and Archives Canada Cataloguing in Publication

Duff, Bob, author
        50 greatest Red Wings / Bob Duff.

Issued in print and electronic formats.
ISBN 978-1-77196-058-8 (bound).--ISBN 978-1-77196-059-5 (ebook)

        1. Detroit Red Wings (Hockey team)--Biography.
2. Hockey players--Michigan--Detroit--Biography. 3. Detroit Red Wings (Hockey team)--History. I. Title. II. Title: Fifty greatest Red Wings.

GV848.D4D94 2014   796.962092'277434   C2013-903214-2
                                           C2013-903215-0

Edited by Dan Wells
Typeset by Chris Andrechek
Cover designed by Gordon Robertson

PRINTED AND BOUND IN CHINA

Photo Credits:
Detroit Times Archive: 16, 20, 49, 116;
Dwayne LaBakas: 10,16, 21, 22, 34, 40, 46, 52, 58, 64, 70, 74, 78, 82, 94, 102, 110, 118, 130, 133, 134, 137, 142, 145, 146, 150, 154, 156, 157, 158, 166, 174, 178, 182, 186, 190, 194, 198, 202, 209, 212, 214, 218, 222, 226,
All other photos courtesy of *The Windsor Star*

CONTENTS

INTRODUCTION

A REPORTER ONCE SUGGESTED TO JACK ADAMS, BACK WHEN he was the mastermind behind the Detroit Red Wings during their glorious run to a record seven successive National Hockey League regular-season championships during the 1950s, that the general manager's hockey club was the New York Yankees of the NHL.

"No," Adams quickly responded. "The Yankees are the Red Wings of baseball."

Through the more than eight decades of this mighty franchise's history, the place now proclaimed as Hockeytown has witnessed numerous great moments, including 11 Stanley Cup titles. Certainly, an equal number of sensational players have donned the Winged Wheel.

Narrowing the list down to the 50 greatest Red Wings of all-time was no easy task, nor was it an assignment that was undertaken with the notion that it would be simply done.

Over the course of this work, and throughout the time that I have covered this team, which dates back to the fall of 1988, I have interviewed, spoken with and gathered opinions on virtually every player mentioned in this book. Often, I was afforded the good fortune to speak directly with many of those who grace this list.

Assessments and advice were also sought from opponents of these players, scouts who studied them in action, coaches and managers who worked with and against them and journalists who covered these talented performers. While the end result may just be one man's opinion, it is nevertheless the culmination of years of gathered research and shared knowledge with some of the finest minds in the game of hockey.

Some choices were easy. Who would disagree with Gordie Howe as the greatest Red Wing of them all? Beyond his immense talent and his one-of-a-kind longevity, the man they call Mr. Hockey could play any style of game you required, and was capable of filling any position on the ice except, perhaps, goaltender.

Quickly, though, the selections grew more difficult. Nicklas Lidstrom at No. 2 will be disputed by those who feel it should be a place reserved for Steve Yzerman. But it is my opinion—one shared by Yzerman, I might add—that Lidstrom deserves to be where he is on the list.

Each of the top three could easily be assigned a No. 1 position with the Red Wings. Howe ranks as the greatest performer, Lidstrom as the finest thinker of the game and Yzerman as the supreme leader in Red Wings' history.

As the list reached its end, the choices became vastly more difficult and without a doubt more open to debate. Weight was given to those who performed with spectacular results at the most important time of the year, during the Stanley Cup playoffs.

Perhaps the hardest part of all came as the end of the list arrived, the last 10 spots on the grid. Some great players—Hall of Famers—fell by the wayside.

Some weren't difficult to put aside. Defenceman Doug Harvey was a seven-time Norris Trophy winner but played just a couple of games as a Red Wing. Goaltender Cecil (Tiny)

Thompson and right winger Charlie Conacher were among the NHL elite in the 1930s, but by the time both came to Detroit their respective careers were on the downturn.

At the other end of the spectrum, left winger John Bucyk's NHL career was barely underway when he was dealt to the Boston Bruins in 1957, where he'd star for the next two decades. Likewise, Adam Oates grew to NHL stardom with St. Louis and Boston after departing from Detroit, where he launched his NHL career.

Earl Seibert was an all-star defender who came to Detroit at the tail end of his NHL career in the 1940s. Roy Conacher led the NHL in goals with Boston before coming to Detroit, and won an Art Ross Trophy in Chicago after he was dealt away by the Wings. George Hay was a 22-goal scorer with the team in 1927-28, but his best years were also before he came to Detroit.

Right winger Andy Bathgate, defenceman Leo Boivin, centre Frank Fredrickson centre Frank Foyston, goaltender Harry (Hap) Holmes, centre Gordon (Duke) Keats, left winger Jack Walker, defenceman Viacheslav Fetisov, centre Bernie Federko, defenceman Reg Noble, left winger Luc Robitaille, centre Darryl Sittler, defenceman Borje Salming, centre Ralph (Cooney) Weiland, left winger Harry Watson and defenceman Brad Park were other Hall of Famers who made cameo appearances in Detroit.

Others were not as easy to exclude from the ranks, but ultimately, their body of work did not warrant inclusion.

Left winger Frank Mahovlich was a 49-goal scorer for the Wings in 1968-69, but his Detroit time was short-lived and the greatest accomplishments of the Big M's career certainly came during his time with the Toronto Maple Leafs and Montreal Canadiens.

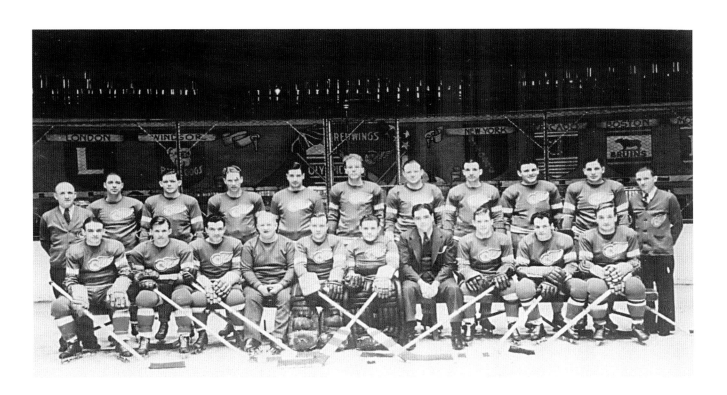

Likewise, though he launched his career as a Red Wing, winning the Calder Trophy and earning First All-Star status during his brief Detroit tenure, Glenn Hall went on to earn acclaim as possibly the greatest goaltender of the decade in the 1960s with the Chicago Blackhawks.

Another who came ever so close to making the cut was defenceman Chris Chelios. But although he was stellar for the majority of nearly a decade as a Red Wing, Chelios wasn't the same all-star Norris Trophy winner who starred for Chicago for so many years. The same could be said for defenceman Mark Howe, who skated the last three of a 22-year major-league career with Detroit.

There were many who shone briefly as Red Wings. Goalie Wilf Cude backstopped Detroit to its first Stanley Cup final appearance in 1933-34. Steve Wochy set Red Wings rookie records with 19 goals and 39 points in 1944-45. Paul MacLean was a 71-point scorer in 1988-89, part of a record-setting forward line with Yzerman and Gerard Gallant. Marian Hossa was a 40-goal scorer in 2008-09, his only season with Detroit.

Defenceman Carl Brewer was an NHL Second All-Star Team selection during the 1969-70 season, his lone campaign for Detroit. Bill (Flash) Hollett set an NHL record for defencemen with 20 goals in 1944-45, but scored just 10 more goals in his other two seasons as a Red Wing. But none of the above in the end warranted inclusion, due to some combination of longevity, talent or contribution to the team and its history.

If you were to assemble an all-time Red Wings team by position based on this top 50 list, it would look like this:

Left Wing	Centre	Right Wing
Ted Lindsay	Steve Yzerman	Gordie Howe
Alex Delvecchio	Sid Abel	Larry Aurie
Brendan Shanahan	Sergei Fedorov	Mickey Redmond
Henrik Zetterberg	Pavel Datsyuk	Igor Larionov

Defence	Defence	Goal
Nicklas Lidstrom	Red Kelly	Terry Sawchuk
Ebbie Goodfellow	Marcel Pronovost	Chris Osgood
Jack Stewart	Bill Quackenbush	

That's an aggregate which could certainly win its fair share of Stanley Cup titles. But maybe you don't agree, you'd tweak things a little bit, or a lot for that matter.

That's fine. In fact, in a sense, it's the whole point of this project.

Ultimately, this top 50 is merely my opinion. Many will disagree and that's not only weclomed, it's encouraged.

The object of this exercise is to open debate and to have fun doing it; but most of all, it's to remember the legends who have skated in the Detroit uniform, embrace the memories that they've made, and the many more to come in the years ahead.

Bob Duff
January, 2015

1 GORDIE HOWE

Right Wing

Born: March 31, 1928, Floral, Saskatchewan
Shot: Both Height: 6-0 Weight: 205 lbs.
Red Wing From: 1946-47 to 1970-71
Elected to Hockey Hall of Fame: 1972
Acquired: Signed to a pro contract October 5, 1945.
Departed: Announced retirement, September 9, 1971.

PERHAPS THE SCARIEST NOTION FOR DETROIT RED WINGS fans to consider is how close they came to knowing Gordie Howe only as an opposition player.

Before the Red Wings discovered the man who would grow to be known by the all-encompassing handle of Mr. Hockey, a nickname he has since trademarked, Howe was invited to try out for the New York Rangers.

In 1943, Howe, 15, attended the Rangers' training camp in Winnipeg.

"I was there four days," Howe recalled. He left for home in Saskatoon without a contract.

Soon after, Detroit scout Fred Pinckney got Howe's name on a C form, committing him to the Red Wings, and he came east to play in the club's junior system.

He was assigned to Detroit's OHA junior club in Galt, but Howe wasn't allowed to play because the Saskatchewan association wouldn't permit him a transfer. He practiced all season with the team and participated in exhibition contests, learning the game from Al Murray, a former NHL defenceman with the New York Americans.

"He came to me and said, 'I've got some news for you and you're not going to like it,'" Howe remembered. "That's

DETROIT HONOURS:

- Stanley Cup champion 1949-50, 1951-52, 1953-54, 1954-55
- Won Hart Trophy 1951-52,1952-53,1956-57,1957-58,1959-60,1962-63
- Won Art Ross Trophy 1950-51,1951-52,1952-53,1953-54,1956-57,1962-63
- Won Lester Patrick Trophy, 1967
- NHL First All-Star Team 1950-51; 1951-52; 1952-53; 1953-54; 1956-57; 1957-58; 1959-60; 1962-63; 1965-66; 1967-68; 1968-69; 1969-70
- NHL Second All-Star Team 1948-49; 1949-50; 1955-56; 1958-59; 1960-61; 1961-62; 1963-64; 1964-65; 1966-67
- Played in NHL All-Star Game 1948, 1949, 1950, 1951, 1952, 1953, 1954, 1955, 1957, 1958, 1959, 1960, 1961, 1962, 1963, 1964, 1965, 1967, 1968, 1969, 1970, 1971
- NHL record holder for most seasons played (26)
- NHL record holder for most games played (1,767)
- NHL record holder for goals (801), assists (1,049) and points (1,850) by a right winger
- NHL record holder for most 20-goal seasons (22) and most consecutive 20-goal seasons (22, 1949-50 to 1970-71)
- Led NHL in goals four times
- Led NHL in assists three times
- Led Stanley Cup playoffs in scoring six times
- First Red Wing to record an 80-point season, (1950-51)
- First Red Wing to record a 90-point season (1952-53)
- First Red Wing to record a 100-point season (1968-69)
- Team captain, 1958-62
- Howe's No. 9 was retired by the Red Wings on March 12, 1972.

when he told me my transfer didn't come through. But he told me if I stayed the year in Guelph, he'd make me into a hockey player and he did."

Howe turned pro in 1945, playing for coach Tommy Ivan with Omaha of the U.S. League. The next spring, Ivan was promoted to Indianapolis of the AHL. Before training camp that fall, Detroit coach-GM Jack Adams told Ivan that Howe would be joining him at Indianapolis.

"No," Ivan said. "He'll be playing for you."

Ivan was right. Howe never played another game in the minor leagues during an amazing quarter-century as a Red Wing, establishing himself as hockey's most enduring combination of ability, longevity, productivity and durability.

"There is no player like him," Howe's former Detroit teammate Bill Gadsby told the Miami News in 1967. "No other player I saw or ever heard of comes close to Gordie.

"Not one of them does so many things as well as Howe."

As much as it was about numbers—Howe is still the NHL's all-time leader in goals, assists and points by a right winger, and his 786-1,023-1,809 totals in a Red Wings uniform remain the club's career standards more than four decades after he played his last game in Detroit—that alone isn't what made Howe the greatest ever to wear the Winged Wheel.

Simply, it was because he could do it all—score or set up the big goal, check the other team's best player, work the power play, kill penalties, or straighten out a troublemaker. He even played defence in a pinch several times during his career.

"There's no doubt that Howe is the greatest player in the history of the game," New York Rangers general manager Murray (Muzz) Patrick told Associated Press in 1963. "In any situation, offensively or defensively, Gordie is just the best there is.

"To be considered a star today, you have to kill penalties when your team is one or two men short, be in on the power play and check effectively as well as being a good scorer.

"Howe does all these things and does them better than anyone else in the game."

He was even the NHL's first ambidextrous shooter, and early in his career, Howe got the better of Montreal's Bill Durnan, the NHL's only ambidextrous goalie. Durnan wore special gloves that could operate as both blocker and trapper, and when Howe broke into the clear on him right-handed, Durnan flipped his stick to what would be Howe's strong side.

Howe followed suit, flipping his stick over to shoot left-handed and fired a shot past the startled Canadiens netminder.

"He crossed Durnan up by shifting to his left side after Durnan had made the change-over," Adams recalled to the *Toronto Star*.

HOWE'S RED WINGS STATISTICS:

	REGULAR SEASON					PLAYOFFS				
Season	GP	G	A	P	PIM	GP	G	A	P	PIM
1946-47	58	7	15	22	52	5	0	0	0	18
1947-48	60	16	28	44	63	10	1	1	2	11
1948-49	40	12	25	37	57	11	8	3	11	19
1949-50	70	35	33	68	69	1	0	0	0	7
1950-51	70	43	43	86	74	6	4	3	7	4
1951-52	70	47	39	86	78	8	2	5	7	2
1952-53	70	49	46	95	57	6	2	5	7	2
1953-54	70	33	48	81	109	12	4	5	9	31
1954-55	64	29	33	62	68	11	9	11	20	24
1955-56	70	38	41	79	100	10	3	9	12	8
1956-57	70	44	45	89	72	5	2	5	7	6
1957-58	64	33	44	77	40	4	1	1	2	0
1958-59	70	32	46	78	57	-	-	-	-	-
1959-60	70	28	45	73	46	6	1	5	6	4
1960-61	64	23	49	72	30	11	3	11	15	10
1961-62	70	32	46	78	57	-	-	-	-	-
1962-63	70	38	48	86	100	11	7	9	16	22
1963-64	69	26	47	73	70	14	9	10	19	16
1964-65	70	29	47	76	104	7	4	2	6	20
1965-66	70	29	46	75	83	12	4	6	10	12
1966-67	69	25	40	65	53	-	-	-	-	-
1967-68	74	39	43	82	53	-	-	-	-	-
1968-69	76	44	59	103	58	-	-	-	-	-
1969-70	76	31	40	71	58	4	2	0	2	2
1970-71	63	23	29	52	38	-	-	-	-	-
Totals	1687	786	1023	1809	1643	154	67	91	158	218

"It was the first time I can ever recall an ambidextrous wingman beating an ambidextrous goalie and was big Bill surprised."

Howe scored against Toronto's Turk Broda in his first NHL game, but took a bit of time to make a name for himself with Adams, who often confused the young Howe with recently-retired Wings star Syd Howe.

"One game, Adams said, 'Syd, get out there,'" Howe recalled. "I didn't move. He looked at me and said, 'I don't care what your name is, get out there.'"

Howe got out there. And he got after it.

In 1948-49, his third NHL season, Howe led all Stanley Cup scorers with eight goals and 11 points in 11 games. "I don't think there has ever been another 21-year-old in his class," Adams said that spring.

By 1950-51, Howe won the first of four straight league scoring titles.

Amazing to think how close it came to never happening for him.

During the opening game of Detroit's 1950 Stanley Cup semifinal series with the Toronto Maple Leafs, Howe tangled with Toronto captain Teeder Kennedy along the boards and fell headfirst into the dasher, suffering life-threatening head injuries.

"Gordie has a deep cut in his right eyeball, a fractured nose, a possible fractured cheekbone and a possible fractured skull," Red Wings team physician Dr. C.L. Tomsu told the *Windsor Star*.

It was touch and go for a couple of days, but Howe pulled through, and was quick to deflect any blame for his injuries away from Kennedy.

"I don't hold Kennedy to blame," Howe said. "He's too fine a player to intentionally hurt anyone. All I remember is chasing him toward the boards. I don't recall being struck or hitting the boards."

Kennedy professed his innocence to the *Montreal Gazette*. "Gordie is one of my friends and I certainly would never do him any harm," Kennedy said.

Howe recovered quickly and was able to attend Game 7 of the final series as the Wings downed the New York Rangers to capture the first Stanley Cup of Howe's career.

"I enjoyed the last three Cups that I won," Howe said. "The first one wasn't much fun."

Steadily, virtually every NHL record became Howe's personal property as he dominated the league like no one before him and over a tenure that none have come close to equaling.

He was 23 when he won his first scoring title and MVP honours, and 35 when he captured both for the sixth time in his career. His 20-point output during Detroit's run to the 1954-55 Stanley Cup stood as the club's single-season playoff scoring mark until 1988.

Howe scored at least 20 goals a record 22 straight seasons, and also established another unequalled NHL mark by finishing among the league's top-10 scorers for 21 consecutive seasons from 1949-50 through 1969-70. Howe

was past his 40th birthday when he enjoyed his best NHL season, garnering 103 points during the 1968-69 campaign.

At the end of the 1969-70 season, Toronto centre Murray Oliver was the active NHL leader in consecutive games played with 240. Howe, 42, was next at 233.

"They ought to bottle his sweat," suggested Hall of Famer King Clancy. "It would make a great liniment for hockey players."

In 1965, Howe became the third player in NHL history to play 20 seasons, and just when he'd be called upon to give up the game was a question that seemed to offer no answer.

Edmonton Journal columnist Terry Jones once asked Howe about how he'd know when he was too old to play? "That's like asking somebody, 'When do you run out of your sexual desires?'" Howe said. "You'll have to ask someone older than me.

"I'll just retire at 65, like everyone else."

For all the accolades and accomplishments, Howe remained a humble man. On Christmas Day, 1956, he set personal bests with three goals and three assists in a 8-1 win over the New York Rangers, but shrugged off the compliments afterward.

"Yes, I guess that's the most I ever made in one game with the Red Wings," Howe told the *Windsor Star*. "But I scored 14 goals and got one assist in a game for King George School when I was in the eighth grade back in Saskatoon.

"We beat the School for the Deaf team 15-0."

Howe worked as a golf pro in the summer months and was also a sensational baseball player who was known to drive balls out of Tiger Stadium during batting-practice stints with the Detroit Tigers.

"He could have been a big-leaguer in anything he did," Adams said.

His scoring exploits were matched by the callous indifference with which Howe viewed the opposition. Wrong him, or one of his teammates, and retribution would be delivered quickly and painfully. In hockey circles, Howe's elbows were viewed as weapons of mass destruction.

"He's big enough at 205 pounds to break your ribs with a twitch of his elbow," Gadsby said.

Howe came by his powerful strength naturally. His father Ab was foreman at a cement yard. Young Gordie started working there and within no time at all could lift a pair of 86-pound cement bags on to a truck simultaneously.

"We laid the foundation for (Saskatoon's) Bessborough Hotel," Howe recalled.

Howe laid out many more during his NHL days.

"Gordie Howe is the dirtiest player who ever lived," former NHL defenceman Carl Brewer lamented to the *Ottawa Citizen*. "A great player, but also the dirtiest.

"He'll gouge your eye out if you give him the chance, carve you up. He's big and tough and uses his size to intimidate people."

Hall of Fame defenceman Pierre Pilote insisted all in the NHL knew to steer clear of Mr. Hockey's personal space.

"To survive in the big leagues, every player made sure he had one foot of the ice around him that belonged to him," Pilote explained. "Gordie carved himself out about three feet of ice and anyone who dared enter his space would be sorry for it."

In fact, the only people who appeared capable of bringing pain to Howe lived within the confines of his family home.

"When I was real young, I liked to get up in the middle of the night and crawl into bed with my parents," recalled Murray Howe, Gordie's youngest son. "My dad had a couple of cracked ribs and had to sleep in a special vest to keep from moving.

"I was a fidgety sleeper and I'd thrash around at night. One time, I guess I rolled over and kicked my dad right in the ribs. I was too young to remember doing it, but they've never let me forget that one."

"We seemed to have a knack for that," added Marty Howe, oldest of the three Howe boys. "Dad would come through the door after a six-game road trip. The three of us would tackle him and naturally, hit him right where his latest injury had occurred.

"Overall, dad had it pretty easy, though. We'd be causing trouble and he'd get to leave on a road trip. Mom would have to handle the discipline."

Mom was Colleen Howe, the one and only love of Gordie's life.

Howe is a believer in fate. He absolutely abides by the theory that everyone has a soulmate.

He found his more than a half-century ago in, of all places, a Detroit bowling alley. It was appropriately named the Lucky Strike, because as far as Howe is concerned that was the biggest stroke of luck in his life.

"I used to go bowling after practice, because I was a young guy and it was the middle of the day and I had nothing else to do," Howe recalled. "I walked in one day and there was this beautiful blonde bowling with these three elderly gentlemen."

It was Colleen.

Howe grilled the proprietor of the alley to gain details about the woman who'd made him swoon, finding out she was a regular there, bowling with her grandfather. The shy Howe desperately wanted to meet her, but the most feared skater in the NHL couldn't muster up the gumption to approach the woman who would ultimately become his wife.

"I was kind of like a stalker there for a while, showing up to bowl, watching her, but never talking to her," Howe said.

Finally, the bowling alley operator introduced the pair. When the two met, Gordie had already won two Hart trophies and three Art Ross trophies, but the ever humble Howe didn't let on about his celebrity. She knew Gordie played hockey, but they dated for a year before Colleen found out the man in her life was the most famous athlete in Detroit.

"I was getting ready to go home for the summer to Saskatoon and we were saying our goodbyes," Howe said. "She wanted me to meet her father."

Before Colleen could finish the introduction, her dad, a huge hockey fan, intervened.

"I know who he is," he said.

Everyone in Detroit knew of Howe and his unmatched exploits.

Early in their marriage, Colleen answered a knock at the door to find a pair of neighbourhood kids had come calling, hockey sticks in tow.

"Hello," they said to Mrs. Howe. "Will you let Gordie come out and play with us?"

Sid Abel, centre of Detroit's famed Production Line between Howe and Ted Lindsay, found out exactly where he rated in Detroit hockey lore when he came upon his son Gerry playing road hockey with some chums.

"As each of the boys announced which NHLer they intended to emulate, Abel, captain of the Red Wings, was stunned to hear his son pronounce, 'I'm Gordie Howe.'"

Even today when Howe attends games at Joe Louis Arena, he must seek refuge in the press box to avoid the throngs of people seeking to get close to this Detroit legend.

"My dad can't sit in the seats, because he gets mobbed non-stop for autographs," said Mark Howe, who followed in his dad's footsteps, playing for the Wings in the 1990s. "It's not that he doesn't appreciate the attention, but he feels badly for the people sitting around him, who never get to see the game."

It's a lifelong love affair that still warms Gordie's heart.

"When you're scoring goals and winning games, that's one thing," he said. "But when they remember you years after, that's really something. "

More than 40 years since he wore his Red Wings sweater for the final time, the man they call Mr. Hockey is still Mr. Red Wing.

And he remains the greatest of them all.

2 NICKLAS LIDSTROM

Defence

Born: April 28, 1970, Vasteras, Sweden
Shot: Left **Height:** 6-1 **Weight:** 190 lbs.
Red Wing From: 1991-92 to 2011-12
Acquired: Selected 53rd overall in June 17, 1989 NHL entry draft.
Departed: Announced retirement, May 3, 2012

A WARM FIRE. A TWINKLE IN THE EYE. HIS HEROES ON THE screen. Hockey night in Vasteras, Sweden wasn't all that different from Hockey Night in Canada.

"They only had one game a week, on cable TV," recalled Nicklas Lidstrom of his homeland's access to National Hockey League broadcasts when he was a youngster.

Those nights were special ones for the young Lidstrom, made even more significant on those rare occasions when the Toronto Maple Leafs and Hall of Fame defenceman Borje Salming, the icon of Swedish hockey, were featured.

"I just saw him play maybe one or two games a year," Lidstrom said of Salming. "They didn't show Toronto much."

That's right. Lidstrom idolized a member of the Leafs, a budding Swedish Legend worshipping another.

"Borje Salming was my big hero growing up," Lidstrom said. "He was my partner in the Canada Cup in 1991. I had a chance to partner up with him, and that was a big thrill for me."

While Salming was the man, there were other Swedish NHLers on the radar of the young Lidstrom.

"I watched Mats Naslund, Hakan Loob, Thomas Steen, Bengt Gustafsson, guys that played in the eighties like Ulf Samuelsson, Tomas Sandstrom," Lidstrom said. "There were a lot of players that we followed."

Keeping track of these players wasn't an easy task. With so few NHL broadcasts in his homeland, Lidstrom often resorted to news reports to keep on top of his favourite players.

"I did follow them, especially the Swedish players," Lidstrom said. "They had their stats in there all the time. Now, with the Internet, which we didn't have back in the eighties, all the kids, all the people back in Sweden are paying attention, and they're good at it."

Clearly, the guy who all young Swedes followed during the last two decades was the man who wore No. 5 for the Red Wings.

DETROIT HONOURS:

- Stanley Cup champion 1996-97, 1997-98, 2001-02, 2007-08
- Won Norris Trophy 2000-01, 2001-02, 2002-03, 2005-06, 2006-07, 2008-09, 2010-11
- Won Conn Smythe Trophy, 2001-02
- NHL First All-Star Team 1997-98, 1998-99, 1999-2000, 2000-01, 2001-02, 2002-03, 2005-06, 2006-07, 2007-08
- NHL Second All-Star Team 2008-09
- Played in NHL All-Star Game 1996, 1998, 1999, 2000, 2001, 2002, 2003
- NHL All-Rookie Team 1991-92
- Olympic gold medallist with Sweden, 2006
- First European born-and-trained captain of Stanley Cup champion, 2008-09
- Red Wings career leader in playoff games (263)
- Shares NHL record for most consecutive years in playoffs (20)
- Won Viking Award as top Swedish player in North America, 1999-2000, 2005-06
- Team captain 2006-12
- Lidstrom's No. 5 was retired by the Red Wings on March 6, 2014.

"He's been my idol and a big role model in my life, and why not?" Chicago Blackhawks defenceman Niklas Hjalmarsson suggested of Lidstrom. "He might be the best defenceman in the world and one of the best of all time. I've tried to copy some of the things he does."

Certainly, no one who's ever teamed with Lidstrom would debate the point regarding Lidstrom's place among the greats of the game.

"He's the best player I've ever played with," long-time Detroit captain Steve Yzerman said.

"He was the best player for us every night," added Wings centre and fellow Swede Henrik Zetterberg, who followed Lidstrom as Detroit captain in 2012.

Long-time Detroit coach Mike Babcock (now in Toronto) ramped up his praise of Lidstrom even further.

"He's a phenomenal player, he's a generational-type player," Babcock said. "Everyone's going to know who he was long after he's done playing."

Babcock is willing to put Lidstrom's resumé up against anyone who's ever patrolled a blue line in an NHL uniform.

"Bobby Orr's probably going to get the most credit and lots of people who played with different people are going to say different things, but to me, the class of man he is, the kind of leader he is, how good he's been for how long, just how impressive he is and the amount of winning he's done, that counts for a lot as well," Babcock said. "To me, he's very special to have had the opportunity to coach. He's a good guy for the coach because he gives you a lot of input and goes about it the right away. He's a great man.

"I've never coached anybody this good, never coached anybody as consistent, as intuitive, who had a great understanding of the game and was tuned into what's going on. He was such a professional, when you talked to him as a coach it was an unbelievable experience for you. He was comfortable to share his thoughts with you."

While Detroit knew almost immediately of Lidstrom's special qualities as a player, it took the rest of the NHL a little longer to catch on to the reality of his greatness.

Though he won seven Norris Trophies as the league's best defenceman, more than anyone in the history of the league save Orr, Lidstrom wasn't honoured with his first Norris until he'd played a decade in the league. But he was 41 when he won his seventh and final Norris, making him the oldest defender to be recognized as the NHL's best.

"It's something that I'm proud of, to have been able to play at a high level for a long period of time," Lidstrom said.

Lidstrom's only sin was his quiet efficiency, which seldom attracted attention.

LIDSTROM'S RED WINGS STATISTICS:

	Regular Season					Playoffs				
Season	GP	G	A	P	PIM	GP	G	A	P	PIM
1991-92	80	11	49	60	22	11	1	2	3	0
1992-93	84	7	34	41	28	7	1	0	1	0
1993-94	84	10	46	56	26	7	3	2	5	0
1994-95	43	10	16	26	6	18	4	12	16	8
1995-96	81	17	50	67	20	19	5	9	14	10
1996-97	79	15	42	57	30	20	2	6	8	2
1997-98	80	17	42	59	18	22	6	13	19	8
1998-99	81	14	43	57	14	10	2	9	11	4
1999-00	81	20	53	73	18	9	2	4	6	4
2000-01	82	15	56	71	18	6	1	7	8	0
2001-02	78	9	50	59	20	23	5	11	16	2
2002-03	82	18	44	62	38	4	0	2	2	0
2003-04	81	10	28	38	18	12	2	5	7	4
2005-06	80	16	64	80	50	6	1	1	2	2
2006-07	80	13	49	62	46	18	4	14	18	6
2007-08	76	10	60	70	40	22	3	10	13	14
2008-09	78	16	43	59	30	21	4	12	16	6
2009-10	82	9	40	49	24	12	4	6	10	2
2010-11	82	16	46	62	20	11	4	4	8	4
2011-12	70	11	23	34	28	5	0	0	0	0
Totals	1564	264	878	1142	514	263	54	129	183	76

"Nick didn't seek out the spotlight and the spotlight doesn't usually shine on guys like him," his former defence partner Larry Murphy said.

Lidstrom's style of play wasn't going to draw rave reviews, or make the nightly highlight packages. He didn't lead the rush like Brian Leetch, or level someone with a devastating body check a la Rob Blake or Chris Pronger. He'd merely perform with steadfast efficiency.

"When you play more physical, (people) notice that a lot more than a guy who plays strong positionally," Lidstrom said. "Both Pronger and Blake had different styles than I did. They're bigger guys and they used that to their advantage. My game was always good positioning and being in the right spot."

A thinking man's defender, Lidstrom always opted for the smart, simple play, making life easier for his teammates in the process.

"You always got the puck on the blade," Zetterberg said of receiving a Lidstrom pass. "The only thing you had to do was be in the right spot. If you were in the right spot, you got the puck. It's easy to forget how spoiled you got from playing with him."

Lidstrom's teammates rarely did what the hockey world too often seemed to do—take him for granted.

"In my opinion, he was one of, if not the best defenceman of our generation," former Detroit defenceman Brad Stuart said. "To still be the elite level of player that he established throughout his career was very impressive, especially to a fellow player, because you can understand a little better just how hard it can be to maintain that level."

Eventually, the rest of the hockey world caught on to Lidstrom's quiet wizardry.

"A classy individual," was how Washington Capitals coach Barry Trotz described Lidstrom. "When you talk about people who exude what a hockey player should be, people like Nick come to the forefront."

Lidstrom footage didn't make play of the day, but night after night, he made the plays that paid off at the end of the day.

"He had so much patience and such an outstanding level of skill," Winnipeg Jets coach Paul Maurice said of Lidstrom. "And it didn't matter what type of game it was— hard-hitting, high skill, grinding—his game never changed. He had tremendous tempo out there."

The subtleties of Lidstrom's game couldn't be appreciated by the average hockey fan seeing him only on occasion. His hand-eye coordination was stunning. Perhaps no one in the history of the game was more adept at keeping pucks in at the blue line. He could beat a goalie with his powerful point shot, but was just as likely to put the puck in a place where it could be easily deflected by a forward in front of the net.

Lidstrom learned every curve of Joe Louis Arena and was a master at utilizing the rink's lively boards to aim a shot just wide of the net and have it bank into the slot to the stick of a waiting teammate.

"You'd see the way Nick played at such a high level and you wanted to be there right with him," former Detroit centre Kris Draper said. "We knew that every time Nick came to the rink, he was going to be one of, if not our best player."

Lidstrom also displayed another trait of the truly great, the ability to take those around him to another level. Lidstrom's partners in 2005-06 (Andreas Lilja) and 2006-07 (Danny Markov) enjoyed career years skating alongside him. In 2007-08, Brian Rafalski netted a career-high 13 goals and equaled his career-best of 55 points playing with Lidstrom.

"Since I got here (in 2005), every one of his defence partners—(Mathieu) Schneider, Lilja, Markov, Rafalski, Ian White—had a career year," Babcock said. "That's not by accident. He was just that good. He made the people around

him better. Other defencemen have some dimensions to their games, but Nick had all the dimensions.

"The only thing he didn't do was cross-check you in the face, so he didn't take penalties. He was on the ice all the time."

That was another amazing aspect of Lidstrom's game, his ability to defend without violating the rulebook. Five times during his NHL career he played the entire season while accumulating fewer than 20 penalty minutes and was a multiple finalist for the Lady Byng Trophy, given to the player who showed the best combination of performance and sportsmanlike play.

"Usually, when defencemen get penalties, it's because of their stick—they cross-check someone at the net, get beat and give the guy a tug," explained former Detroit coach Dave Lewis, an ex-NHL rearguard. "Nick was such a good positional player he didn't have to rely on that."

When he took the ice for the 2012 Stanley Cup playoffs, Lidstrom was playing in his 20th straight NHL post-season, tying Larry Robinson, another legendary defenceman, for the all-time record. In those two decades, Lidstrom played 263 playoff games, a Red Wings club record.

In the spring of 2008 he established another NHL mark, becoming the first European-born and trained captain to lead his team to the Stanley Cup when the Wings ousted the Pittsburgh Penguins in six games.

"For him to be the first was huge in Sweden," said former Toronto captain and fellow Swede Mats Sundin.

"It was a great honour," Lidstrom agreed, "but still not as important as the team goal."

Lidstrom didn't fit the popular image of the captain. Those fascinated by the role of the on-ice leader tend to think it's all about fire-and-brimstone speeches.

Rafalski, who won three Cups skating in a defence pairing alongside a Hall of Fame captain, felt nothing could be further from reality. Scott Stevens, his partner and captain for two titles with the New Jersey Devils, was already inducted into the hockey shrine. Lidstrom will join him there when he first becomes eligible in 2015.

Stevens put fear into opponents with his punishing hits. Lidstrom frustrated opponents with the league's best positioning and most active and accurate stick. Otherwise, Rafalski saw mirror images in the two.

"You've got a Hall of Famer back there, that's a good cornerstone to build around," Rafalski said. "Obviously, they were two different-style players, but both very dominating at what they did—Scotty through physical play, Nick by controlling the game.

"As leaders, they were both pretty similar. Scotty wasn't real vocal in the locker room, either. They both led by example on the ice. They'd go out there and they'd do what they had to do on the ice."

Others questioned whether a European could lead an NHL team. As Canadian as they come, Mark Messier won six Cups and remains the only man to captain two different teams to the Stanley Cup—the Edmonton Oilers (1989-90) and the New York Rangers (1993-94). Messier didn't buy into the antiquated notion that Europeans can't lead.

"He was the prototypical leader by example," Messier said of Lidstrom. "I don't know Nick well enough to know what he did behind the scenes in the dressing room, but if you talk about a consistent leader, he was the same guy game in and game out. He was consistent in his personality so that when the guys looked at him, he was always going to be the same guy.

"He had some tough shoes to fill with Yzerman leaving there and he stepped in and they didn't miss a beat."

Since Lidstrom retired in the summer of 2012, the Wings have been left with an equally difficult void to be filled.

"He played in all positions—power play, penalty kill, even strength, four on four," Detroit defenceman Brendan Smith said of Lidstrom. "Whatever it was, he dominated.

"You can't replace a guy like Nick Lidstrom. Nobody in the NHL can."

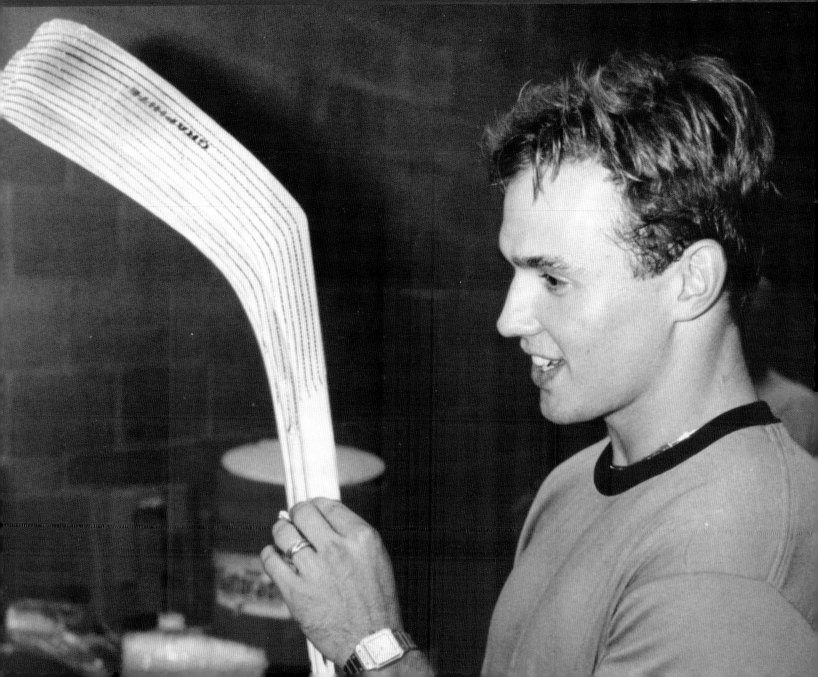

3 STEVE YZERMAN

Centre

Born: May 9, 1965, Burnaby, British Columbia
Shot: Left **Height:** 5-11 **Weight:** 185 lbs.
Red Wing From: 1983-84 to 2005-06
Elected to Hockey Hall of Fame: 2009
Acquired: Selected fourth overall in June 8, 1983 NHL entry draft.
Departed: Announced retirement, July 3, 2006.

FORGET THE NUMEROUS 100-POINT SEASONS, INCLUDING his team-record 65-goal, 155-point campaign of 1988-89. They might serve as the measure of Steve Yzerman's talent, but they are the not the measure of the man.

When his former teammates talk about Yzerman, they talk about his will, his desire to win, and above all of his accomplishments on the ice.

"That's the one thing you always knew," said former Detroit centre Kris Draper of the club's longtime captain. "Through an 82-game season and playoffs, you were going to face adversity. And usually when we faced adversity, Stevie was the guy who stepped up and kind of calmed the waters.

"He was always a calming influence on us."

They especially talk about the iron will of Stevie Y during Detroit's run to the Stanley Cup in the spring of 2002. He played all season on a right knee in desperate need of repair and they witnessed the pain their captain endured up close.

"He was suffering a lot," remembered former Detroit forward Tomas Holmstrom said. "He couldn't play as well as he wanted to.

"There was a lot of pain that he was going through, especially with his knee. You could see how much it hurt him. Before he had the bad knee, he could do so much with the puck. And even with the bad knee, he could be our best player still."

DETROIT HONOURS:

- Stanley Cup champion 1996-97, 1997-98, 2001-02
- Won Lester B. Pearson Award, 1988-89
- Won Conn Smythe Trophy, 1997-98
- Won Selke Trophy, 1999-2000
- Won Bill Masterton Memorial Trophy, 2002-03
- Won Lester Patrick Trophy, 2006
- Named to NHL First All-Star Team, 1999-2000
- Named to NHL All-Rookie Team, 1983-84
- One of only four players in NHL history (along with Alex Delvecchio, Nicklas Lidstrom and Stan Mikita) to play more than 20 NHL seasons with just one team
- Team captain 1986-2006
- Holds club record for goals (65), assists (90) and points (155) in a season
- Holds club record for points by a rookie (87 in 1983-84)
- Led NHL in shorthanded goals in 1989-90 (seven), 1990-91 (eight), 1991-92 (seven)
- Led NHL in shots on goal (388) and even-strength goals (45) in 1988-89
- Won Canada Cup with Canada, 1984
- Won Olympic gold medal with Canada, 2002
- Won silver medal at World Championship with Canada, 1985, 1989
- Yzerman's No. 19 was retired by the Red Wings on January 2, 2007.

And yet he persevered and led the way, carrying the Wings to their third Stanley Cup in six seasons. Of all his years that he wore the crown as hockey's ultimate leader, this was perhaps Yzerman's finest hour.

Even those who led the Wings before him couldn't help but be impressed.

"I think Steve Yzerman is what every athlete should be," former Detroit captain Ted Lindsay said. "Being captain, it's a recognition of leadership. A quality that you have to hold your team together, make them perform as a unit. I think Steve Yzerman would be the best illustration. Steve Yzerman didn't kick any butt.

"He used to show guys how to do it. I think this is where lots of mistakes are made by people who think a guy gets in the dressing room and he makes a big show. That's not true leadership. You do it by leading by example."

You do it the way Yzerman did it for so many years.

Ask him about those 2002 playoffs and Yzerman will downplay what he accomplished while basically skating on one leg.

"All I did was play the games," Yzerman recalled. "At the time, I didn't realize it, but it was the beginning of the end for me.

"I played on a line with (Brendan) Shanahan and (Sergei) Fedorov. We played the trap, so I would glide around and force the play one way or another and then they would do most of the work."

Yzerman would play three more seasons in Detroit, retiring after the 2005-06 campaign with 1,755 career points, good for sixth place on the NHL's all-time list. He captained the Red Wings for an NHL-record two decades.

How large is Yzerman's legend?

When Justin Bieber played the St. Pete Times Forum in 2011, Yzerman took his young daughters to see the Canadian teen idol, but Bieber only had eyes for Stevie Y, pointing out to the crowd how honoured he was to be in Yzerman's presence.

"That was one of the few times I've been recognized in Florida," shrugged Yzerman, who has served as general manager of the Tampa Bay Lightning since 2010.

Even today's stars on ice sometimes still struggle to speak of Yzerman without awe in their voice.

"He was my idol growing up," Philadelphia Flyers forward Vincent Lecavalier said. "I wore his jersey, and went and watched him play against Montreal.

"I've seen the type of captain he was, and the leader he is as a GM. He brings a lot of respect and class. When you speak to him, he's so respectful. He makes everyone around him better."

YZERMAN'S RED WINGS STATISTICS:

Season	REGULAR SEASON					PLAYOFFS				
	GP	G	A	P	PIM	GP	G	A	P	PIM
1983-84	80	39	48	87	33	4	3	3	6	0
1984-85	80	39	50	89	58	3	2	1	3	2
1985-86	51	14	28	42	16	-	-	-	-	-
1986-87	80	31	59	90	43	16	5	13	18	8
1987-88	64	50	52	102	44	3	1	3	4	6
1988-89	80	65	90	155	61	6	5	5	10	2
1989-90	79	62	65	127	79	-	-	-	-	-
1990-91	80	51	57	108	34	7	3	3	6	4
1991-92	79	45	58	103	64	11	3	5	8	12
1992-93	84	58	79	137	44	7	4	3	7	4
1993-94	58	24	58	82	36	3	1	3	4	0
1994-95	47	12	26	38	40	15	4	8	12	0
1995-96	80	36	59	95	64	18	8	12	20	4
1996-97	81	22	63	85	78	20	7	6	13	4
1997-98	75	24	45	69	46	22	6	18	24	22
1998-99	80	29	45	74	42	10	9	4	13	0
1999-00	78	35	44	79	34	8	0	4	4	0
2000-01	54	18	34	52	18	1	0	0	0	0
2001-02	52	13	35	48	18	23	6	17	23	10
2002-03	16	2	6	8	8	4	0	1	1	0
2003-04	75	18	33	51	46	11	3	2	5	0
2005-06	61	14	20	34	18	4	0	4	4	4
Totals	1514	692	1063	1755	924	196	70	115	185	82

During Yzerman's first season in charge, the Lightning came within a goal of reaching the Stanley Cup final.

"He brought so much credibility, coming from such a great organization," said New York Rangers forward Martin St. Louis, a Lightning that season. "As a player, and as management, he's seen how it should be. It was a hall of fame career that he had in Detroit, and he's a well-respected guy in hockey."

He's also a player that the Wings readily admit they weren't entirely certain about when they selected him from the Ontario Hockey League's Peterborough Petes with the fourth pick of the 1983 NHL entry draft.

"Some of our scouts were disappointed that we didn't get (Sylvain) Turgeon or (Pat) LaFontaine," recalled Nick Polano, who was Detroit's coach at the time.

Yzerman, mistakenly called *Why*-Zerman by most everyone in the Red Wings' camp during his rookie season, didn't impress anyone with his performance in the off-ice conditioning drills that fall.

Then, he donned his skates.

"He was far and away our best player," Polano said. "As an 18-year-old."

Yzerman set a club rookie record with 87 points that first season and just kept getting better, recording six straight 100-point seasons between 1987-88 and 1992-93.

Putting up numbers was never difficult for Stevie Y. He holds 18 marks in the Detroit record book. Putting up a Stanley Cup banner in the JLA rafters proved Yzerman's most daunting task.

It was the only thing missing from Yzerman's resumé. He was a dozen years into his career before the Wings reached the Cup final series, and played 14 seasons as an NHLer before he finally got to lift Lord Stanley's mug aloft.

The Stanley Cup was always Yzerman's No. 1 priority. "It's the only award that matters," Yzerman said. "By far, the most rewarding thing is going through four rounds of the playoffs and winning the Stanley Cup."

Being on top has always been what it's all about for Yzerman. And he'll employ whatever means necessary to attain that goal. His old teammates would marvel at the unparalleled competitiveness with which Yzerman approached the game.

He was nastier than bipartisan politics. More ornery than the Tasmanian Devil. This captain accepted no passengers on his ship. Those not willing to pay the price were cast adrift. He made certain of that.

Former Detroit defenceman Chris Chelios, who wore the C with pride for years in Chicago, described Yzerman as "the ultimate captain."

"No one competes more than him," Chelios said of Yzerman. "He's been like that ever since I've known him."

A leader by example, Yzerman was not a touchy-feely captain. His sense of humour was biting, his temper explosive. Beloved

by Red Wings fans on a level exceeded only by Gordie Howe, Yzerman shared Howe's distaste for the opposition.

Yzerman is such a competitor that he admits he can't turn it off when he goes home. Card games. Monopoly. Scrabble. It doesn't matter. In Yzerman's mind, only one person can be No. 1.

"I have to win at everything," he said. "It's cost me some friends."

Has it cost him any sleep? Hardly. And it certainly never cost him any fans.

Even those who starred with other Detroit sports franchises bowed in reverence to what Yzerman meant to the city.

"I think if you look at this area's sports teams, tradition has always been a big part of it," former Detroit Lions tackle Lomas Brown said. "You look at guys like (Al) Kaline, Lou (Whitaker) and Tram (Alan Trammell) with the Tigers and Steve Yzerman with the Wings. People see that loyalty to one team and identify with those players."

Everyone in the Motor City identified with Stevie Y.

"There were so many intangibles that Steve brought to this team," ex-Wings player and coach Dave Lewis said. "It's hard to put his value into words. What he did on the ice, what he did in the locker room, the players simply enjoyed being around him, even when he was grumpy at times."

An engaging conversationalist when he wants to be, Yzerman can speak on virtually any topic with some sense of authority. Except himself.

Consider his reaction when the city of Detroit renamed the road leading up to Joe Louis Arena Steve Yzerman Drive on Jan. 2, 2007, the same night the Wings retired Yzerman's No. 19 sweater.

"That's kind of neat, but I kind of wish my name was Smith or Jones, because in 20 years, no one's going to remember how to pronounce it," Yzerman joked. "It took me 20 years to get everyone around here to pronounce it right."

That humble, self-deprecating reaction is Yzerman at his best. Even as they raised the No. 19 banner to the rafters, he couldn't accept his status as a Detroit hockey legend. Watching his number—with a C appropriately affixed to the upper left corner of the banner—join the digits of Terry Sawchuk (1), Ted Lindsay (7), Gordie Howe (9), Alex Delvecchio (10) and Sid Abel (12)—Yzerman wondered aloud what all the fuss was about.

"It's a tremendous honour for me, but I don't think of myself as being among them," Yzerman said. "Those are the players that built the league."

Yzerman was the guy who rebuilt the long-forlorn home of the Dead Wings into Hockeytown.

"For years, he was the team," Lindsay said.

The lore of Yzerman had as much to do with the way he carried himself as it did with the way he carried the team.

"The reason people fell in love with Stevie is because of his class," Detroit GM Ken Holland said. "The person you saw on the ice was the person you saw off the ice—a caring, hard-working person with a great passion for the game and for his family and friends."

And someone who holds a firm belief that he'd done nothing exceptional in 22 years as a Wings player. "Look at the great players I played with," Yzerman said, downplaying his role. "All of the accolades that came my way were made possible by those great players."

It was typical Yzerman. "He never wanted to stand out from the other players," recalled Dallas GM Jim Nill, who launched his Detroit career as Yzerman's teammate. "He just wanted to be one of the guys.

"When I think of Steve, I think of competitiveness and intensity, the will to win. He was going to win no matter what."

It's a description that everyone who crossed paths with Yzerman shares. "You won't come across a better player or a better person," former teammate Tim Taylor said.

Always uncomfortable in the spotlight, when the NHL first released action figures of its players in the mid-1990s, Yzerman was among those to be featured.

"I'm not a movie star," he said with a shrug. "I'm not a rock 'n' roll singer. I'm just a hockey player.

"All of the Spice Girls have dolls, too. I don't want to be lumped into that category."

Those who watched him operate on a daily basis admired the way Yzerman never let the fame go to his head or deter him from his objective.

"He's a classy guy," Lindsay said.

"He put great demands on himself," Detroit senior vice-president Jimmy Devellano said.

"He just does the right thing time in and time out, even when the right thing is very hard to do," former Detroit coach Mike Babcock said. "Most of us go for the path of least resistance. That's not Steve Yzerman."

It's what took him to Tampa Bay, when Yzerman could have easily stayed with Detroit and worked in the Wings' front office forever.

"This is exciting and a little bit scary for me, but it's something I wanted to do." Yzerman said. "I'd been sheltered in Detroit for a long time and they've protected me. It was really safe for me in Detroit, really comfortable for me in Detroit.

"I hadn't gone outside of Detroit my entire life. I was stepping out on my own for the first time really since I was 18 years old.

"I loved living there, I loved playing there. I moved on to this different part of my career with nothing but great feelings for the organization, and the city, and the state."

Red Wings fans feel the same way about Yzerman. Stevie Y will always be their guy.

4 TERRY SAWCHUK

Goal

Born: December 28, 1929, Winnipeg, Manitoba
Died: May 31, 1970
Shot: Left Height: 5-11 Weight: 180 lbs.
Red Wing From: 1949-50 to 1954-55; 1957-58 to 1963-64; 1968-69
Elected to Hockey Hall of Fame: 1971
Acquired: Signed to pro contract November 5, 1947.
Departed: Traded to Boston Bruins by Detroit with Marcel Bonin, Lorne Davis and Vic Stasiuk for Gilles Boisvert, Norm Corcoran, Warren Godfrey and Ed Sandford, June 3, 1955.
Reacquired: Traded to Detroit by Boston Bruins for Johnny Bucyk, June 10, 1957.
Departed: Claimed by Toronto Maple Leafs from Detroit in NHL Intra-League Draft, June 9, 1964.
Reacquired: Traded to Detroit by Los Angeles Kings for Jim Peters Jr., October 15, 1968.
Departed: Traded to New York Rangers by Detroit with Sandy Snow for Larry Jeffrey, June 17, 1969.

ONE OF THE GREATEST NETMINDERS EVER TO STRAP ON A pair of pads?

Absolutely.

One of the most tragic figures ever to play in the National Hockey League?

Definitely.

This was the paradox that was the life of Terry Sawchuk. On the ice, no one stopped the puck more effectively than Sawchuk.

Away from the rink, perhaps no player who ever skated in the NHL was touched as often and as deeply by injury and tragedy as Sawchuk, who died in 1970 at the age of 40 from a pulmonary embolism, caused by internal injuries suffered in a scuffle with New York Rangers teammate Ron Stewart.

"He was always injured," recalled Jimmy Skinner, who coached Sawchuk with both the Windsor Spitfires and Detroit Red Wings.

Growing up in the Winnipeg suburb of East Kildonan, tragedy visited Sawchuk's life long before the NHL ever became a possibility. He inherited his first pair of goal pads from his oldest brother Mike, who died suddenly of a heart ailment at the age of 17. Another brother, Roger, died of pneumonia.

By the time he was 14, Sawchuk held down two jobs—one in a foundry, the other with a sheet metal company—to help the family make ends meet while his dad Louis was off with a broken back suffered after a fall from a scaffold.

DETROIT HONOURS:

- Stanley Cup champion 1951-52, 1953-54, 1954-55
- Won Vezina Trophy 1951-52, 1952-53, 1954-55
- Won Calder Trophy 1950-51
- Selected to NHL First All-Star Team 1950-51, 1951-52, 1952-53
- Selected to NHL Second All-Star Team 1953-54, 1954-55, 1958-59, 1962-63
- Played in NHL All-Star Game 1950, 1951, 1952, 1953, 1954, 1959, 1963
- Won Lester Patrick Trophy, 1971
- Elected to Manitoba Hockey Hall of Fame, 1985
- Red Wings all-time leader in shutouts (85) and wins (352)
- Led NHL in wins 1950-51, 1951-52, 1952-53, 1953-54, 1954-55
- Led NHL in shutouts 1950-51, 1951-52, 1954-55
- Led Stanley Cup playoffs in shutouts 1951-52, 1954-55
- Sawchuk's No. 1 was retired by the Red Wings on March 6, 1994.

Bob Kinnear, the Red Wings scout who discovered Sawchuk, knew early of this double-edged life that he led—how tragedy followed him, and yet when he strapped on the pads and stood between the posts, perfection was his constant companion.

"What is that rhyme?" Kinnear asked the *Vancouver Sun*. "Wednesday's child is full of woe? Terry was born on a Wednesday and he had a lot of troubles, but as far as I was concerned, was a wonderful kid."

Kinnear recalled how he found Sawchuk, barely into his teens, and realized almost instantly he was watching a child prodigy at work.

"The Red Wings asked me to scout for them in Winnipeg around 1944 and gave me the money to build an outdoor rink in East Kildonan," Kinnear recalled. "I had a 10-team house league and Terry's older brother Mike came out and he played goal.

"Terry followed him and he played defence. Then Terry's brother died suddenly. After that, I suggested to Terry that he try playing goal and he brought the equipment and he was great from the time he put the pads on.

"I wrote so many glowing letters on Terry to (Detroit GM) Jack Adams that Jack asked me to bring Terry to Detroit. Terry was only 14 then.

"He worked out with the Wings and afterward I was talking to Adams when Jack Stewart came along. Stewart was the best defenceman in the league then and he told Adams that Terry was going to be great. He was right."

Many feel Sawchuk's hard life accounts for his well-documented mood swings. Remembered as someone who had a quick wit and who loved practical jokes, Sawchuk could also be sullen and downright ugly at times, especially with the media and autograph seekers.

"He was a very low-key guy," Skinner remembered. "And he could be moody and surly when he played. He didn't talk much. You had to really get to know him to get him to talk."

In 1947, the Wings brought Sawchuk east to play junior with Skinner's Spitfires, but it was a short apprenticeship.

| SAWCHUK'S RED WINGS STATISTICS: | | | | | | | | | | | |
| REGULAR SEASON | | | | | | PLAYOFFS | | | | | |
Season	GPI	MIN	GA	SO	W-L-T	GAA	GPI	MIN	GA	SO	GAA	W-L
1949-50	7	420	16	1	4-3-0	2.29	-	-	-	-	-	-
1950-51	70	4200	139	11	43-13-13	1.99	6	463	13	1	1.68	2-4
1951-52	70	4200	133	12	44-14-12	1.90	8	480	5	4	0.63	8-0
1952-53	63	3780	119	9	32-15-16	1.89	6	372	20	1	3.23	2-4
1953-54	67	4004	129	12	35-19-13	1.93	12	751	20	2	1.60	8-4
1954-55	68	4080	132	12	40-17-11	1.94	11	660	26	1	2.36	8-3
1957-58	70	4200	206	3	29-29-12	2.94	4	252	19	0	4.52	0-4
1958-59	67	4020	207	5	23-36-8	3.09	-	-	-	-	-	-
1959-60	58	3480	156	5	24-20-14	2.69	6	405	19	0	2.81	2-4
1960-61	37	2150	112	2	12-16-8	3.13	8	465	18	1	2.32	5-3
1961-62	43	2580	141	5	14-21-8	3.28	-	-	-	-	-	-
1962-63	48	2775	117	3	22-16-7	2.53	11	660	35	0	3.18	5-6
1963-64	53	3140	138	5	25-20-7	2.64	13	677	31	1	2.75	6-5
1968-69	13	641	28	0	3-4-3	2.62	-	-	-	-	-	-
Totals	734	43556	1782	85	352-243-132	2.45	85	520	209	11	2.41	46-37

"He was only 17, but even then, he was outstanding," Skinner said.

Sawchuk played just four games with Windsor. "A few games into the season, (Detroit GM) Jack Adams calls me and says 'I've got some bad news Jim, we've got to move Sawchuk to Omaha.' I wasn't surprised, though, because I figured he should have been there in the first place."

He posted a league-leading 3.21 goals-against average with Omaha and was named USHL rookie of the year. In the fall of 1948, as the Wings arrived in Saskatoon for training camp, there was speculation that Sawchuk might supplant Harry Lumley as Detroit's goalie.

"In all my hockey I have never seen a young goalie handle himself as well as Sawchuk," Detroit coach Tommy Ivan told the *Canadian Press*. "Why that Terry is terrific and while we tentatively have him booked for our farm club at Indianapolis, the way he's going here in Saskatoon would lead me to believe he's ready for the NHL right now."

The Wings stuck with their original plan and Sawchuk won the Dudley (Red) Garrett Memorial Trophy as the AHL's top rookie with Indianapolis. The next season, he went 8-0 in the playoffs as Indianapolis earned the Calder Cup as AHL champions, earning a seven-game call-up to the Red Wings.

Despite winning the Stanley Cup in 1949-50, Adams opted to deal Lumley to Chicago and make Sawchuk his No. 1 goalie, and the moved paid enormous dividends.

No netminder in the history of the NHL put together a start to their career that can match what Sawchuk did for Detroit. Sawchuk garnered 56 shutouts over his first five seasons, leading the NHL in wins and posting a GAA under 2.00 in each of those seasons. He was the NHL rookie of the year in 1950-51 and won three Vezina Trophies and two Stanley Cups during this five-year span.

"I saw a lot of the greats—(Jacques) Plante, (Bill) Durnan, (Gump) Worsley—but to my mind, I never saw anyone better than Sawchuk," Skinner said. "Reflexes, angles—he had it all and he also had a lot of guts. He was fearless in the net and extremely confident.

"He'd always say to the guys, 'Get me a couple and we'll win.' And he meant it. He didn't say it in a bragging kind of way. He was just that confident."

A chubby kid when he first turned pro, Sawchuk got the message early about the importance of physical conditioning and heeded it to the extreme.

"I'm down to 198 pounds, the lightest I've been in three years and that's no accident," Sawchuk told *Associated Press* during Detroit's 1951 training camp. "I reported to training camp at 220 pounds—10 pounds more than my rookie weight—and I could see that didn't enhance my popularity with the boss, Jack Adams."

Sawchuk was well aware of Lumley's fate and wasn't interested in opening the door to another Detroit goalie prospect. "I wasn't going to let that happen to me," he said. "So I put on a sweat jacket and laid off the bread and potatoes and I feel fine. Last year I sort of tired near the end of a game. No more."

Sawchuk was meticulous in his game preparation, both at and away from the rink. "I stay away from movies and television screens during the season and I don't read any more than I have to," he said. "I'll play the game over in bed, but I won't pick up a paper."

Sawchuk's play during the 1952 playoffs as the Wings won the Stanley Cup in the minimum eight games was a once-in-a-lifetime performance. He posted four shutouts, a 0.63 GAA and a .977 save percentage.

"Uke (as Sawchuk was known) was the best goalie I've ever seen," former Detroit captain Ted Lindsay said. "If you threw a handful of rice at him, he'd catch every kernel."

Shortly after that amazing performance, Sawchuk checked himself into hospital to undergo surgery for bone chips in his right elbow. "I didn't say anything about it," Sawchuk said at the time. "I didn't want people to think I was alibiing in case I didn't play well in the playoffs."

The issue stemmed from a childhood football injury in which Sawchuk had damaged the elbow and never had it treated, leaving him with one arm that wasn't fully functional. Sixty bone chips were removed from his right elbow through three different operations.

"He couldn't lift his arm to comb his hair," recalled long-time teammate Marcel Pronovost. "He'd have to hold the comb out and tilt his head down to drag the hair through the comb."

Eventually, his right arm was two inches shorter than the left, forcing Sawchuk to invent the crouching style of goal that made him so successful. Sawchuk was one of the first netminders to adopt the crouch, situating himself low in the net to see around and under bodies and pick up screen shots.

"He was in the crouch, but he never left his feet," Skinner said. "You wouldn't see him go down so quickly like the goalies do today."

Over the course of his career, Sawchuk assembled a punishing legacy. He took 400 stitches to the face. Another 175 stitches were required to close a gruesome cut when Toronto forward Bob Pulford skated across his hand. Three tendons were severed in Sawchuk's glove hand.

"It's been so long, you forget about them," Sawchuk said of the number of times he'd been sewn back together.

Not to mention how frequently he was broken to bits. Sawchuk suffered seven broken ribs, three broken fingers, a broken blocker hand, and a broken left instep. He underwent surgery to have two discs removed from back. Twice he broke his nose. He separated his right shoulder and endured a pinched nerve in his left shoulder.

Sawchuk once described himself as, "one great big aching bruise," suggesting that, "I spend my summers in the hospital." He often fretted about what he'd do with his life if his numerous injuries eventually caught up with him and ended his playing days.

"When I was with Omaha of the U.S. League, I nearly lost the sight of my right eye from a high stick," Sawchuk recalled. "I had three stitches taken in the eyeball. It was bandaged for three weeks. I said to myself then, 'What am I going to do for a living?' I had no answer. I still wouldn't if I couldn't play hockey."

Sawchuk sometimes endured crises of confidence, fearing he wasn't good enough to maintain his position in the NHL. "He got himself in trouble through his insecurities," said Pronovost, who remembered seeing both sides of Sawchuk at the rink.

"One time, a young boy got hit with a puck during a game. They brought him in the dressing room afterwards and Terry got his stick signed by all the players and gave it to the boy. Then he turned to me and said, 'If you tell the press about this, I'll kill you.'

"That's the way he was. He liked to present himself as this moody, aloof person, because then people would leave him alone."

Perhaps it was this level of insecurity that led the Wings to cast Sawchuk adrift shortly after he won them the Stanley

Cup in the spring of 1955. "He won't be playing for Detroit next year," Montreal Canadiens forward Bernie (Boom Boom) Geoffrion told the *Montreal Gazette* during the 1955 final. "He has a sign on his house right now that says, 'House for sale.' I predict Sawchuk will be sold or traded to Boston."

In fact, Sawchuk was dealt to the Bruins that summer in an NHL-record nine-player deal, the Wings handing their goaltending reigns to Glenn Hall. "I first heard the rumour on the radio. Then Boston phoned me to tell me they were my new owners," an unhappy Sawchuk said.

"We had to make a decision between Terry Sawchuk and Glenn Hall," Adams told *Canadian Press*. "Hall is more advanced than Sawchuk when he joined us and all the players insist Glenn has been NHL material for the past year."

Two years later, Adams did a 180 and reacquired Sawchuk, who had left the Bruins midway through the 1956-57 season battling mononucleosis, exhaustion and a nervous breakdown.

"Terry is too good to stay out of the game," Adams told *Associated Press*. "This is his home, this is where he got his start, this is where he belongs and we're very happy to have him back." Added Sawchuk: "I'm very happy to be back home and back in hockey."

Detroit didn't reach the same heights during Sawchuk's second tour of duty, and by the start of the 1960-61 season Wings coach Sid Abel opted for a rotation in net of Sawchuk and Hank Bassen. But Sawchuk caught fire in the second half of the season, leading the Wings to their first Stanley Cup final appearance in five years. "I feel like my old self again," Sawchuk said.

In 1962, he donned a mask and led the Wings to back-to-back Cup final appearances. "I don't know what it is really, but I feel I am playing better with a mask," Sawchuk said. "Maybe it's the extra confidence that it gives me."

Early during Detroit's 1964 semifinal series with Chicago, Sawchuk suffered a punched nerve in his left shoulder. He checked into Detroit Osteopathic Hospital and was placed in traction. The next day, Sawchuk checked out of hospital, went to Olympia Stadium, shut out the Blackhawks 3-0, then returned to hospital and was again placed in traction.

"My shoulder pained me during the game and twice I dropped my stick," Sawchuk told *UPI*. "But it was worth it to get the shutout. Now I'll stay in hospital until just prior to game time."

After the season concluded, with Toronto beating Detroit in a seven-game final series, Sawchuk was left unprotected and moved to the Leafs for the $20,000 draft price.

"We're on a youth movement," Abel explained to the *Windsor Star*. "We have four young goaltenders and Roger Crozier was going to start for us anyway. So we had to lose him to protect our youngsters."

A saddened Sawchuk reluctantly again accepted his fate. "I had a little hunch this would happen," Sawchuk said. "But what are you going to do? I'm not happy but I'll report. I have to leave Detroit, my home."

With Toronto, Sawchuk would lead the Leafs to the 1967 Stanley Cup before he was let go to Los Angeles in the NHL expansion draft. After one season with the Kings, he was dealt back to the Wings for a third tour of duty with Detroit.

Sawchuk mentored Crozier and Roy Edwards during the 1968-69 season, playing just 13 games before being traded to the New York Rangers, where his life would take one final horrific turn.

Sawchuk died on May 31, 1970, from complications from injuries suffered in a scuffle with Stewart. The Hockey Hall of Fame waived the mandatory three-year waiting period for election, inducting Sawchuk in 1971.

His sensational career and tragic life were both at an end, and Sawchuk's old teammates found difficulty in trying to make sense of it all.

"For a man who seemingly (had) everything, he was a very sad individual, which is too bad," Gordie Howe said.

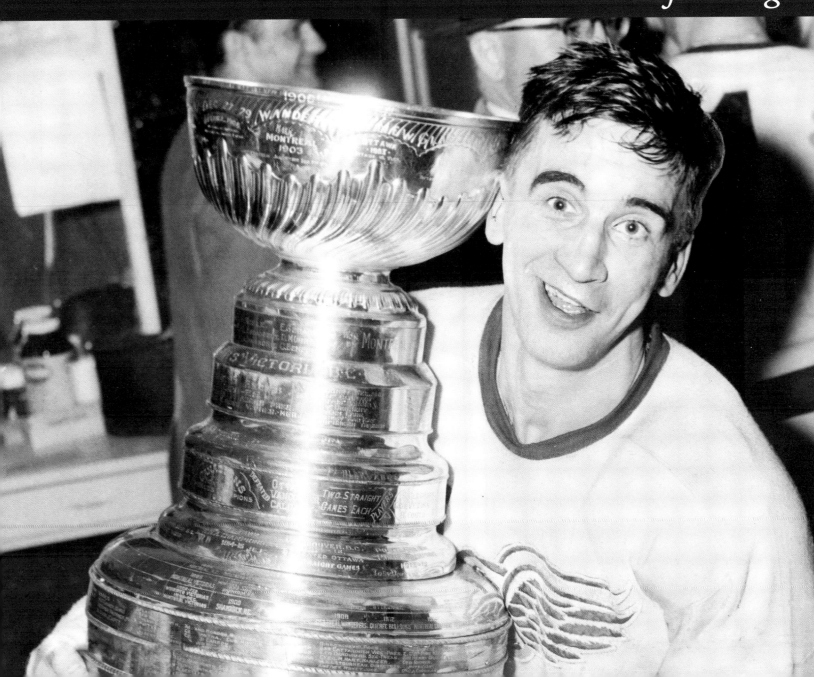

5 TED LINDSAY

Left Wing

Born: July 29, 1925, Renfrew, Ontario
Shot: Left Height: 5-8 Weight: 163 lbs.
Red Wing From: 1944-45 to 1956-57; 1964-65
Elected to Hockey Hall of Fame: 1966
Acquired: Signed to pro contract October 18, 1944.
Departed: Traded to Chicago Blackhawks by Detroit with Glenn Hall for Johnny Wilson, Forbes Kennedy, Bill Preston and Hank Bassen, July 20, 1957.
Reacquired: Rights purchased from Chicago Blackhawks by Detroit, October 14, 1964.
Departed: Announced retirement from hockey, April 15, 1965.

THEY CALLED HIM TERRIBLE TED, BUT WHEN THE DETROIT Red Wings' chief scout Carson Cooper turned up to check out Lindsay in action for the junior Toronto St. Michael's Majors, he saw a man who would become the heart and soul of the franchise.

The night they scouted Lindsay in action, St. Mike's fell 5-3, but Lindsay recorded a double hat trick, scoring all three of his team's goals and dropping the gloves for fistic encounters on three other occasions. Even though his build was slight, his game was stout. The Wings were sold on Lindsay and added him to the club's negotiating list.

In the spring of 1944, Lindsay led all scorers in the OHA Jr. A playoffs with 13 goals and 19 points in 12 games. After eliminating St. Michael's, the Oshawa Generals added Lindsay to their roster in their successful pursuit of the

Memorial Cup against the Trail Smoke Eaters. He potted another seven goals and nine points in seven Memorial Cup games with the Generals.

That fall, Lindsay went to training camp with the Red Wings and never looked back. He was signed to a pro contract and jumped directly into the Detroit lineup, without any minor-league seasoning. Lindsay scored in his second NHL game against the New York Rangers and didn't take long to make an impression.

"I especially like that kid Ted Lindsay that they got from St. Michael's College," Montreal Canadiens defenceman Leo Lamoureux expressed to the *Windsor Star* after meeting the Wings. "He's going to be a real hockey player or I miss my guess."

Lindsay came to his hockey talent genetically. His father Bert was a star goaltender who played for the Victoria

DETROIT HONOURS:

* Stanley Cup champion 1949-50, 1951-52, 1953-54, 1954-55
* Won Art Ross Trophy 1949-50
* Selected to NHL First All-Star Team 1947-48, 1949-50, 1950-51, 1951-52, 1952-53, 1953-54, 1955-56, 1956-57
* Selected to NHL Second All-Star Team 1948-49
* Played in NHL All-Star Game 1947, 1948, 1949, 1950, 1951, 1952, 1953, 1954, 1955, 1956, 1957
* Team captain 1952-56
* Led NHL in goals, 1947-48
* Led NHL in assists, 1949-50, 1956-57
* Led Stanley Cup playoffs in points, 1951-52
* Led Stanley Cup playoffs in assists, 1948-49
* Led Stanley Cup playoffs in goals, 1951-52
* First player to score 200 goals in a Red Wings uniform
* Lindsay's No. 7 was retired by the Red Wings on November 10, 1991.

Aristocrats in the 1913-14 Stanley Cup final, and also tended goal for one of hockey's most star-studded aggregates, the 1908-09 Renfrew Creamery Kings, whose lineup included future Hall of Famers Cyclone Taylor, Newsy Lalonde, and the Patrick brothers, Frank and Lester.

The elder Lindsay played in the NHL for the Montreal Wanderers (1917-18) and Toronto Arenas (1918-19), meaning that when Ted took the ice with the Wings, he became the first son of an original NHLer to play in the league.

Early in Lindsay's career, he drew the assignment of checking Montreal star Maurice (Rocket) Richard, the NHL's top goal scorer, and he was effective in this chore, much to Richard's ire. In 1990, three decades after his last game against Lindsay, the Rocket placed Lindsay at left wing on his all-time team, but did so through gritted teeth. "Lindsay had a big mouth," Richard explained. "I still despise him 30 years later."

It was an attitude that tended to be unanimous among Lindsay's opponents. They all admired his competitive streak and his unbreakable determination, but they dreaded the thought of having to deal with it.

"Lindsay was a great digger," former Detroit goalie John Ross Roach once explained to the *Windsor Star*. "He'd go fight for that puck and dig it out for you. Lindsay would play it any way you wanted. If you wanted to fight, he could fight."

Detroit reached the 1944-45 Stanley Cup final, losing to Toronto in seven games, and as rookie Lindsay potted 17 goals and drew comparisons to a Detroit legend.

"In a few years Lindsay will be as good a winger as Larry Aurie was," Detroit GM Jack Adams told the *Montreal Gazette*. "I believe he is further advanced right now than Larry was at the same stage of his career."

Lindsay was among the first of a series of players who would be groomed by the Wings to form the core of an NHL powerhouse that dominated the league from the mid-1940s through the mid-1950s. There was Harry Lumley and later Terry Sawchuk in goal, and Bill Quackenbush, Red Kelly and Marcel Pronovost on defence. Gordie Howe would soon join Lindsay along the forward line.

Lindsay led the NHL with 33 goals in 1947-48 and Detroit coach Tommy Ivan struck hockey gold when he put Lindsay and Howe alongside veteran centre Sid Abel in what would become the Wings' Production Line. Detroit reached successive Stanley Cup finals in 1947-48, 1948-49 and 1949-50, finally lifting hockey's Holy Grail when they beat the New York Rangers in 1950.

During the 1949-50 campaign, Lindsay (23-55-78), Abel (34-35-69) and Howe (35-33-68) finished 1-2-3 in the NHL scoring race, the only time in league history that linemates from a Stanley Cup championship team finished as the NHL's top scoring trio.

"We instinctively knew where the opposition was," Lindsay said of the Production Line. "We just understood each other. We knew where to go, so we consequently were efficient."

"We played together until we knew each other's every move," added Howe, who described Lindsay as "the No. 1 left wing of all-time."

LINDSAY'S RED WINGS STATISTICS:

Season	Regular Season					Playoffs				
	GP	G	A	P	PIM	GP	G	A	P	PIM
1944-45	45	17	6	23	43	14	2	0	2	6
1945-46	47	7	10	17	14	5	0	1	1	0
1946-47	59	27	15	42	57	5	2	2	4	10
1947-48	60	33	19	52	95	10	3	1	4	6
1948-49	50	26	28	54	97	11	2	6	8	31
1949-50	69	23	55	78	141	13	4	4	8	16
1950-51	67	24	35	59	110	6	0	1	1	8
1951-52	70	30	39	69	123	8	5	2	7	8
1952-53	70	32	39	71	111	6	4	4	8	6
1953-54	70	26	36	62	110	12	4	4	8	14
1954-55	49	19	19	38	85	11	7	12	19	12
1955-56	67	27	23	50	161	10	6	3	9	22
1956-57	70	30	55	85	103	5	2	4	6	8
1964-65	69	14	14	28	173	7	3	0	3	34
Totals	862	335	393	728	1423	123	44	44	88	181

Detroit checking winger Marty Pavelich, Lindsay's long-time friend and business partner, felt that playing on Lindsay's line helped Howe develop his famous aggressive streak.

"I always said that being with Teddy helped him become a better hockey player," Pavelich said. "Teddy was so aggressive that I think that Gordie got caught up in that, too."

Howe doesn't debate Lindsay's contribution to his greatness. "I don't know who started that, but I think Ted Lindsay helped me," Howe said. "His stick was on the ice only half the time, but what a tough, little guy."

Lindsay didn't need any instruction on the ways of nastiness. "He'd fight his mother if he lost," Howe said.

Along with Hall of Famer Nels Stewart one of only two players in NHL history to have led the league in scoring and in penalty minutes during a single season, Lindsay retired as the NHL's career penalty-minute leader with 1,808 minutes, a title he held into the 1970s.

"I had the idea that I should beat up every player I tangled with and nothing ever convinced me it wasn't a good idea," Lindsay said of his style of play. "You had to play tough in those days, or they'd run you out of the building."

Lindsay's face is chiseled with the scars of his many hockey wars, which resulted in over 700 stitches and so many broken noses he says he lost count. But Lindsay could give it out as well as he took it. "You cut him for five (stitches) and he would cut you for 10," Pavelich said.

Naturally, it didn't make Lindsay many friends around the league, not that he sought out companionship from his foes. "You'd get to the All-Star Game and Ted Lindsay would walk by and grunt," Hall of Fame right winger Andy Bathgate said. "That's the only words you'd get out of him."

Former Toronto forward Howie Meeker explained once to a Vancouver magazine the subtle difference between the brutality of Howe and Lindsay. "Howe would stare you straight in the eyes and give it to you," Meeker said. "Lindsay would stare you straight in the back and give it to you."

Some of Lindsay's most epic battles were with former Boston and Toronto winger Bill Ezinicki, like Lindsay an undersized dynamo who gave no quarter and asked none.

"Lindsay and Ezinicki were going at it every game," recalled Hall of Fame Detroit defenceman Marcel Pronovost.

Their bloodiest bout came Jan. 25, 1951, and when it was done, Ezinicki lay unconscious on the ice with a broken nose, minus a tooth and cut for 19 stitches.

"Lindsay was the toughest guy who ever played hockey," Hall of Fame referee Bill Chadwick told *Associated Press*. "He never backed off from anybody.

"He had as many fights as any guy who ever played the game. When Lindsay took a penalty it was never a cheap one. It was for fighting or for giving it to some guy in the corner of the rink."

Led by the Production Line, Detroit won another Stanley Cup in the spring of 1952, and when Abel left in the summer to take over as player-coach of the Chicago Blackhawks, the Wings named Lindsay to succeed him as captain.

"Being captain, it's a recognition of leadership," said Lindsay, who on December 21, 1952 became the first Red Wing to score 200 career goals. "A quality that you have to hold your team together, make them perform as a unit."

Under Lindsay's guidance the Wings captured two more Stanley Cups in 1953-54 and 1954-55, and by the end of the 1954-55 season had finished atop the regular-season standings for a record seven consecutive seasons.

"It was a unit," Lindsay said of that Detroit dynasty. "We had great skaters. We had great puckhandlers. A lot of people think we were all old fogies back in those days who couldn't skate. We had guys who could skate with anybody today.

"To win seven league championships in a row, nobody's ever going to defeat that record in hockey. Nobody will ever win it seven years in a row. Not with 30 teams."

After the 1950 Game 7 win over the New York Rangers in the Cup final, an excited Lindsay scooped the Stanley Cup off its perch on a table at centre ice and skated around the rink, much to the delight of a capacity Olympia Stadium crowd.

"I was well aware who paid my salary and it wasn't (Wings owner) Mr. (James) Norris, it was the fans," Lindsay said.

"I saw the Cup just sitting there, no one was around it, so I picked it up and brought it to the fans.

"I wanted to be respectful to the people who paid my salary."

There was no doubt that the Wings followed their leader, who wore No. 7. "Lindsay was a bit mouthy and hard to handle, but he gave you everything on the ice and demanded his teammates do the same," former Detroit coach Jimmy Skinner said.

Now he was about to ask those he'd wronged between the boards throughout his career to follow him.

During the 1956-57 season, Lindsay held clandestine meetings with key players from other NHL teams, including Montreal's Doug Harvey and Toronto's Tod Sloan and Jim Thomson, to discuss plans to organize a players' association.

"Some of the owners are for us and some are fighting us, but I think our chances of recognition are good," Lindsay told *Associated Press*. "We're not looking for any trouble. We just want to make playing in the league more attractive for Canadian and American players."

It was an uphill fight and one that eventually failed, but Lindsay's efforts nonetheless laid the groundwork that ultimately led to the formation of the NHLPA in 1967.

"Don't ask me why I did it," Lindsay said. "I was one of the better hockey players in the world and I was having one of my best years as a Red Wing at the time.

"I felt a responsibility, because I saw fellows being sent down. The clubs could send you home—they could send me home—and they didn't owe you five cents.

"That's not right."

In 2010, the NHLPA recognized Lindsay's efforts by renaming its player-of-the-year trophy the Ted Lindsay Award.

"I see Ted Lindsay one or two times a week and I love to hear the stories of when he played and what he went through with the players' association," former Red Wings defenceman Chris Chelios said. "He was all about doing the right thing.

"Every player that has played owes him a lot for the sacrifices that he made."

Among those sacrifices was the loss of his Red Wings sweater. Adams replaced Lindsay as captain with Red Kelly

to start the 1955-56, season and even though Lindsay posted career-high 30-55-85 totals in 1956-57 he was dealt to Chicago that summer.

"I had my best year ever as a Red Wing the year I was traded," Lindsay recalled. "I was traded because of the union. But I did it, and I knew what it was gonna cost me. They were gonna hang me.

"I didn't play hockey because of Jack Adams, I played hockey because I loved it. Just like all the guys."

News of the deal shook the NHL and touched off a war of words between the fiery winger and the club's equally snarly GM.

"It got to the point where I couldn't take it anymore," Lindsay said. "The fans in Detroit are the greatest and my relations with the players have been wonderful. But I've had enough."

Adams told *United Press* that the move was simply a hockey trade and there was nothing personal between him and Lindsay.

"All these wild rumours about personal differences between Lindsay and myself are without foundation," Adams claimed. "My job is to afford the hockey fans of Detroit and Michigan with the best possible team. I would be unfaithful to those fans if I hadn't done what I feel is best for the team."

When the war of words escalated, his tune quickly changed. "There is no place in sports for a disloyal and selfish athlete," Adams told the *Windsor Star* of Lindsay. "He is apparently putting himself above hockey."

Joining the woeful Blackhawks, Lindsay's veteran leadership helped mold a young Chicago team, including Bobby Hull, Stan Mikita, Glenn Hall and Pierre Pilote, into the club that would win the Stanley Cup in 1960-61 at the expense of the Red Wings, though Lindsay wouldn't be a part of it.

He announced his retirement from the game in the summer of 1960. "Either I'm slowing up or these players are getting faster," Lindsay said. But it turned out there was still a fire burning in his belly.

In the fall of 1964, he made a comeback with the Red Wings. Proving he hadn't mellowed, in his first NHL game in four years, Lindsay was handed a 10-minute misconduct

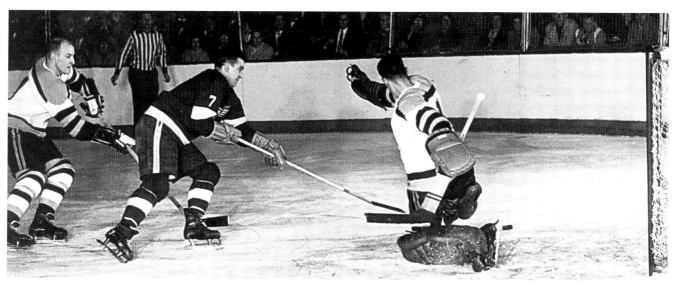

and a $25 fine for verbal abuse of referee Vern Buffey.

"Lindsay's command of the English language is quite startling," remarked Leafs defenceman Bob Baun.

Later in the season, again in a game involving Toronto and Buffey, Lindsay was fined $75 for misconduct and assessed a game misconduct penalty but insisted he wouldn't pay his fine, going as far as to announce that he wouldn't stand for NHL president Clarence Campbell's "kangaroo court." Eventually, Lindsay relented, wrote a letter of apology to Campbell and paid the fine. "I didn't want to hurt the club," he explained.

The Wings finished the season in first place for the first time since Lindsay had left Detroit, and he posted respectable 14-14-28 numbers. "Even at the age of 39, Lindsay's been a godsend for us," said Detroit coach-GM Abel, Lindsay's old linemate. "Ted was one of the best players on my club late in the season and during the playoffs."

Lindsay retired for good after the season. "This won't mean a lot to everyone, but I ended up a Red Wing and that means a lot to me," Lindsay said. He was inducted into the Hockey Hall of Fame in 1966, one of the rare times that the Hall waived its three-year waiting period.

A decade later, he would once more return to Detroit, this time when he was hired as GM of the Wings in 1977.

"I asked Ted, 'Can you bring us a winner?' And without hesitation, he said, 'Yes,'" Wings owner Bruce Norris told the *Pittsburgh Post-Gazette*.

True to his word, Lindsay guided the Wings to a playoff appearance in 1977-78, the first post-season action seen in Detroit since 1970.

In 1991, the Wings honoured Lindsay by raising his No. 7 to the Joe Louis Arena rafters and for once, the old tough guy was overcome by sentiment.

"If I had two wishes, one would be that my mother and father were here to be part of this, because it was their upbringing which made it all possible," Lindsay said as the No. 7 banner was unveiled.

Lindsay then cast his eyes towards a pair of skates the Wings presented to him as a gift. "My second wish would be that I could put on these skates and don that Red Wing uniform one more time."

Still a regular in the Red Wings dressing room even into his late 80s, Lindsay follows a daily workout regimen.

"Hockey has been wonderful to me," Lindsay said. "The game and the people in it have made my life a good one.

"I love the game and think it's the greatest game in the world."

6 RED KELLY

Defence

Born: July 9, 1927, Simcoe, Ontario
Shot: Left **Height:** 5-11 **Weight:** 180 lbs.
Red Wing From: 1947-48 to 1959-60
Elected to Hockey Hall of Fame: 1969
Acquired: Signed to pro contract September 9, 1947.
Departed: Traded to Toronto Maple Leafs by Detroit for Marc Reaume, February 10, 1960.

MIDWAY THROUGH THE 1953-54 NHL SEASON, BOSTON Bruins coach Lynn Patrick was asked by a reporter who he thought was the best player in the NHL—Detroit Red Wings' right winger Gordie Howe or Montreal Canadiens' right winger Maurice (Rocket) Richard.

"Neither," Patrick answered quickly. "I'll take Red Kelly.

"Kelly is the best all-around performer in our league. Sure, Howe and Richard are good, but Red is not only great on defence, he can score, too. In my opinion, he's the big reason Detroit has won five straight (regular season) championships.

"When Kelly rushes up the ice, it's something to see. He sparks Howe and Ted Lindsay and the others. When we play the Wings, we go out to stop him. We feel there's a better chance of winning that way."

Choosing between Montreal and Detroit for the Cup that spring, Patrick added, "The Wings have Kelly and that might be the difference."

He was right. The Wings did edge Montreal in a seven-game final series, and it was Kelly's game-tying goal that sent the deciding game to overtime, where Tony Leswick netted the Stanley Cup winner.

That spring, Kelly would be the first winner of the James Norris Memorial Trophy, a new award commissioned in honour of the long-time Red Wings owner to be presented annually to the NHL's best defenceman.

Few argued with the decision to go with Kelly. He was a near unanimous selection garnering 162 of a possible 180 votes.

"You've got to go all the way back to Eddie Shore to find one in his class," New York Rangers general manager Frank Boucher, who started in the NHL in 1921, told *Associated Press.* "Shore was more spectacular than Kelly because of the way he skated. He was a weaver—something like a broken field runner in football—and he was a showman. But I doubt if he was any more effective.

"Remember, this is the fifth year in a row that the Red Wings figure to take the pennant and in that space of time they traded away two outstanding defencemen in Bill Quackenbush and Leo Reise. Yet as long as they've got Kelly, they don't seem to be weakening their defence.

"The red head attacks like a great forward and defends like an even greater defenceman. There's nobody like him for taking the pressure off his own team and in a few seconds applying it to the other guys."

High praise indeed for a player who was supposed to be too slow to make the grade in the NHL.

"Toronto scouts thought I would never play 20 games in the NHL," recalled Kelly, who played his junior hockey in

---

DETROIT HONOURS:

- Stanley Cup champion 1949-50, 1951-52, 1953-54, 1954-55
- Won Norris Trophy 1953-54
- Won Lady Byng Trophy 1950-51, 1952-53, 1953-54
- Selected to NHL First All-Star Team 1950-51, 1951-52, 1952-53, 1953-54, 1954-55, 1956-57
- Selected to NHL Second All-Star Team 1949-50, 1955-56
- Played in NHL All-Star Game 1950, 1951, 1952, 1953, 1954, 1955, 1956, 1957, 1958, 1960
- Team captain, 1956-58.

the Toronto system with the the St. Michael's Majors, where Hall of Fame NHLer Joe Primeau, a member of the Maple Leafs' Kid Line in the 1930s, was Kelly's coach.

"Kelly wasn't much of a skater, but he was very strong," Primeau told the *Windsor Star*. "He had the big arms and legs of a ploughboy. He kept on getting better and better. His skating seemed to improve with every passing week."

It was with St. Michael's where Kelly made the conversion from forward to defence.

"Kelly started out as a left winger when he moved up to our junior A team," Primeau explained. "We lost a couple of defencemen to injuries, so we decided to shift a couple of our forwards—Eddie Sandford and Kelly—to defence. Sandford was out of his natural element as a defenceman, but Kelly took to the job like a duck takes to water."

St. Mike's was a powerhouse club. The Majors reached the Memorial Cup final in 1945-46 but lost to the Winnipeg Monarchs. The following spring, they were back in the Memorial Cup final and this time emerged victorious, sweeping the Moose Jaw Canucks in the best-of-seven final. Kelly collected five goals and 10 points in nine Memorial Cup games that season.

By this point in time, Kelly's hockey future was already secured by the Red Wings.

Detroit scout Carson Cooper, who scooped up Detroit left winger Ted Lindsay from the same St. Michael's squad in 1944, pounced on Kelly when the Leafs determined his skating wasn't of NHL caliber. A Maple Leafs scout bet Copper $20 that Kelly wouldn't play 20 games his rookie season. He played the entire 60-game schedule and was still playing in the NHL two decades later.

In fact, Kelly jumped directly into the Detroit lineup without a single game of minor-league seasoning, an accomplishment that was rare for any player, but almost unheard of where defencemen were concerned.

He played in the Stanley Cup final in each of his first three NHL seasons, finally tasting success in the spring of 1950 when the Wings downed the New York Rangers in a seven game final series. And Kelly won his first title playing much of the playoffs out of position.

In the opening game of Detroit's semifinal series with Toronto, Detroit's Howe suffered serious head injuries after crashing head first into the boards while trying to check Leafs captain Teeder Kennedy. With Howe lost for the playoffs, Detroit coach Tommy Ivan opted to shift Kelly up to forward, playing him in Howe's right wing spot alongside Lindsay and Sid Abel on Detroit's famed Production Line.

"We seemed to come together after that," Kelly said of the club's response to losing their star player. "The first two years, (Toronto) had bounced us in four straight games (in the 1948 and 1949 Cup final series), after we had gone seven games with Montreal in the semifinals."

Having made the move from forward to defence as a junior, adapting to a new position didn't present much of a challenge to Kelly. "There's no adjustment necessary," he said. "It's all part of the game of hockey. Each player knows

KELLY'S RED WINGS STATISTICS:										
	REGULAR SEASON					PLAYOFFS				
Season	GP	G	A	P	PIM	GP	G	A	P	PIM
1947-48	60	6	14	20	13	10	3	2	5	2
1948-49	50	5	11	16	10	11	1	1	2	10
1949-50	70	15	25	40	9	14	1	3	4	2
1950-51	70	17	37	54	24	6	0	1	1	0
1951-52	67	16	31	47	16	5	1	0	1	0
1952-53	70	19	27	46	8	6	0	4	4	0
1953-54	62	16	33	49	18	12	5	1	6	0
1954-55	70	15	30	45	28	11	2	4	6	17
1955-56	70	16	34	50	39	10	2	4	6	2
1956-57	70	10	25	35	18	5	1	0	1	0
1957-58	61	13	18	31	26	4	0	1	1	2
1958-59	67	8	13	21	34	-	-	-	-	-
1959-60	50	6	12	18	10	-	-	-	-	-
Totals	837	162	310	472	253	94	16	21	37	35

he has to backcheck and cover for his teammate. There's nothing scientific about that.

"You might set up plays differently, depending on the individual strategies of the respective coaches. That's when it may take a while to learn how to play defence.

"I was fortunate that when I started to play on defence with the Wings I played with all-stars such as Bill Quackenbush and Black Jack Stewart. Those were guys you could learn from. I remember one day Quackenbush said to me, 'Red, you're young, you do the skating. I'll be directing.' And that's what we did."

Quackenbush, Kelly's first defence partner in Detroit, also schooled him in the ways of playing the position without incurring penalties. In 1948-49 Quackenbush played the entire

60-game season without drawing a single penalty, becoming the first defenceman to earn the Lady Byng Trophy as the NHL's best combination of sportsmanlike play and ability.

"He showed me the subtle things you could do to avoid taking penalties, things like body positioning and using your stick to take the puck off an opponent," Kelly said.

The young redhead learned his lessons well. Kelly would be awarded the Lady Byng three times with the Wings, in 1950-51, 1952-53 and 1953-54. Up until 2011-12, when Florida's Brian Campbell won the award, Quackenbush and Kelly were the only defenceman to win the Lady Byng.

Detroit general manager Jack Adams immediately traded Quackenbush after his Lady Byng win, and Kelly, who also won the Lady Byng playing centre for Toronto in 1960-61, thinks people are under a misconception of what the award stands for.

"I never thought of the Lady Byng being about penalty minutes," Kelly said. "People look at the penalty minutes aspect, but to me, it's an award which goes to a player who displays sportsmanship. Don't tell me about a player's penalty minutes. Tell me how many goals are scored against the team when he is on the ice. I'll bet it's not too many.

"That's what matters, not that he doesn't get penalties, but that he doesn't get penalties and still gets the job done."

Lindsay, one of Detroit's more rugged players along with Howe and defencemen like Marcel Pronovost and Black Jack Stewart, felt this variation of themes played a significant role in the team's continued run atop the standings.

"That's what made our hockey club so successful," Lindsay said of their differing ways. "We had the right mix of styles and personalities."

The Red Wings of that era certainly got the job done. From 1948-49 through 1954-55, the club finished first overall in the NHL regular-season standings for a record seven consecutive seasons, winning the Stanley Cup four times and playing in a five Cup final series during this span of dominance.

"They were the things you dreamed about," Kelly said. "You never knew they were going to happen and then they

did happen. There were just so many good times that it would be difficult to pick just one outstanding moment."

Perhaps the most remarkable one was Detroit's finish to the 1954-55 campaign. The Wings trailed first place Montreal by as much as 10 points, but they lost just one of their last 16 games, finishing the regular season with a 12-game unbeaten run and a nine-game winning streak to track down the Canadiens.

It all came down to a home-and-home series starting in Montreal, the first game after the NHL had suspended Richard for the remainder of the season when he touched off a brawl in Boston and later attacked a game official.

On Montreal Forum ice, Detroit raced to a quick 4-1 lead by the end of the first period, when fan unrest ignited into a full-scale riot and the game was forfeited to the Red Wings.

"The (New York) Yankees had won (a North American sports record) six (straight regular-season titles) and we knew that," Kelly said. "We were trying to win that seventh one.

"We had the riot in Montreal and then we had to play the last game against them in our rink and we couldn't lose."

Back on home ice at Olympia Stadium, the Wings blasted the Canadiens 6-0. "We had to win both games and we did," Kelly said.

It proved to be huge, because in a seven-game Stanley Cup final series between the Red Wings and Canadiens, the home team won all seven games, Detroit taking the title with a 3-1 verdict in Game 7 at Olympia Stadium.

Kelly recalls that Detroit dynasty with a warm sense of fondness. "A bunch of us came in together and we had a strong sense of friendship," he said. "There were no egos. We were all close friends."

Within a few years, Kelly's sense of family in Detroit would be shattered. Insisting his all-star rearguard was slowing down, Adams dealt Kelly and young forward Billy McNeill to the New York Rangers on Feb. 5, 1960 for defenceman Bill Gadsby and agitating winger Eddie Shack.

"Kelly had lost his drive with us," Adams proclaimed.

Kelly certainly had no drive to move to New York and immediately announced his retirement. "A fellow has to quit sometime and now looks like a good time to me," Kelly said.

McNeill quickly followed suit and the deal was placed in limbo.

"My feelings were hurt," Kelly recalled of the trade to New York.

The root of Adams' decision to move Kelly appeared to be a magazine article that appeared earlier in the month in which Kelly was quoted as saying the team had ordered him to play late in the 1958-59 season, as Detroit fought for a playoff position, even though he was skating on a fractured ankle.

"In the story I was supposed to have said I played with a broken ankle last season," Kelly told the *Windsor Star*. "What I said was I had a broken bone below the ankle.

"There's no doubt about that. I saw the X-rays. But nobody forced me to play."

Clarence Campbell, president of the NHL, stepped in to try and arbitrate a settlement to the situation. "Kelly has been a great credit to the game and I personally feel he has many years of service left," Campbell said.

Adams was in no mood to forgive. "I will not take Kelly or McNeill back regardless of any future decision on their part," he said.

The deal was voided, but five days later, Kelly was shipped to the Leafs, the team that didn't want him all those years ago, in exchange for defenceman Marc Reaume.

Kelly felt he'd been betrayed by his old boss. "Jack Adams called me into his office one day and said he was going to groom me to be his successor," Kelly told *Canadian Press*. "But I was gone to Toronto two years later."

The Leafs converted Kelly to centre and he played in six more Stanley Cup finals with them, winning four more titles, two of them at the expense of the Red Wings, which delighted Kelly. "I'm finished with that town, particularly Jack Adams and his hockey team," Kelly told the *Montreal Gazette*. "If I never get back there again, it will be too soon."

Kelly's eight Stanley Cup wins are the most of any player who never played for the Canadiens. He's also the only active NHL player to have served as a Member of Parliament. Kelly

sat as a Liberal in the House of Commons from 1962-65, winning two elections in the York-Scarborough Ontario riding, and was actively involved in the development of the Canadian flag.

He retired as a player following Toronto's 1966-67 Cup triumph over Montreal, moving into coaching, where he helmed the Los Angeles Kings, Pittsburgh Penguins and the Leafs.

Kelly was elected to the Hockey Hall of Fame in 1969, was made a member of the Order of Canada in 2001 and long ago patched up his differences with Detroit.

"It's a great city with great fans," Kelly said. "And a great sports town."

7 SID ABEL

Centre/Left Wing

Born: February 22, 1918, Melville, Saskatchewan
Died: February 8, 2000
Shot: Left Height: 5-11 Weight: 170 lbs.
Red Wing From: 1938-39 to 1942-43; 1945-46 to 1951-52
Elected to Hockey Hall of Fame: 1969
Acquired: Signed to pro contract October 21, 1938.
Departed: Traded by Detroit to Chicago Blackhawks for cash and named player-coach of the Blackhawks, July, 29, 1952.

WHEN HE ARRIVED FOR TRAINING CAMP WITH THE DETROIT Red Wings in the fall of 1938, Sid Abel didn't exactly cause jaws to drop among the club's hockey operations staff. He was long-legged, skinny and physically didn't look very durable.

Goldie Smith, the scout who'd recommended Abel to Detroit coach-GM Jack Adams, simply nodded toward Abel's solid resumé of amateur work. In 1936-37, he scored seven goals in nine Memorial Cup games with the Saskatoon Wesleys. He followed up that performance with six goals in seven Allan Cup games for the Flon Flon Bombers in 1937-38.

That was enough to convince Smith that Abel was a player, and soon everyone in hockey would learn that Sid was definitely able.

He wasn't the best player to ever lace up his skates for the franchise, but few gave as much for as long and in as many capacities to the team as Abel would over his more than four decades of service to the Red Wings.

"You don't have to be great to win in this league," Abel told the *Windsor Star*. "You just have to work and battle for 60 minutes every game."

Abel captained the team for seven years, wearing the C for three Stanley Cup championships, tied with Steve Yzerman for the most in franchise history. Abel coached the Wings for a dozen years, guiding them to four Stanley Cups finals. He served as the general manager of the club for eight years, and later in life held forth as an analyst on Red Wings broadcasts well into the 1980s.

"He was the finest man that ever walked in a hockey rink," said former Detroit defenceman Gary Bergman, who played for Abel when he coached the Wings and grew to be a close friend.

Splitting his first two pro seasons between the Red Wings and their American League affiliates in Pittsburgh and Indianapolis, Abel finally made the NHL grade for good

47

DETROIT HONOURS:

- Stanley Cup champion 1942-43, 1949-50, 1951-52
- Won Hart Trophy 1948-49
- Selected to NHL First All-Star Team 1948-49, 1949-50
- Selected to NHL Second All-Star Team 1941-42, 1949-50
- Played in NHL All-Star Game 1948, 1949, 1950
- Team captain, 1942-43; 1946-52
- Led NHL in goals, 1948-49
- Led Stanley Cup playoffs in goals, 1949-50
- Led Red Wings in scoring, 1948-49
- Led Red Wings in assists, 1941-42
- Named NHL player of the year for 1949 by Sport Magazine
- Abel's No. 12 was retired by the Red Wings on April 29, 1995.

in 1940-41. Although he'd gain his most fame as centre on Detroit's Production Line between Gordie Howe and Ted Lindsay, it was as a left winger on the Wings' Liniment Line alongside Don Grosso and Eddie Wares that Abel would first come to prominence.

He produced 18 goals and 49 points in 1941-42 and earned NHL Second All-Star Team status on left wing that season. Detroit reached the Stanley Cup final in each of Abel's first three full NHL seasons. Early into his career, Adams recognized Abel's leadership qualities, and he was named captain of the Wings to begin the 1942-43 campaign.

"We all think Abel is the greatest guy in the world," Detroit forward George Gee told *Associated Press*. "Any of us would skate right through the backboards if he told us to."

Leading Detroit to a Stanley Cup final sweep of the Boston Bruins that spring, Abel produced five goals and 13 points in 10 playoff games. "I always felt that was my most memorable moment as a player," Abel said of that 1942-43 Cup triumph. "I was captain of that team and it was my first Cup."

After the season, Abel enlisted in the Royal Canadian Air Force and spent the next three years aiding the war effort during the Second World War. He returned to the Detroit lineup late in the 1945-46 season and immediately picked up where he'd left off in terms of leadership.

The Wings were a team in transition and young players who would become the core of the club's next dynasty—people like Lindsay, Howe, defencemen Red Kelly and Marcel Pronovost and goalie Terry Sawchuk—were either already in Detroit, or on their way to the big club.

Abel became a father figure to many of them as they got their feet wet in the NHL.

"I remember the first time I was in Sid Abel's company," Howe recalled. "I was nervous.

"I learned a lot from him from just listening. When I was around Sid, that's the way it was. He was our captain and our leader. He won in every aspect of the game."

At the time, Abel was one of the few Detroit players who had married, and even in matrimony there was a Red Wings connection. His wife, the former Gloria Morandy, worked as Adams' secretary.

"He was my father figure, my father away from home," Lindsay told the *Windsor Star* of Abel. "I was young; I was away from my father. Gordie and I used to go to their place for dinner.

"Gloria was like a mother to us. She was a wonderful lady who would cook all of us up some wonderful spaghetti dinners. It was a consoling thing for us."

Howe felt he got to see both sides of Abel. "Sid had a soft heart, but when he hit the ice he was very much a machine," Howe said.

When Detroit coach Tommy Ivan put the two young stars on Abel's wing in the late 1940s, there was instant chemistry as the Wings soared to the top of the NHL standings in 1948-49. Abel led the league with 28 goals and was awarded the Hart Trophy as the NHL's most valuable player. He was also selected to the NHL First All-Star Team at centre that season, becoming the first player to be selected to the all-star teams at two different positions.

| | ABEL'S RED WINGS STATISTICS: | | | | | | | | | |
| | REGULAR SEASON | | | | | PLAYOFFS | | | | |
Season	GP	G	A	P	PIM	GP	G	A	P	PIM
1938-39	15	1	1	2	0	6	1	2	2	2
1939-40	24	1	5	6	4	5	0	3	3	21
1940-41	47	11	22	33	29	9	2	2	4	2
1941-42	48	18	31	49	45	12	4	2	6	8
1942-43	48	18	24	42	33	10	5	8	13	4
1945-46	7	0	2	2	0	3	0	0	0	0
1946-47	60	19	29	48	29	3	1	1	2	2
1947-48	60	14	30	44	69	10	0	3	3	16
1948-49	60	28	26	54	49	11	3	3	6	6
1949-50	69	34	35	69	46	14	6	2	8	6
1950-51	60	23	38	61	30	6	4	3	7	0
1951-52	62	17	36	53	32	7	2	2	4	12
Totals	570	184	279	463	366	96	28	30	58	79

"He's a take-charge guy on the ice," Adams told the *Montreal Gazette* of Abel. "He needles Howe and Lindsay into giving everything they've got. Guys like him come along about once every 10 years."

Abel found it humorous that he would finish as the NHL's leading goal scorer. "I couldn't shoot a puck," he told the *Montreal Gazette*. "Why I used to get some goals because my shot was so slow, the goalie would reach out his hand and it wouldn't be there yet.

"I had a weak wrist—at least I thought it was weak—and I used to tape it up for the games for support, but with all that, I still couldn't break a pane of glass."

In 1949-50, Lindsay, Abel and Howe finished 1-2-3 in NHL scoring, launching a stretch of five straight seasons in which one of the members of the line would top the NHL scoring race. Add in Lindsay (1947-48) and Abel's (1948-49) stints as NHL goal-scoring leaders and for seven successive seasons, one of the Production Line led the league in a major production department.

The unit was looked upon as Howe and Lindsay raising Cain in the corners and getting the puck to Abel in the slot, and often that was indeed the case. The trio displayed an uncanny knack for always knowing where one another were on the ice. Abel would carom a shot off the boards right to the stick of the incoming Howe or Lindsay. "It took other teams about four years to figure out that play," Howe said.

"Sid always said he was limited in his talent," long-time Red Wings broadcaster Budd Lynch said. "He said, 'I just threw the puck in the corner and told them to go get it.'"

Abel could keep the fiery Lindsay in check and ignite a fire under the sometimes laconic Howe. Compared to the roughhouse tactics frequently deployed by Howe and Lindsay to gain an advantage on the ice, Abel was a pacifist, but he was hardly a Lady Byng Trophy contender.

"People don't realize how rough he was. Sid Abel was a rough, big guy, " Howe said, recalling a famous scrap between Abel and Montreal's ornery Maurice (Rocket) Richard.

"I got into a fight with Rocket Richard one time and Sid stuck his nose in." Howe knocked Richard to the ice with a punch, to the delight of Abel, who skated over to taunt the Montreal star.

"Today, if you called someone what Sid called Rocket, you'd get called up before a judge," Howe said. "Sid was leaning towards Rocket and Rocket bopped him in the nose. Just before Rocket hit him, Sid said, 'You've got to be tired,' and took him on. I couldn't help but laugh. Afterwards, Sid told me, 'Hell, if you tire them out, I'll fight anybody.'"

The punch left Abel's nose a twisted, bloody mess, forever earning him the nickname 'Old Bootnose.'

Detroit won another Stanley Cup in 1951-52, then the Production Line was broken up forever when Abel left the Wings to take over as player-coach of the Chicago

Blackhawks. In his first season there, Abel guided the Blackhawks into the playoffs for the first time in nine seasons, taking the eventual Cup champion Canadiens to a decisive seventh game before falling in the semifinals.

Abel's Detroit days, though, were long from being done. When illness overcame Red Wings coach Jimmy Skinner and he was forced to step down in early January 1958, Adams reached out to Abel, who'd been let go by the Blackhawks in 1954, to take over behind his old team's bench. Abel's first game as coach was a 2-1 loss at Montreal in which Skinner joined him behind the bench to help ease the transition. "I was never so nervous in my life," Abel told the *Montreal Gazette*.

His first home game as coach was a 3-2 win over the Toronto Maple Leafs, and already Abel was getting a taste for what drove Skinner out of the position. "This coaching is a lot tougher than playing," Abel told the *Windsor Star*. "A

couple of times in the third period I almost jumped on the ice myself when the Leafs were in our end."

With his patented dark suits, fedora and trademark horn-rimmed glasses, Abel struck a familiar figure behind the Detroit bench and a warm and welcoming note in the Red Wings' dressing room, where he was viewed as a players' coach.

"Sid was the best at relating to guys," Bergman recalled. "He knew when to kick you in the (butt) and when to pat you on the back. When he looked you in the eye and told you something, you knew it was the truth."

He preferred giving his players time off over seeking to whip them into shape, often taking his players to the racetrack as opposed to the rink.

"When you're forced to put on a uniform every day of the week it gets to be a chore," Abel told the *Montreal Gazette*. "In my last few years, I practiced only when I felt I needed it.

"I believe if you treat players the right way, you get more out of them. Most coaches believe you have to drive players to have them produce. I don't buy that. I'd rather have a happy hockey player than one who hates my guts."

The approach seemed to work. Abel guided the Wings to seven playoffs appearances as coach and to four trips to the Stanley Cup final, though none ended successfully. "Most of my memories as a coach were heatbreakers," Abel admitted.

Regardless, in 1964-65, he guided the club to first overall in the NHL for the first time since 1956-57 and the last time until 1994-95. After Detroit's first place-clinching victory, Abel got a telegram from Michigan governor George Romney noting that many had picked the team to miss the playoffs. "It just goes to show you the polls can be wrong," was Romney's message.

As well, Detroit's 1965-66 Stanley Cup final appearance under Abel's direction was the last time the Wings would play in a final series until the spring of 1995. Between 1958-77, Abel was the only Detroit coach to win a playoff game.

Shortly after the conclusion of the 1961-62 season, Abel wondered if it was all over for him when he was called to the office of Wings owner Bruce Norris. Instead, another new chapter was about to be written.

Adams, the club's GM since 1927, was retiring and Abel was to be his replacement, which at first he found uncomfortable. "Everything I have ever done in hockey has been with Mr. Adams," he told the *Windsor Star*. "I played for him, I coached for him, and I followed in his footsteps as general manager."

Norris couldn't think of a better choice to follow the legacy Adams had established in Detroit. "He has been a credit to this organization in every capacity and we have been pleased and fortunate to be associated with him," Norris told *Associated Press* of Abel's credentials.

Deposed as GM in 1971, Abel went to St. Louis and later Kanas City in both coaching and management roles before returning to Detroit in the broadcast booth.

As the Detroit franchise sunk into it's 'Dead Wings' era, missing the playoffs in 15 of 17 seasons between 1966-67 through 1982-83, Abel's no-nonsense approach won him cult-hero status among Red Wings fans and saw him called on the carpet by management more than once due to his refusal to sugarcoat the club's many deficiencies. "Sid's voice is in my head forever," former Wings forward and current team broadcaster Mickey Redmond said.

George Baier, a disc jockey with Detroit's WRIF-FM, paid tribute to Abel's style by creating an on-air character based after him entitled "Sid Disabled."

A self-proclaimed rink rat, early in his playing days Abel would often stay after games and join fans in public skating sessions at Olympia Stadium. "I was just looking to meet girls," he claimed. He endeared himself to arena staff, always taking time to talk hockey with the workers, and Abel never turned down an autograph request from a fan.

"He was about as wonderful a person as you would ever want to meet," Wings team statistician Greg Innis said.

In April of 1995, the Wings held a pre-game ceremony to retire Abel's No. 12 sweater. The large red banner with the No. 12 emblazoned across it rose to the Joe Louis Arena rafters and settled in its proper place, between Nos. 9 (Howe) and 7 (Lindsay).

"To go up there between my old buddies Gordie and Ted again is a very touching moment," Abel said.

Five years later, heart disease claimed Abel's life at the age of 81.

8 SERGEI FEDOROV

Centre

Born: December 13, 1969, Pskov, Russia
Shot: Left Height: 6-1 Weight: 200 lbs.
Red Wing From: 1990-91 to 2002-03
Acquired: Selected 74th overall in June 17, 1989 NHL entry draft.
Departed: Signed as a free agent by Anaheim Ducks, July 19, 2003.

HE COULD MAKE THE PUCK DANCE LIKE A PUPPET ON A string. He could skate with the speed of a race car and manoeuver through opponents like a piece of paper blowing in the breeze. Without the puck, he was capable of frustrating the most skilled players in the game.

There only seemed to be one thing that Sergei Fedorov couldn't do during his tenure as a Detroit Red Wing and that was win over the fans to his side.

Citing his list of accomplishments—he's the only Red Wing to win the Hart Trophy as NHL MVP in the past 50 years, and was twice awarded the Selke Trophy as the NHL's best defensive forward—there was no doubting Fedorov's ability at both ends of the ice.

Looking at what he did just to play for the team, the courage he showed by walking away from the Soviet national team during the 1990 Goodwill Games in Seattle to pursue his dream of playing in the NHL, it was difficult to fathom that people would question Fedorov's commitment. Yet this was frequently the case.

Over his Detroit career, Red Wings fans remained cool towards Fedorov. Some resented him for his five-month contract holdout in 1997-98. With others, it's simply Don Cherry-like jingoism.

Fedorov once stated that if his name was Sam Jones, people wouldn't be as harsh in their criticism. He might have had a point.

DETROIT HONOURS:

- Stanley Cup champion 1996-97, 1997-98, 2001-02
- Won Hart Trophy, 1993-94
- Won Selke Trophy, 1993-94, 1995-96
- Won Lester B. Pearson Award, 1993-94
- Selected to NHL First All-Star Team, 1993-94
- Selected to NHL All-Rookie Team, 1990-91
- Played in NHL All-Star Game, 1992, 1994, 1996
- Led Stanley Cup playoffs in points, 1994-95
- Led Stanley Cup playoffs in assists, 1994-95, 1995-96
- Led Stanley Cup playoffs in goals, 1997-98
- Led Red Wings in goals, assists and points, 1993-94, 1995-96
- Led Red Wings in goals, 2000-01
- Led Red Wings in assists and points, 2002-03
- Won silver medal with Russia at 1998 Nagano Winter Olympic Games
- Won bronze medal with Russia at 2002 Salt Lake City Winter Olympic Games
- Played for Soviet Union in 1991 Canada Cup
- Played for Russia in 1996 World Cup of Hockey.

Regardless, it would be folly to suggest he was not one of the greatest players ever to wear the winged wheel. The accolades may not have always been there, but the talent and the numbers always were.

Former NHL defenceman Jamie Macoun remembered how excited he was to be traded by the Toronto Maple Leafs to Detroit in 1998 and be offered the chance to team up with Fedorov.

"There was a lot of relief, knowing I didn't have to defend against him anymore," Macoun said. "He had such great ability and great talent, and you just gained so much more respect for what he could do, getting the chance to watch him on a daily basis.

"His speed was unbelievable and he could turn on a dime."

Larry Murphy, another defenceman who joined the Wings from Toronto, just smiled when asked about his memories of Fedorov. "You mean Mr. Impact?" Murphy said. When a big goal was needed, or a one-goal lead was in need of being maintained, Fedorov was the guy the Wings counted on to get the job done.

"He was outstanding, but it's not like we were ever surprised by that fact," Murphy said. "He always played that well for us. That was just Sergei doing his thing."

A seeming longshot to play in Detroit when the Wings drafted him in 1989 while he was still behind the Iron Curtain, Fedorov was whisked away from the Soviet national team while they were in Seattle in July of 1990.

"It was a mutual kind of thing," recalled former Red Wings vice-president Jim Lites, who was a key player in helping get Fedorov to Detroit. "Sergei had talked to lawyers in the U.S. and was well aware of what had to be done."

Bryan Murray, at the time Detroit's coach and general manager, experienced a similar situation during his days as coach of the Washington Capitals when Michal Pivonka fled Czechoslovakia to play for the Capitals.

"It was very much the same, but I think Fedorov had more going for him," Murray said. "He was very dedicated. He had that drive to be successful.

"I'd seen him at the World hockey championships. The thing that I liked about him that was not very common with European players in that era was that he was very willing to go into traffic or into the corners to make a play."

Murray's assessment was proven correct when Fedorov, in a foreign country, with no family support and unable to speak the language, finished with 31-48-79 totals in 77 games during the 1990-91 campaign, coming in second behind Chicago Blackhawks goalie Ed Belfour in the Calder Trophy balloting for the NHL's rookie of the year.

Fedorov wasn't surprised that his transition seemed so seamless. "I was 20, but I came from an entirely different background, the Soviet system," he said. "I had four years of playing for (legendary coach) Viktor Tikhonov at Red Army. I already had many big competitions under my belt."

His numbers progressed steadily with each passing season. "My first year over here, I came to the United States and lived the good life for first time," Fedorov said. "After that, I must do a little more for the team. I had responsibilities."

FEDOROV'S RED WINGS STATISTICS:

	Regular Season					Playoffs				
Season	GP	G	A	P	PIM	GP	G	A	P	PIM
1990-91	77	31	48	79	66	7	1	5	6	4
1991-92	80	32	54	86	72	11	5	5	10	8
1992-93	73	34	53	87	72	7	3	6	9	23
1993-94	82	56	64	120	34	7	1	7	8	6
1994-95	42	20	30	50	24	17	7	17	24	6
1995-96	78	39	68	107	48	19	2	18	20	10
1996-97	74	30	33	63	30	20	8	12	20	12
1997-98	21	6	11	17	25	22	10	10	20	12
1998-99	77	26	37	63	66	10	1	8	9	8
1999-00	68	27	35	62	22	9	4	4	8	4
2000-01	75	32	37	69	40	6	2	5	7	0
2001-02	81	31	37	68	36	23	5	14	19	20
2002-03	80	36	47	83	52	4	1	2	3	0
Totals	908	400	554	954	587	162	50	113	163	113

It was the 1993-94 season when Fedorov exploded into prominence. After a herniated disc pushed Detroit captain Steve Yzerman to the sidelines in late October, Fedorov stepped forward and took a step up.

He collected 120 points, second in the NHL to Wayne Gretzky, and turned heads around the league. Hockey people knew Fedorov was a good one. Now, they debated whether anyone in the game was better.

"That's the best hockey player in the world," an NHL scout suggested while watching Fedorov tear up the league. Such sentiments were echoed in the Red Wing dressing room, where Fedorov continued to amaze everyone on a daily basis.

"That is just an exceptional hockey player," Detroit coach Scotty Bowman said at the time. "He might be the best player in the NHL right now."

Even the Great One bowed in reverence. "As far as I'm concerned, Sergei Fedorov is probably the best player in the game," Gretzky said.

That opinion was affirmed when Fedorov was awarded the Hart Trophy as league MVP at the end of the season. Fedorov was the first Red Wing to win the Hart since Gordie Howe in 1962-63.

"When such things were said about me, I felt good about it," Fedorov recalled of the lofty praise. "It made me feel proud to hear that people thought such things about me."

Defining Fedorov's game wasn't an easy task. He didn't fit into any specific mold. "I didn't play American style, I didn't play Soviet style," he said. "I think that good players build their own style."

Stopping him was an equally difficult assignment. "He was not the kind of guy you could put one man on," former NHL coach Ron Wilson said. "He was going to get free."

Though his offensive totals were always impressive, they did not leave much of an impression on the man who compiled them.

"Everybody wanted to talk about points, but I did not worry about points," Fedorov said. "The game is not about points and what happens in the offensive zone. The game is about what you do without the puck."

Hockey people were in agreement that Fedorov's responsibility when his team was looking to stop the opposition was also without parallel. His two Selke Trophies as the NHL's best defensive forward included 1993-94, making Fedorov the only player in NHL history to win the Hart and Selke in the same season.

"I just worked hard and tried to be better every day," Fedorov said. "I liked playing against the big lines. I liked to be challenged. I liked to have the important job to do."

It seemed that winning the Selke meant as much to Fedorov as the Hart, supposedly the single most important individual honour in the game.

"Hockey is a lot of little things," Fedorov explained. "You have to have pretty good responsibility in your defensive zone. If you have fast players who can handle the puck, if you take care of your own end of the ice and do not give up the puck in the neutral zone, then the goals will come, because you have the speed and the puck control and you are not making the mistakes which will cost your team a goal.

"If you work hard and take care of your own end, the points will come. And it does not matter who gets the goals, as long as we got the goals. What mattered was winning."

It was suggested by his detractors that winning didn't mean as much to Fedorov as it did to other players on the Wings, citing as Exhibit A his 1997-98 holdout, when he missed the first half of the NHL season in a contract dispute with the club as the Wings sought to defend their first Stanley Cup title since 1955.

In truth, the sitting out ate Fedorov up inside. "Deep down in my head, I always wanted to keep playing for the Red Wings," said Fedorov, who got his wish when the Wings matched a six-year, $38-million offer sheet from the Carolina Hurricanes, even though it meant paying him $28 million in bonuses that season, including a $12-million bonus for leading Detroit to the conference finals.

"I had no idea where I'd be," Fedorov remembered of the prolonged negotiations, which lasted until late February. "For a long time, I didn't feel I'd ever be in Detroit again."

While he was waiting for his contract situation to be resolved and living life in hockey limbo, Fedorov would sometimes talk with his Red Wings teammates.

"They'd say, 'Don't worry about it,'" Fedorov remembered. "'Everything will work out. You'll be back. We're going to repeat and you're going to be a big part of it.'"

How right they were. Fedorov returned and the Wings steamrolled their way to a second straight Stanley Cup as he led all playoff scorers with 10 goals, tying a franchise playoff record.

Fedorov's goal with 4:51 left in regulation in Game 3 of the 1998 Cup final series at the MCI Center gave Detroit a 2-1 win over the Washington Capitals and a 3-0 lead in the series.

The goal was pure Fedorov. Bearing down on Washington defenceman Calle Johansson, Fedorov faked inside, stepped to the outside and rifled a shot past Caps goalie Olaf Kolzig.

"He turned nothing into a game-winning goal," Detroit centre Kris Draper remembered. "We had a good year going, but when we got Sergei back, we were ready for a great run. He was a gamebreaker."

Some suggested he made the game look easy, but Fedorov would laugh when he'd hear such a notion.

"It looked maybe easy, but I don't think anything about hockey is easy," Fedorov said.

What impressed teammates and opponents even more about Fedorov beyond his uncanny natural ability was his work ethic. "He was a guy who was committed to working hard," former Detroit teammate Stu Grimson said.

Those close to Fedorov felt that people mistook his lack of outward expression for a lack of passion.

"His greatness was that he was a cerebral player," suggested Ken Hitchcock, who coached Fedorov toward the end of his career with the Columbus Blue Jackets. "He played with limited emotion, but tremendous positional play with and without the puck.

"He managed the games. He organized the line he played with and he organized the defence pair. He was always in a position to get you out of trouble. He was always there. He was there for wingers; he was there for the D. He'd go in and pull it off the boards when you were in trouble. You'd get spinning and he'd just go in and settle it down in our zone."

There was little Fedorov couldn't do on the ice. He could work as a checking centre, or on a scoring forward line. He could quarterback a power play, or create havoc as half a penalty-killing tandem.

When injuries crippled the Wings' back end one season, Bowman filled the void by dropping Fedorov back to the defence. Bowman felt Fedorov could have won a Norris Trophy had he stayed in the position, because his ability to pass the puck was so top notch.

"Thanks, Scotty, I guess," Fedorov said. "That's quite a compliment."

About the only place Fedorov didn't look comfortable was between the pipes, recalling his brief fling as a netminder as a youngster in Russia. "I played the first period and was minus-two,'" remembered Fedorov, who quickly answered "No thank you" when asked if he would have liked to add goaltending to his NHL resume.

"I came back as a forward for the last two periods and we won that game 18-2. I played on the same team with (former NHLer) Roman Oksiuta and we each scored six or seven goals."

Fedorov won another Stanley Cup with the Wings in 2001-02, but a year later when his contract was up, the Wings let him go and he signed with the Anaheim Ducks. He also played in Columbus and then Washington before leaving the NHL for good after the 2008-09 season.

Fedorov spent three seasons in the Russian KHL, then in 2012, took over as general manager of the Red Army team in that league, the same club he played for from 1986-90.

Fedorov the GM admitted he's thriving on the challenge of assembling his own club. "Enjoying it? Yes," Fedorov said. "Learning all the time? Yes. Involved in every aspect of the team? Yes.

"The hockey part of it is not new to me. I learned a lot about the game and how it works from my time in North America and in terms of experience, I am using those lessons and that experience to help me now."

Though he's a long way from Hockeytown, Fedorov still fondly recalls his time in Detroit.

"I spent my best years there and we won a few championships there," Fedorov said.

9 ALEX DELVECCHIO

Centre/Left Wing

Born: December 4, 1932, Fort William, Ontario
Shot: Left **Height:** 6-0 **Weight:** 195 lbs.
Red Wing From: 1950-51 to 1973-74
Elected to Hockey Hall of Fame: 1977
Acquired: Signed to pro contract March 24, 1951.
Departed: Retired as player and named coach of Detroit, November 7, 1973.

IN 2011, NICKLAS LIDSTROM ADDED TO DETROIT'S dominance as a one-team city for pro athletes when he played his 20th NHL season, all with the Red Wings.

Lidstrom became the sixth Detroit player from one of the four major North American sports—NHL, NBA, MLB and NFL—to have played 20 seasons all in one city. "I did not know that," said Lidstrom, who joined Red Wings Alex Delvecchio (24) and Steve Yzerman (22), Detroit Tigers Al Kaline (21) and Alan Trammell (20) and Detroit Lions kicker Jason Hanson (21). "I guess I'm in some nice company then."

Later in the season he played his 1,550th NHL game, all with the Wings, surpassing longtime Wings captain Delvecchio to acquire the NHL record for games played by a player whose career was spent entirely with one team. In fact, Detroit players hold down the top three spots in this unique category—Lidstrom (1,564), Delvecchio (1,549) and Steve Yzerman (1,514).

"It means a lot to me," Lidstrom said after breaking the record. "Mr. Delvecchio was down here during the last game. I had a chance to meet him. It means a lot to me to be able to play with one team throughout my career and moving up, especially moving ahead of such a legend as Alex Delvecchio."

Delvecchio was proud to pass on his mark to a fellow Red Wing. "He's a great hockey player," Delvecchio said. "To be truthful, I didn't even know I had any record for playing games. All I wanted to do was play hockey. But I can't think of a better person to beat it than Nick. I wish him all the best. He's a good player. He's not that rough and tough on the ice, but he handles himself, checks well and has a great shot. He's just a leader out there."

So was the guy that Wings teammates playfully nicknamed Fats because of the seemingly ever-present baby fat in Delvecchio's cheeks. But the man who would play nearly a quarter century with the Red Wings was hardly a baby when he launched his hockey career. Delvecchio was 12 when he played his first organized hockey in his hometown of Fort William, Ont.

Within three years, Delvecchio was attending the Wings' training camp as a wide-eyed 15-year-old with big dreams. "I guess they thought highly of me, because I was able to

59

DETROIT HONOURS:
* Stanley Cup champion 1951-52, 1953-54, 1954-55
* Won Lady Byng Trophy 1958-59, 1965-66, 1968-69
* Selected to NHL Second All-Star Team 1952-53, 1958-59
* Played in NHL All-Star Game, 1953, 1954, 1955, 1956, 1957, 1958, 1959, 1961, 1962, 1963, 1964, 1965, 1967
* Won Lester Patrick Trophy, 1974
* Team captain, 1962-73
* Holds Red Wings consecutive games played record of 548
* Delvecchio's No. 10 was retired by the Red Wings on November 10, 1991.

play a couple shifts with Gordie Howe and Ted Lindsay," Delvecchio recalled. "Sid Abel was their centre iceman, so they had their line, but it still meant so much to me."

Detroit assigned Delvecchio to its Oshawa junior affiliate in the Ontario Hockey Association, where he was schooled in the ways of the game by Larry Aurie, a Red Wings legend who was a key player on the club's back-to-back Stanley Cup winners in 1935-36 and 1936-37.

"I left the Lakehead when I was 18 to play with the Oshawa Generals and the next year I turned pro with Detroit," Delvecchio said.

The Wings called him up for a game against Montreal toward the end of the 1950-51 season. Delvecchio, who'd finished his OHA season with Oshawa with a league-leading 72 assists and 121 points, was rushed to Detroit when the Generals' season ended, signing his first NHL contract in the lobby of Olympia Stadium.

He remembered that he hardly saw the ice, but that didn't seem to matter to Delvecchio. He was in the NHL, after all. "The players were great guys," recalled Delvecchio. "They welcomed you as someone who could help the team, not as someone who was going to take your job."

After just six games of seasoning with Detroit's American League affiliate in Indianapolis the next season, Delvecchio was summoned to the Red Wings, where he'd play for the next 23 years.

"It was unbelievable," Delvecchio recalled of making the NHL. "You'd ask yourself, 'How can this be?' It was an awesome feeling, playing with guys like Terry (Sawchuk), Gordie, Teddy, Sid, Leo Reise and Bob Goldham on defence."

The veteran Wings took Delvecchio under their wing and offered a helping hand to the rookie, but with a subtle approach.

"We did a lot of train travel and after the games, you always met and had a discussion of what went on and who was causing problems," Delvecchio said. "It just helped you in your next game.

"If you had a bad game, they didn't bring it up at all. They just let it slide. You knew if you had to try better next game."

That didn't seem to be an issue for Delvecchio, who produced 15 goals and 22 points as Detroit won the Stanley Cup in 1951-52. The next season, his 43 assists were second on the team behind Howe, and Delvecchio's 59 points were third after Howe and Lindsay.

"Years ago playing in the NHL, there was a lot of pride involved," Delvecchio said. "You had to play to survive. If

DELVECCHIO'S RED WINGS STATISTICS:										
		REGULAR SEASON				PLAYOFFS				
Season	GP	G	A	P	PIM	GP	G	A	P	PIM
1950-51	1	0	0	0	0	-	-	-	-	-
1951-52	65	15	22	37	22	8	0	3	3	4
1952-53	70	16	43	59	28	6	2	4	6	2
1953-54	69	11	18	29	34	12	2	7	9	7
1954-55	69	17	31	48	37	11	7	8	15	2
1955-56	70	25	26	51	24	10	7	3	10	2
1956-57	48	16	25	41	8	5	3	2	5	2
1957-58	70	21	38	59	22	4	0	1	1	0
1958-59	70	19	35	54	6	-	-	-	-	-
1959-60	70	19	28	47	8	6	2	6	8	0
1960-61	70	27	35	62	26	11	4	5	9	0
1961-62	70	26	43	69	18	-	-	-	-	-
1962-63	70	20	44	64	8	11	3	6	9	2
1963-64	70	23	30	53	11	14	3	8	11	0
1964-65	68	25	42	67	16	7	2	3	5	2
1965-66	70	31	38	69	16	12	0	11	11	4
1966-67	70	17	38	55	10	-	-	-	-	-
1967-68	74	22	48	70	14	-	-	-	-	-
1968-69	72	25	58	83	8	-	-	-	-	-
1969-70	73	21	47	68	24	4	0	2	2	0
1970-71	73	21	34	55	6	-	-	-	-	-
1971-72	75	20	43	65	22	-	-	-	-	-
1972-73	77	18	53	71	13	-	-	-	-	-
1973-74	11	1	4	5	2	-	-	-	-	-
Totals	1549	456	825	1281	383	121	35	69	104	29

you'd have injuries, sickness, or anything, you didn't want to sit out because if they took you out you might not get back in. You'd be out of a job.

"In the old days, you could be bawled out, yelled at and threatened. You can't do that now."

The players lived in fear of retribution for any miscreant deed. "I remember one time, Gordie called and said, 'Let's go skiing,'" Delvecchio recalled. "We weren't supposed to ski. It was in our contracts.

"I had everything all packed and was ready to go, but then I thought, 'If Gordie Howe breaks his leg skiing, the team will forgive him. If I break my leg skiing, they might not be as forgiving.'

"I called Gordie and told him he'd better go by himself."

Delvecchio, who negotiated every one of his contracts on his own without the help of an agent until 1970, remembered what it was like to talk contract in that era, if talking was in fact the appropriate term.

"I'll tell you, when you sat down with the late Jack Adams, there wasn't too much negotiating, but he was always fair," Delvecchio said.

When Abel left the Wings in 1952 to take over as player-coach in Chicago, Detroit coach Tommy Ivan inserted Delvecchio into his spot between Howe and Lindsay on the team's top forward line.

"They didn't bring me up to replace Sid," Delvecchio told *NHL.com*. "We were on the Red Wings together for a year before they traded him to Chicago. I wasn't trying to replace Sid, just become a member of the Red Wings. I worked hard and wanted to be a regular with the team and eventually when I got to play with Gordie and Ted, that just made me try harder. I wanted to be excellent and an asset to their careers.

"I probably had the greatest hockey player in history on my line in Gordie Howe. He could do so many things with the puck and he could score goals. The older guys on the team, Bob Goldham and Marty Pavelich, just told me to get the puck to the big guy and don't worry about my scoring.

Then I had Ted Lindsay on the other side and he could put the puck in the net too, a scoring champion one year. I just concentrated on feeding those guys."

It turned into a long-running relationship. Delvecchio was Howe's centre almost exclusively from that day until Howe retired from the Red Wings after the 1970-71 season.

Over the years, there were several changes to the third party in the group. When Lindsay was dealt to Chicago in 1957, several wingers got try-outs. In 1958-59, Abel, now Detroit's coach, shifted Delvecchio to left wing and moved Norm Ullman into the centre spot on the line.

It led to a huge campaign for Delvecchio, who was voted to the left wing position on the NHL's Second All-Star Team. He'd already been named an NHL Second All-Star at centre in 1952-53.

On top of his all-star selection, Delvecchio, who garnered just six penalty minutes all season, was awarded the Lady Byng Trophy as the NHL's most impressive package of gentlemanly play and productivity.

During his 24-season career, Delvecchio was assessed just 383 penalty minutes, or 15 less than Bob Probert's 1987-88

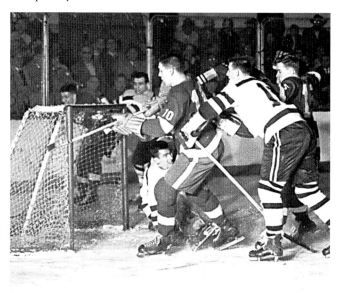

Detroit club record. "I think I had maybe five fights my whole career," Delvecchio said, crediting Aurie for setting him on the straight and narrow when it came to committing fouls and Adams for reinforcing the notion once he got to Detroit.

"Larry told me I was no value to the Generals in the box," Delvecchio said. "And when I got up to Detroit, Adams said the same thing when I took a few chippy, foolish penalties. Adams told me, 'If you want to stay here, you'd better stay out of that box.' I sure wanted to stay, so I forgot the chippiness."

Delvecchio's clean play earned him two more Lady Byngs during his playing days, but not everyone was impressed. After his first Byng win, amidst rumours he was about to be shipped to Toronto for a package of players, Maple Leafs coach and GM Punch Imlach lit into Delvecchio's style of game.

"Do you think I'm crazy enough to give up four players for one?" Imlach asked *Associated Press*. "Is Delvecchio that good? He didn't score 20 goals and he didn't get more than a couple of penalties. So what was the guy doing?

"My only conclusion is that Delvecchio was doing nothing. I don't care who it is, no player in this league can go through 70 games and get only a couple of penalties. He's bound to trip or board someone.

"I don't want any Lady Byng winners on my club. I'll fine any player who wins the Byng Trophy."

That was fine with the Wings, who were delighted to have Delvecchio in their lineup, one of the most durable and consistent players in the game. He captained the Wings from 1962-73, longer than any player in team history other than Yzerman. Delvecchio scored at least 20 goals in 13 of his 24 campaigns. He registered 50 or more points 17 times. "Alex was the most underrated player in the game," Hall of Famer Phil Esposito said.

A broken ankle early in the 1956-57 season cost Delvecchio 22 games on the sideline, but he returned with a vengeance. Delvecchio launched a club-record consecutive games streak of 548 upon his return and missed just 16 games the remainder of his playing days.

Almost all of those games were played skating alongside Howe. Delvecchio was Howe's centre when he set the club record with 49 goals in 1952-53, and he assisted on Howe's 700th tally. He also centred Howe and Frank Mahovlich in 1968-69, when Howe produced the first 100-point season in Red Wings history.

"He is an all-star without a title," Howe said of Delvecchio, but it was a mutual admiration society.

"I wouldn't have done half of what I have done without him," Delvecchio told *Sport Magazine* of playing in Howe's shadow. "And I guess he couldn't have done half of what he has done without me.

"Being associated with a guy like Gordie and guys like Frank Mahovlich and Ted Lindsay, they just made you play better. If you wanted to stay with them, you'd better learn how to play the game."

In 1970, new Detroit coach Ned Harkness experimented with Howe on defence but quickly scuttled the idea when he saw how it was affecting Delvecchio's game. "It's like

taking Alex's right hand away from him when Gordie isn't playing on the line," Harkness told *United Press*.

When he started the 1969-70 season by going 30 games without scoring, Delvecchio pondered retirement, but soon reconsidered. "The retirement business last spring was only a tentative thought," Delvecchio told the *Windsor Star* in 1970. "In my mind, I know now I can play another year or two."

Milestones were coming his way fast and furious. In 1966, he became the fifth player in Stanley Cup history to collect 100 points. On Dec. 15, 1968 against the Minnesota North Stars, Delvecchio became the third NHL player to record 600 assists. On Feb. 16, 1969 Delvecchio became the third NHLer to record 1,000 points, with an assist in a 6-3 victory over the Los Angeles Kings. Then on Oct. 28, 1970 he scored his 400th and 401st goals in 5-3 win over Boston, becoming the sixth NHLer to do so. Howe picked up his 1,000th assist on the second goal.

Finally, on Nov. 26, 1972 Delvecchio scored a goal against California's Gilles Meloche for his 1,220th point to move into second on the NHL's all-time scoring list behind Howe. "Forget about me ever being No. 1," Delvecchio said at the time. "I'll have to be happy with No. 2."

By now, Howe was gone, but Delvecchio soldiered on. In 1972-73, he was Mickey Redmond's centre as Redmond set a Wings club record, becoming the franchise's first 50-goal scorer. "Certainly Alex was a big factor in Redmond getting 52 goals," Detroit coach Ted Garvin told *Associated Press*, a fact Redmond doesn't debate.

"Alex deserved a lot of the credit for any success I had," Redmond said. "He got you the puck; he laid it right in there on your stick. He was terrific."

Delvecchio's 71 points in 1972-73 remain the third-highest total ever posted in an NHL season by a player 40 or older, trailing only Howe's 103 points in 1968-69 and the 86 points posted by Boston's John Bucyk in 1975-76. That summer, Delvecchio turned down a lucrative offer to join Howe in Houston, where he was launching a comeback with the WHA Aeros, signing on for another tour with the Wings.

With the Wings floundering early into the 1973-74 campaign, the Wings fired Garvin and named Delvecchio as replacement. "I've joined the ulcer department," Delvecchio joked.

Wings owner Bruce Norris felt Delvecchio was the sort of leader who would be capable of getting the team headed in the right direction. "The high morale on this team is directly attributable to Delvecchio," Norris said, a sentiment that was echoed by GM Harkness.

"We picked Alex because of his leadership," Harkness said. "He is a statesman in hockey. He has the charisma to turn the club around."

The next season, Delvecchio replaced Harkness as GM. "Well, I tried to be a GM," laughed Delvecchio, who didn't succeed at the task and was replaced in 1977 by his old linemate Lindsay.

"It takes a different breed to be coach or GM," Delvecchio said. "You can't play hockey forever … only Gordie Howe can do that."

Inducted into the Hockey Hall of Fame in 1977, Delvecchio had been a Red Wing forever, a fact that was given the ultimate acknowledgement in 1991 when his No. 10 sweater was retired and lifted into the Joe Louis Arena rafters.

"This is a tremendous honor," Delvecchio said as he stood at the podium with his family. "I've been inducted into the Hall of Fame, I've won Stanley Cups, but this is better."

Delvecchio remains in the Detroit area. He's run his own promotions company for many years, is active in the club's alumni association and is often seen at Wings games.

"A great sports town," Delvecchio said of Detroit. "And not just for hockey. I'm surprised at how many people remember Alex Delvecchio."

10 PAVEL DATSYUK

Centre

Born: July 20, 1978, Sverdlovsk, Russia
Shoots: Left **Height:** 5-11 **Weight:** 197 lbs.
Red Wing From: 2001-02 to present
Acquired: Selected 171st overall by Detroit in June 27, 1998 NHL Entry Draft.

THE DETROIT RED WINGS LOVE TO TALK ABOUT THE amazing talents of Pavel Datsyuk, but there's one feat he performs that they insist everyone must see to believe, and it has nothing to do with pucks.

During the club's annual charity golf tournament, Datsyuk will tee up the ball and then pace off 10 yards directly behind the ball. He'll stop, turn, run toward the golf ball and hammer it 250 yards down the heart of the fairway.

The Happy Gilmore drive.

That's hand-eye coordination.

That's Datsyuk.

"He makes unbelievable moves that we've never seen before," former Detroit defenceman Mathieu Dandenault said.

On the golf course and, most especially, on the ice.

"I don't know of a player in the NHL who handles the puck as well as Pavel and does the creative things that he does," former Detroit teammate Brendan Shanahan said. "It's a part of the game we're losing, because most coaches don't allow their players to try the things that Pavel can do."

While many bench bosses in the hockey world seek to turn hockey into a paint-by-numbers game, Datsyuk remains an abstract artist, a Picasso with puck and stick.

"What he's capable of on the ice, it's remarkable," former Detroit teammate Kris Draper said. "You don't know what he is going to do. You don't know where he's going to go. All you try to do when you play with him is get open and stay out of his way."

At the rink, no one's capable of mimicking the moves mastered by Datsyuk. "It's entertaining," Shanahan said, before paying Datsyuk the ultimate compliment. "I'd buy a ticket to watch him play."

Opponents bow in equal reverence to the way Datsyuk can make the puck dance. "He's a leader for them on offence and defence," former NHL goalie Martin Biron said. "He works so hard in his own end to get the puck back. He's a difference maker."

"He's such a dynamic player," added long-time defenceman Ed Jovanovski. "He's strong on his skates and he's got more moves than a lot of guys in this league. You have to pay attention to where he is at all times."

DETROIT HONOURS:

- Stanley Cup champion 2001-02, 2007-08
- Won Lady Byng Trophy, 2005-06, 2006-07, 2007-08, 2008-09
- Won Selke Trophy, 2007-08, 2008-09, 2009-10
- Named to NHL Second All-Star Team, 2008-09
- Played in NHL All-Star Game, 2004, 2008, 2012
- Led NHL in plus/minus, 2007-08
- Played for Russia in 2002, 2006, 2010 and 2014 Winter Olympic Games, winning bronze medal at 2002 Salt Lake City Winter Games
- Played for Russia in 2005 World Cup of Hockey
- Played for Russia in 2003, 2005, 2010 and 2012 World Championship, winning gold medal in 2012, silver medal in 2010 and bronze medal in 2005
- Led Red Wings in goals, assists and points, 2003-04, 2005-06, 2006-07, 2007-08, 2008-09
- Led Red Wings in goals and points, 2009-10, 2012-13

The kids would label what Datsyuk is capable of doing with a puck as "sick," but New York Rangers defenceman Keith Yandle is willing to up the adjective ante on Datsyuk's dangling efforts. "The guy is disgusting," Yandle said with admiration. "It is fun to watch him, but not fun to play against him."

People still talk about the magical play Datsyuk attempted to execute on a Detroit goal scored during the 2011 Stanley Cup playoffs against the Coyotes.

Bursting into the clear down the right wing, as he cut to the net, Datsyuk fired a shot on goal between his legs. Coyotes' goalie Ilya Bryzgalov snaked out his right pad to parry the drive, but kicked it directly onto the waiting stick of Darren Helm, who buried it into the twine.

How many NHLers would have the courage … nay, the bravado, to snap a shot between their legs in a Stanley Cup game? "Maybe a handful of guys," former Wings captain Nicklas Lidstrom estimated. "Not more than that.

"We'd see him in practice all of the time, trying different things. He's not shy to try them in games, either.

"He's very strong. He can lean on guys and have one hand on his stick to fight them off for the puck. With his determination, other players might hang onto the puck, but they won't make that next play. He will, because of his awareness of where the puck should go. He's just that special of a player."

Draper could only imagine one place where he'd ever try to make a patented Datsyuk play with the puck. "On my son in ball hockey—that's about it," Draper said.

Datsyuk actually chastised himself for trying it on such a significant stage. "It was a stupid thing," he said. "It worked, though. Now it's more confidence for me. Maybe next time, I try more easy way to score."

Like desperate defenders seeking a method to foil him, it's easy to become mesmerized by Datsyuk's numbers. He produced back-to-back 87-point seasons in 2005-06 and 2006-07, then followed up with consecutive 97-point campaigns in 2007-08 and 2008-09, helping the Wings win another Cup at the expense of Sidney Crosby, Evgeni Malkin and the Pittsburgh Penguins in the spring of 2008.

Chicago Blackhawks forward Marian Hossa was Datsyuk's linemate with the Wings in 2008-09, one season after Crosby was his centre in Pittsburgh. "They're different players," Hossa said in comparing the two. "Sidney is more a skater and Pavel is more a playmaker."

Hossa also found Datsyuk to be the more unpredictable playmaker. Hossa learned quickly not to try and anticipate, just be ready to react when riding shotgun with Datsyuk. "He's a great passer," Hossa said.

"He always gets the puck to you. You just have to make sure you get open. You don't even have to say anything, he sees you even when you're behind him. Basically, you just get ready for the shot."

Hossa just can't understand why Datsyuk isn't more often classified among the NHL elite. "To tell you the truth, I don't know why he isn't mentioned more in the league," Hossa said. "(Washington forward Alexander) Ovechkin, Crosby, Malkin, he's right there. I don't know why people think (he's not a candidate for the Hart Trophy)."

Around Detroit, there's no debate about Datsyuk's status within the NHL hierarchy. "He does everything pretty

	DATSYUK'S RED WINGS STATISTICS:									
	Regular Season					Playoffs				
Season	GP	G	A	P	PIM	GP	G	A	P	PIM
2001-02	70	11	24	35	4	21	3	3	6	2
2002-03	64	12	39	51	16	4	0	0	0	0
2003-04	75	30	38	68	35	12	0	6	6	2
2005-06	75	28	59	87	22	5	0	3	3	0
2006-07	79	27	60	87	20	18	8	8	16	8
2007-08	82	31	66	97	20	22	10	13	23	6
2008-09	81	32	65	97	22	16	1	8	9	9
2009-10	80	27	43	70	18	12	6	7	13	8
2010-11	56	23	36	59	15	11	4	11	15	8
2011-12	70	19	48	67	14	5	1	2	3	2
2012-13	47	15	34	49	14	14	3	6	9	4
2013-14	45	17	20	37	6	5	3	2	5	0
2014-15	63	26	39	65	8	7	3	2	5	2
Totals	887	298	571	869	214	152	42	71	113	51

quietly, without a lot of fanfare, and I think he likes that," Wings defenceman Niklas Kronwall said. "At the same time, we understand how important he is in this room and we appreciate the work he does at both ends."

Defenceman Ian White, who joined the Wings in 2011, was impressed by Datsyuk's one-of-a-kind skill from afar, but it was even more astonishing seeing the show live and up close.

"He seems to do that kind of thing every game, so that's why he's one of the best in the world," White said. "I don't know if he's better than I thought, but it's neat to see how good he really is, day in, day out. I've always regarded him as the best player in the world and to get to see him do it every game is quite amazing."

Beyond his unparalleled skill, Datsyuk's value also comes via his tremendous defensive skills. He annually leads the NHL in takeaways and three years in a row was awarded the Selke Trophy as the NHL's top defensive forward. Seemingly equipped with his own personal Romulan cloaking device, Datsyuk will stealthily sneak up on an opposing puck carrier, then make off with the disc like a pickpocket snapping up an unsuspecting mark's wallet.

"Most of the time, a player doesn't even know he's coming," Kronwall said of Datsyuk's puck-stealing capabilities. "He's so smooth (in the way he skates) and he just waits for the right moment to get in there with the stick. He's not one of those guys who's always there hooking, hooking and trying all the time.

"He just waits for the right moment. Boom, one try and the puck is his and off he goes. It just looks ridiculous sometimes."

Instantly, he turns a defensive situation into an offensive opportunity for the Wings. "That's where it usually starts," Detroit forward Johan Franzen said. "He backchecks and steals the puck and creates turnovers."

Teammates and opponents alike share similar views of Datsyuk's impact on the NHL. "I can't think of somebody who is a more complete (player) than Pavel," Hossa said.

"He has the ability to control the puck. He plays well defensively in our zone. I think he's the best all-around player in the world right now."

Former Detroit defenceman Chris Chelios was a rookie when Wayne Gretzky was in his prime in the mid-1980s, and he skated in the NHL well into his 40s, but insists he saw no one else in the game that was comparable to Datsyuk.

"How he comes back, backchecks and competes in his own end (are the most impressive aspects of his game)," Chelios said. "Then to be the first guy back and the first guy up the ice with the puck, he's carrying a load. It's amazing. In all my years, I don't think I've seen a forward that can do it like he does it."

His talent wows them, but it's Datsyuk's work ethic that truly amazes his teammates. "The words that come to mind (for Datsyuk) are pure determination," Draper said. "He's a dominant force at both ends of the rink."

His commitment to the little details of the game, when with his tremendous skill level he could easily fall back on his talent and still be among the game's best, sets an example for all of his teammates to aspire toward.

"He's the best two-way player in hockey, bar none," former Detroit coach Mike Babcock said. "He's an incredible, incredible player, better without the puck than he is with the puck, if you can actually imagine that. That's because of his commitment without the puck and his faceoffs and his strength and his battle level. All the intangible things he has beside his skill set and his vision. Those things are God-gifted. The other stuff he's earned."

For Babcock, who coached Datsyuk for a decade in Detroit, what Datsyuk accomplishes defensively is what separates him from most other offensive stars in the game. "He's just a great, great player and he continues to be a dominant player in the league offensively and defensively."

In Datsyuk's case, often the best defence is his incredible offensive skills. "We'd like Pav to have the puck for 18 or 20 minutes like he normally does," Babcock said. "That's a great concept. When he has the puck, they don't have it.

"It's not even playing defence, you just have the puck. You don't have to worry about it. Plus, you're faster coming out of your zone. You're faster in the neutral zone."

Datsyuk has earned four Lady Byng Trophies thanks to his ability to play such a sensational all-around game within the framework of the rules. "Maybe my lady will be waiting for me again in Las Vegas," Datsyuk joked as he left to attend the NHL awards show in 2010, when he won his record fourth straight Lady Byng.

Not that he should be considered soft by any means. Just ask Anaheim Ducks forward Corey Perry, the 2010-11 Hart Trophy winner, who was beat handily by Datsyuk when the two fought during the season opener in 2007. "Just part of the game," Datsyuk remembered. "I have lots of text messages from Russian fans about it."

That night, Datsyuk recorded what's known in hockey as a Gordie Howe hat trick—a goal, an assist and a fight in the same game—and his performance resonated in the Detroit dressing room. "When our guys see Pav committed physically, there's a message there to our guys that no one gets off the hook," Babcock said.

"He's a feisty little player," Lidstrom said. "He can take care of himself."

In 2010-11, for the only time of his career, Datsyuk was a Hart Trophy finalist, voters finally recognizing that there may be no stronger two-way puck presence in the game. "He's a tremendous athlete, a real hard-working star in the league," Former NHL coach Randy Carlyle said. "He's one of those guys that continually has an impact on the game, even if he's not putting points on the board."

The Wings know full well what Datsyuk brings to the table and they can't wait for that table to be set.

"When he has the puck, he makes the other team play defence," Lidstrom said. "Even if doesn't score, he makes them turn around and have to play defence. He works so hard defensively. He has a lot of takeaways."

Babcock marvels as much at Datsyuk's will as he does at his amazing skills. "Watch Pavel Datsyuk play and you talk about how skilled he is," Babcock said. "When I watch Pavel Datsyuk play, all I think about is how much will he has and how determined he is.

"The best of the best are ultra-competitive and they bring it every single day. They don't have it every day, but

they bring it. Those guys are our best players and they drive our bus.

"You don't have to get them started or beg them to play. They come to play every night."

Opponents recognize that to stop the Wings, they must find a way to contain Datsyuk. "He's a catalyst for them," Ottawa right winger Bobby Ryan said.

"He creates another dynamic to the game," added Anaheim forward Andrew Cogliano.

A dynamic the Wings have grown accustomed to having on their side of the ice. "Pav does it all year for us, as he has year after year," Kronwall said.

Datsyuk joined Detroit in 2001-02, playing a third-line role between future Hall of Famer Brett Hull and Boyd Devereaux, as the Wings captured the Stanley Cup during his rookie season. "He's the smartest player I've ever played with," Hull said. And perhaps the most creative mind ever to play the game.

When practice ends, most players head for the relief of the dressing room. In Detroit, they stick around to see what new tricks Datsyuk has learned, because this is the time of day when this mad puck scientist conducts his experiments.

"He does things with the puck that no one has ever seen before," Kronwall said. "Mostly he's just skating around by himself (at the end of practice). You can see him just playing and having fun with the puck, constantly trying new things."

When it transfers into something sensational, like the many Datsyukian dekes that today are staple downloads on YouTube, everyone simply shakes their head in disbelief. "When he does something like that you can see the whole bench go, 'Wow!'" Kronwall said.

Datsyuk admits he rarely scripts his moves. Each rush is an individual journey and he has no idea where his moments of genius come from.

"I don't know all my moves myself," Datsyuk said. "Maybe some come in a dream. I don't know where."

He doesn't spend nearly the amount of time pondering the end result of his highlight-reel scoring forays. "I'm happy when I beat a defenceman, but for it to be special, I

have to finish and score," Datsyuk said. "If you don't score, no one will remember because they won't show it on TV."

Datsyuk admits he started developing his unique style trying to survive on the rink as an undersized child. While some players study videotape to unlock clues for improving their game, Datsyuk envisions opportunities from a variety of sources, including watching how his young daughter would entertain herself during playtime.

"I see how kids play," Datsyuk said. "How suddenly she moves to the side."

He also doesn't obsess over his goaltender-embarrassing moves the way his fans do. Datsyuk isn't one to put much thought into what he'd call his signature sleight of hand with the puck.

"The name is, 'It's a goal,'" joked Datsyuk. "There's not much else you want to name a move."

Datsyuk leaves them guessing on the ice and leaves them laughing off the ice. Datsyuk's sense of humour is glib and very Yakov Smirnov-like.

"He is a funny guy," Wings captain Henrik Zetterberg said. "He always has something smart to say."

Datsyuk is unpredictable, on and off the ice.

If linemates can't figure out Datsyuk's next move, pity the poor goaltenders that make their living by trying to stop Datsyuk's dazzlers. "He amazes us every single game," said Wings goalie Jimmy Howard, who admits that he's been embarrassed many times by Datsyuk. "He does it in practice. He does it in games.

"One night in Chicago, he stickhandled through four guys. You're standing down at the other end and it's like, 'Wow. Thank you he's on my side.' In practice, I usually give it to him, razz him a bit, after I actually stop him."

Datsyuk tries to vary his breakaway bids, so that netminders can't get a read on him. "I don't want them to know my moves," he said.

He's not nearly as guarded about his unique tee-off talent. "You come to the golf course," he said of his Happy Gilmore-like prowess with a driver. "I will show you."

11 NORM ULLMAN

Centre/Left Wing

Born: December 26, 1935, Provost, Alberta
Shot: Left **Height:** 5-10 **Weight:** 175 lbs.
Red Wing From: 1955-56 to 1967-68
Elected to Hockey Hall of Fame: 1982
Acquired: Signed pro contract Sept. 23, 1954.
Departed: Traded by Detroit to Toronto Maple Leafs with Floyd Smith, Paul Henderson and Doug Barrie for Frank Mahovlich, Pete Stemkowski, Garry Unger and the NHL rights to Carl Brewer, March 3, 1968.

HIS GAME WAS MORE METHODICAL THAN COLOURFUL. He seldom smiled and said even less.

All Norm Ullman did was score big goals, time and time again.

The soft-spoken, somewhat shy Ullman was overshadowed during his Detroit Red Wings days by more luminous stars such as Gordie Howe, Alex Delvecchio, Ted Lindsay, Terry Sawchuk, Red Kelly and Marcel Pronovost, but that wasn't because he didn't shine as an NHLer.

"Hello," was considered a lengthy conversation with Ullman, jokingly referred to as "Noisy Norm" by his teammates. He was known to play an entire round of golf without uttering anything other than "nice shot."

"I don't mind talking to one or two people, but not a crowd," Ullman explained to *Canadian Press*. "It's just not my nature."

Instead, he relied upon his ability to play the game to make him stand out in the crowd.

Red Wings scout Clarence Moher first spotted Ullman as a 14-year-old playing for the Edmonton Maple Leafs.

"Normie isn't a great skater, but he is a great hockey player," Moher told the *Calgary Herald*.

Moher established Ullman as his benchmark when scouting. Any other prospect he'd see would eventually lead him to say "He's no Norm Ullman."

Ullman made it clear in junior hockey with the Edmonton Oil Kings that he possessed star quality. He led the Western Canada Junior League in scoring in both 1952-53 and 1953-54 and was also the top scorer in the playoffs and Memorial Cup playdowns during the latter campaign. After the season, Ullman was awarded the Gene Carrigan Memorial Trophy as the Edmonton junior athlete who best combined sportsmanship and ability.

He turned pro at the age of 18, and after one season with the Western Hockey League's Edmonton Flyers, Ullman jumped into the lineup of the defending Stanley Cup champion Red Wings in the fall of 1955.

By the 1956-57 season, he was being tried at centre between Gordie Howe and Ted Lindsay on Detroit's top forward line, and finished the season with 19 goals and 52

DETROIT HONOURS:

+ Named to NHL First All-Star Team, 1964-65
+ Named to NHL Second All-Star Team, 1966-67
+ Played in NHL All-Star Game, 1955, 1960, 1961, 1962, 1963, 1964, 1965, 1967, 1968
+ Led NHL in goals, 1964-65
+ Led Stanley Cup playoffs in assists and points, 1962-63
+ Led Stanley Cup playoffs in goals and points, 1965-66
+ Led NHL in even-strength and game-winning goals, 1964-65
+ Set Stanley Cup record with two goals in five seconds, April 11, 1965.

Ullman's quiet nature made him a success at negotiating contracts with tight-fisted Red Wings general manager Jack Adams, and it frustrated Adams to no end.

"He won't say anything," Adams complained to the *Edmonton Journal*. "He just sits there while you talk. If he'd just argue.

"He won't say a thing until I offer the contract he wants."

Always a steady contributor, Ullman's fortunes took a quantum leap forward during the 1964-65 season as Detroit finished in first place. He led the NHL with 42 goals and finished second in the league scoring race with 83 points. The performance earned Ullman the Hockey News player-of-the-year award and runner-up status to Chicago's Bobby Hull in the voting for the Hart Trophy.

He also led the NHL with 10 game-winning goals. "It's a tremendous feeling to score a game-winning goal," Ullman told *Canadian Press*." The guys jump all over you and pat you on the back.

"There's nothing like it."

points. In 1957-58, Ullman scored 23 times, the first of sixteen 20-goal campaigns he'd enjoy during his 20 NHL seasons.

"You like to score at least 20 goals and they expect me to score about 30," Ullman told *Canadian Press*.

Ullman's career remained upward in motion. In 1960-61, now working on a line with Howe and Alex Delvecchio, he set a club record with points in 14 straight games. An excellent stickhandler, he was considered among the NHL's top two-way forwards and perhaps the game's most determined forechecker.

"He always was a good defensive player," Detroit coach Sid Abel told *Canadian Press*. "I've never seen a better forechecker, but I don't know why he's so good at it. He always gets his 20 goals or more, so you have to say he's been pretty good on offence, too.

"He seldom slaps the puck or tips a goalie when it's coming. He's always snaring loose pucks and beats goalies by shooting when they are not expecting a shot."

ULLMAN'S RED WINGS STATISTICS:

Season	Regular Season					Playoffs				
	GP	G	A	P	PIM	GP	G	A	P	PIM
1955-56	66	9	9	18	26	10	1	3	4	13
1956-57	64	16	36	52	47	5	1	1	2	6
1957-58	69	23	28	51	38	4	0	2	2	4
1958-59	69	22	36	58	42	-				
1959-60	70	24	34	58	46	6	2	2	4	0
1960-61	70	28	42	70	34	11	0	4	4	4
1961-62	70	26	38	64	54	-				
1962-63	70	26	30	56	53	11	4	12	16	14
1963-64	61	21	30	51	55	14	7	10	17	6
1964-65	70	42	41	83	70	7	6	4	10	2
1965-66	70	31	41	72	35	12	6	9	15	12
1966-67	68	26	44	70	26	-				
1967-68	58	30	25	55	26	-				
Totals	875	324	434	758	552	80	27	47	74	61

In the playoffs that spring, Ullman established a Stanley Cup record. "I scored two goals in five seconds," recalled Ullman of Detroit's April 11, 1965 semifinal game against Chicago. "It's still a playoff record in the NHL.

"After the first goal, I took the faceoff and the puck went over to the boards by their blue line. (Chicago forward) Eric Nesterenko picked it up, peeked over his shoulder to pass it to the other defenceman and I skated between, picked it up and scored.

"When you think about it, it really sounds impossible. I was pretty lucky. It's still one of my best memories."

He seemed to save his best nights for playoff games against the Blackhawks. When Detroit beat Chicago 4-2 in Game 5 of the 1963 semifinals, Ullman figured in all four goals, scoring twice and setting up the other pair. He garnered 13 points in Detroit's 1964 semifinal triumph over the Blackhawks, and twice registered five-point games against Chicago in post-season play.

Ullman led all Stanley Cup scorers with six goals and 15 points in 1965-66 as Detroit reached the final for the fifth time in his Red Wings career, coming out short of a title on all five occasions. In 1965-66, he received votes at both centre and left wing in the NHL All-Star balloting.

"He was intelligent," former NHL referee Bruce Hood said of Ullman. "He could read everything on the ice, set up any play and handle the puck well.

"He was there all the time."

Away from the rink, Ullman was known to be a wise investor and was jokingly referred to as the NHLer with the most money in the bank. Perhaps that played a role in his election as president of the NHLPA on Jan. 18, 1968.

Whether the latter development played a role in Ullman's sudden departure from Detroit late in the 1967-68 season is a matter that remains up for debate. He'd been a contract holdout in training camp, and even though he'd scored 30 goals in just 58 games, the Wings shipped him to Toronto in a multi-player deal that brought all-star left winger Frank Mahovlich to Detroit.

"I wasn't really too surprised," Ullman told *Canadian Press* after the trade, insisting the Wings were disappointed with his efforts. "They had been on me the last two or three months. They apparently thought I hadn't been playing as well as in past years.

"I might have been a little slower, but I didn't think I'd been playing that badly."

The Leafs were certainly delighted by their acquisition of Ullman. "He's the best all-around hockey player I've seen in 10 years," Toronto coach Punch Imlach told *United Press*.

About the only thing that Ullman was guilty of as an NHLer was bad timing. He arrived in Detroit the fall after the club won its final Stanley Cup for 42 years and was dealt to Toronto the season following the Maple Leafs most recent Cup triumph.

"A lot of it is being in the right place at the right time," Ullman said. "If I had been a few years older, I might have played on those Detroit Cup teams in the early 1950s."

Ullman played seven seasons with the Leafs and then two more back home with the World Hockey Association's Edmonton Oilers before hanging up his skates for good in 1977, 22 years after he'd first broke into the NHL with the Red Wings.

12 EBBIE GOODFELLOW
Centre/Defence

Born: April 9, 1906, Ottawa, Ontario
Died: September 10, 1985
Shot: Right Height: 6-0 Weight: 175 lbs.
Red Wing From: 1928-29 to 1942-43
Elected to Hockey Hall of Fame: 1963
Acquired: NHL rights traded to Detroit by New York Americans for Johnny Sheppard and $12,500, April 14, 1928
Departed: Declined position as coach of Indianapolis (AHL) to enter private business, October 11, 1943.

IT WAS ONCE SAID OF EBBIE GOODFELLOW THAT HIS IDEA OF tact in a hockey game was to skate up to an opposition player and knock him flat on his back. On the ice, Goodfellow was reported to be equipped with a winning smile, a shattering bodycheck and a world of speed.

He certainly carried the physique to be a star. At the age of 20 he stood six feet tall and weighed 180 pounds, leading the Ottawa City League in scoring while playing for the Ottawa Montagnards. That performance caught the eye of Jack Adams, a former Ottawa Senators star who'd recently assumed the role as coach and general manager of the Detroit Cougars.

Adams wanted Goodfellow in his fold, but there were two issues to be dealt with. In 1924, Goodfellow had signed a contract with the Saskatoon Sheiks of the Western Canada Hockey League. Though he'd declined to report, the Saskatoon club, now members of the minor-pro Prairie Hockey League, held firm to Goodfellow's pro rights.

That turned out to be merely the first hurdle in getting Goodfellow to Detroit. Adams soon found out that the New York Americans had placed Goodfellow on their NHL negotiating list, so he was required to trade forward Johnny Sheppard and $12,500 to the Amerks to finally secure Goodfellow, though he was certain the investment would prove to be worth every penny.

"I liked the way he was put together and decided to gamble on him," Adams said.

It seemed a pricely sum, but the cost paid immediate dividends when Goodfellow, a centre, led the Canadian Professional League in scoring with 26-8-34 totals for the Detroit Olympics, the Cougars' farm club.

Coming up to the big leagues for the 1929-30 campaign, Goodfellow made a seamless adjustment to the NHL. Establishing a Detroit mark with 25 goals and 48 points in 1930-31, his second NHL campaign, Goodfellow set a club record with four goals against Toronto's Benny Grant in a 10-1 win on Christmas Day, 1930. He led the league in scoring for most of the season until he was nipped at the wire by Montreal Canadiens centre Howie Morenz.

The Boston Bruins were so impressed with Goodfellow's work that they were willing to part with $50,000 to acquire his services from Detroit, but the offer was declined.

Aside from his skill level, Goodfellow—nicknamed Poker Face for his seemingly permanently-etched scowl that would

DETROIT HONOURS:

- Stanley Cup champion 1935-36, 1936-37, 1942-43
- Named to NHL First All-Star Team, 1936-37, 1939-40
- Named to NHL Second All-Star Team, 1935-36
- Played in NHL All-Star Game, 1937, 1939
- Team captain 1934-35, 1938-39 to 1941-42
- Led Detroit in goals and points, 1930-31, 1931-32

have made him the ideal candidate to fill a role as an extra in any 1930s gangster movie—was also considered among the tougher players of his era. He was known around the league as the NHL's best one-punch fighter.

During a game against Toronto late in the 1932-33 season, Goodfellow crashed the Maple Leafs net and was welcomed to the goal crease by a rap across the head from Toronto's Lorne Chabot. The two dropped their gloves and went at it and both were penalized. In those days, goaltenders served their own infractions and Goodfellow and Chabot resumed their bout in the penalty box. Police were required to break up the combatants.

The Leafs and Wings staged an exhibition tour of Western Canada in the mid-1930s, and as exhibition games tend to be, the affairs were somewhat tame. Toronto defenceman King Clancy suggested to Goodfellow that they stage a fight in the next game in Trail, B.C. to liven up the festivities.

"We were in the corner and to start things off, I kind of gave Ebbie a dig with my elbow," Clancy explained to the *Ottawa Citizen*. "The next thing I know, he turns around and hits me so hard I go flying on my back to the ice.

"Next thing you know, everyone is into it and it's a real battle. The next time Ebbie hits me, though, it was on the shoulder and he says, 'All right King, we got it going real good. Take it easy.'

"I didn't think he'd take it so serious, or I might have never gone along with the stunt."

Detroit became the Falcons and then, in 1932, the Red Wings and there were also changes in the offing for Goodfellow. In the midst of a three-game losing streak during the 1933-34 season in which the Wings had been outscored 17-4, owner James Norris held a six-hour meeting with Adams on Jan. 2, 1934 and when they were done, several changes to the club were announced.

The Wings exchanged defencemen with the Montreal Maroons, sending Stew Evans to Montreal for Teddy Graham. Goaltender Wilf Cude was acquired on loan from the Montreal Canadiens, and forward Wilf Starr was recalled from the Olympics.

To make room for Starr on the front line, Adams also revealed plans to convert Goodfellow from centre to defence. During Detroit's previous game, an 8-1 loss to Toronto, Adams had experimented with Goodfellow along the blue line and deemed it a success.

Moving players from forward to defence was not uncommon in those days. Prominent forwards and future Hall of Famers such as Reg Noble, Babe Siebert and Hooley Smith made the adjustment smoothly, but did it late in their careers after losing some of their speed. Goodfellow was in the prime of his playing days, just 27, when he was moved back to the rearguard.

"Goodfellow made the adjustment to defence fairly early in his career," former Detroit defenceman Bill Quackenbush told the *Montreal Gazette* in 1963.

He was also an immediate hit. "Ebbie Goodfellow played a bang-up game on the defence," wrote Vern DeGeer in the *Border Cities Star* after Detroit's 3-1 victory over the New York Rangers in Goodfellow's blue-line debut. "The husky

GOODFELLOW'S RED WINGS STATISTICS:										
	Regular Season					Playoffs				
Season	GP	G	A	P	PIM	GP	G	A	P	PIM
1929-30	44	17	17	34	54	-	-	-	-	-
1930-31	44	25	23	48	32	-	-	-	-	-
1931-32	48	14	16	30	56	2	0	0	0	0
1932-33	41	12	8	20	47	4	1	0	1	11
1933-34	48	13	13	26	45	9	4	3	7	12
1934-35	48	12	24	36	44	-	-	-	-	-
1935-36	48	5	18	23	69	7	1	0	1	4
1936-37	48	9	16	25	43	9	2	2	4	12
1937-38	30	0	7	7	13	-	-	-	-	-
1938-39	48	8	8	16	36	6	0	0	0	8
1939-40	43	11	17	28	31	5	0	2	2	9
1940-41	47	5	17	22	35	3	0	1	1	9
1941-42	9	2	2	4	2	-	-	-	-	-
1942-43	11	1	4	5	2	-	-	-	-	-
Totals	557	134	190	324	511	45	8	8	16	65

former Detroit centre took his new duties seriously. He used his weight and his long reach with telling effect to bump rushing puck carriers and break up combination plays."

Detroit's fortunes also took a turn for the better. With Goodfellow and Doug Young in the Wings' top defence pairing, they reached the Stanley Cup final in 1934. But when Detroit skidded out of the playoff picture the following season, Toronto GM Conn Smythe inquired about what it would require to land Goodfellow for his team. When Adams asked for winger Hec Kilrea and defenceman Clancy, talks quickly broke off.

It turned out to be a break for the Wings, who'd beat Clancy and the Leafs in the 1935-36 Stanley Cup final for Detroit's first title. Goodfellow was selected to the NHL's Second All-Star team that season and was a First-Team choice in 1936-37 as the Wings defended their title.

Adams discarded several of his veterans toward the end of the decade as Detroit rebuilt, but hung on to Goodfellow, and in the 1939-40 season the veteran finished second on the club in scoring with 28 points, earned another First Team All-Star nod and was also voted the Hart Trophy as the NHL's most valuable player, the first time a Red Wing had been so honoured.

"He was the rallying force of the team," Adams said.

Knee injuries slowed Goodfellow over the final two seasons of his career, and in 1941 Adams named Goodfellow a playing assistant coach. "He'll run (the club) when I find it necessary to be elsewhere," Adams explained to the *Windsor Star*. "I'm sure that Goodfellow will be as great a coach as he has been a hockey player. I will help him to get things organized this season and render any assistance I possibly can."

Detroit's new dump-and chase style of hockey became all the rage that season as the team reached the Stanley Cup final despite a fifth-place finish. "Detroit turned out to be a remarkably well-coached club in that style of play—that constant pressure hockey of shooting the puck in ahead of them and forechecking," Boston GM Art Ross said after the Wings swept his team in the semifinals. "Whoever is responsible for coaching the Red Wings, Adams or Goodfellow, did a splendid job."

In 1943, his playing days done, Goodfellow was offered the head coaching position with Detroit's AHL farm club in Indianapolis, but he declined, citing a desire to retain his job as a tool and die salesman with a Royal Oak, Mich. manufacturing firm.

"The offer was a generous one, but I don't feel that I wish to pull up stakes here," Goodfellow told *United Press*. "I have a home here and a good position in industry with opportunity for promotion."

Eventually, Goodfellow did return to coaching, guiding the fortunes of the junior Windsor Spitfires, the AHL's St. Louis Flyers and the NHL's Chicago Blackhawks.

An outstanding golfer, during his playing days Goodfellow served as a caddie superintendant at the prestigious Oakland Hills Country Club in Bloomfield Hills, Michigan, where teammate Tommy Filmore was assistant pro.

In 1959, he helped organize the Detroit Alumni Association, a group whose charity work continues today. Goodfellow also served 21 years on Hockey Hall of Fame's selection committee.

Living in retirement in Sarasota, Fla., cancer claimed Goodfellow's life at the age of 79.

13 BRENDAN SHANAHAN

Left Wing

Born: January 23, 1969, Mimico, Ontario
Shot: Right Height: 6-3 Weight: 218 lbs.
Red Wing From: 1996-97 to 2005-06
Acquired: Traded to Detroit by Hartford Whalers with Brian Glynn for Keith Primeau and Paul Coffey and a 1997 first round draft choice (Nikos Tselios), October 9, 1996.
Departed: Signed as a free agent by New York Rangers, July 9, 2006.

THE FINAL PIECE OF THE PUZZLE. THE MAN WHO PUT them over the hump and ended Detroit's decades-long Stanley Cup drought.

That was the way Brendan Shanahan was viewed when the Red Wings acquired the big winger's services from the Hartford Whalers early into the 1996-97 NHL season, and it proved to be an accurate take when that spring, Shanahan scored nine goals and 17 points in 20 games as the Wings won the Stanley Cup for the first time since 1954-55.

It was an impressive performance by him, but an even more astonishing effort by those who pegged Shanahan as the missing part, because labels do not affix easily to this man.

In his prime a leader on the ice and in the dressing room, it was an easy task to explain what Shanahan the player was all about. A prototypical power forward, he possessed the presence of Eric Lindros, the shot of Brett Hull and the toughness of Bob Probert.

Off the ice, things don't fall so neatly into place. "Let's just say Brendan is a man with many facets," said former Detroit teammate Doug Brown, who has known Shanahan since the two were rookies with the New Jersey Devils in 1988.

"What am I about?" Shanahan asks rhetorically. "When I'm on the plane with the other guys, playing cards, I'm a card shark, doing card tricks.

"When I'm playing paintball, I like to sneak up on guys and pick them off. When I'm with my family, I'm quiet, because I'm the youngest. When I'm with my friends, I'm a joker, because I'm the funny guy in the bunch."

It's Shanahan's wicked sense of humour which has made it even more difficult to get a grasp on what makes him tick. When *Sports Illustrated* portrayed him as a Shakespearian scholar after he had recited word for word a passage from one of Shakespeare's plays, Shanahan simply caught the magazine in another of his famous shenanigans.

"We did that play in high school and I just remembered the lines," Shanahan said. Shanny's summer, a section that appeared in his bio in the team media guide each season, was the stuff legends are made of.

DETROIT HONOURS:

- Stanley Cup champion, 1996-97, 1997-98, 2001-02
- Selected to NHL Second All-Star Team, 2001-02
- Played in NHL All-Star Game, 1997, 1998, 1999, 2000, 2002
- Won King Clancy Memorial Trophy, 2002-03
- Played for Canada in 1998 and 2002 Winter Olympic Games, winning gold medal at the 2002 Salt Lake City Winter Games
- Scored Stanley Cup-winning goal, 2001-02
- Played for Canada in 2006 World Championship
- Led Red Wings in goals, 1996-97, 1997-98, 1998-99, 1999-2000, 2001-02, 2005-06
- Led Red Wings in points, 1996-97, 2001-02

According to its lore, Shanahan served as Ireland's backup goalkeeper at the 1994 World Cup, appeared in the movie Forrest Gump, failed a screen test for the role of Dino in The Flintstones, worked as a ball boy during Andre Agassi's matches at the U.S. Open, and played saxophone in the Canadian Jazz Festival.

None of it is true. "I'm just a quiet Canadian kid who spends his summer in the Muskokas," Shanahan said. "I saw some of the exciting stuff some of the other guys were doing in the summer and just figured I ought to liven up my life a little bit."

His ability to utilize some Irish blarney to spin a tall tale has always made it difficult to know when to take Shanahan at face value and when to recognize you're being played.

Consider Shanahan's explanation for his powerful shot. Want to shoot the puck like him? Then this spud's for you. Author of 656 career NHL goals, including a half-dozen 40-goal seasons, Shanahan insisted that the secret to his powerful shot and lightning-quick release was mashed potatoes.

"My mom made me mash potatoes when I was a little kid," Shanahan explained. "I'm eight years old and my forearms are throbbing from mashing potatoes for half an hour."

Believe it or not, Shanahan also claimed that he employed the same recipe to school youngsters on the art of the heavy shot. "That's how I teach shooting at my hockey school," Shanahan said. "Here you go guys. Mash some potatoes."

As glib and irreverent as he could be about his life outside of hockey, Shanahan never did anything to mock the game he loved. "I can be a happy-go-lucky guy, but I'm very serious about my hockey," Shanahan said. "My whole life, all I wanted to be was a hockey player."

That dream came true when the Devils selected Shanahan second overall in the 1987 NHL entry draft. He broke into their lineup at the age of 18 and helped them to the 1988 Eastern Conference final. Further stops in St. Louis and Hartford brought individual success, including a pair of 50-goal seasons and a 100-point campaign, but the ultimate hockey dream didn't come to fruition for Shanahan until he arrived in Detroit.

"They just didn't understand what it meant to be a hockey player," Shanahan said of Hartford. "St. Louis was a pretty good hockey town, but even it doesn't compare to Detroit. You quickly got a sense of the passion here, of how much the people in this city care about their hockey team."

Shanahan delivered equal levels of passion, leading the team in goals six times and in points twice. He still fondly recollects making his Red Wings debut the night he was traded to Detroit and how his teammates instantly made it clear that he was one of them. "The guys held up going out for warm up until I was suited up," Shanahan remembered. "They wanted to make sure I felt like I was part of the team."

He netted the Stanley Cup-winning goal for Detroit against the Carolina Hurricanes in 2002, one of three times while with the Wings that Shanahan earned the honour of lifting Lord Stanley's mug aloft.

"When I scored a big goal in a big game like that, the lift it gave my teammates meant more to me than the individual accomplishment," Shanahan said. "I feel sorry for individual athletes like figure skaters and tennis players, because I don't

| SHANAHAN'S RED WINGS STATISTICS: | | | | | | | | | |
| REGULAR SEASON | | | | | PLAYOFFS | | | | |
Season	GP	G	A	P	PIM	GP	G	A	P	PIM
1996-97	79	46	41	87	131	20	9	8	17	43
1997-98	75	28	29	57	154	20	5	4	9	22
1998-99	81	31	27	58	123	10	3	7	10	6
1999-00	78	41	37	78	105	9	3	2	5	10
2000-01	81	31	45	76	81	2	2	2	4	0
2001-02	80	37	38	75	118	23	8	11	19	20
2002-03	78	30	38	68	103	4	1	1	2	4
2003-04	82	25	28	53	117	12	1	5	6	20
2005-06	82	40	41	81	105	6	1	1	2	6
Totals	716	309	324	633	1037	106	33	41	74	131

think their sense of accomplishment can compare to when a group comes together and becomes a team.

"To me, that's what the Stanley Cup is all about."

Shanahan left the Wings following the 2005-06 season, skating for the New York Rangers and New Jersey Devils before retiring as a player in 2009. Later that year, he was named the NHL's vice-president of hockey and business development. In 2011, he took over from former Detroit defenceman Colin Campbell as the man who doled out NHL discipline. In 2014, Shanahan was named president of the Toronto Maple Leafs.

As for the future, Shanahan says his ultimate dream would be to run with the bulls at Pamplona, Spain, but no one really knows whether they should believe him.

14 LARRY AURIE

Right Wing

Born: February 8, 1905, Sudbury, Ontario
Died: December 11, 1952
Shot: Right **Height:** 5-6 **Weight:** 148 lbs.
Red Wing From: 1927-28 to 1938-39
Acquired: Selected from London (CANPRO) in inter-league draft, September 26, 1927.
Departed: Named coach of Pittsburgh (IAHL), October 3, 1938.

NEXT TO THE REASONS BEHIND THE OCTOPUS-throwing tradition, the mystery of sweater No. 6 may be the most oft-asked question in terms of Detroit Red Wings lore.

For many years, if you looked in the National Hockey League Guide and Record Book, it would list Larry Aurie's Detroit sweater No. 6 as being retired.

No Red Wing player has worn No. 6 since 1959.

Yet, it will not join the others in a place of honour. It's caught up in a technicality.

"It was never officially retired," former Red Wings media relations director Bill Jamieson explained. "The papers were never filed with the league. (Detroit coach-GM) Jack (Adams) just took it out of circulation."

When Aurie left the Wings in 1938 to serve as coach of the club's Pittsburgh farm team, Adams made the move to take Aurie's number out of service.

"It wouldn't seem right for anyone else to wear it," Adams said.

The only Red Wing to wear No. 6 since that time was Cummy Burton from 1957-59. He is Aurie's nephew.

In 2000, the number was removed from Detroit's list of retired sweaters and there was thought given to reintroducing No. 6 to the Red Wings lineup, which would have proven to be a terrible shame, for Aurie was the first legitimate superstar to play for the club.

"We were going to bring it back into circulation," Jamieson recalled. "Then, we decided those were Jack's wishes and elected not to do so."

Aurie played 11 seasons with Detroit. He joined the club in 1927, Detroit's second season in the NHL, the year Olympia Stadium opened and the first season that Adams was in charge of the team. Aurie is among a unique few players to have suited up under all three of Detroit's nicknames—Cougars, Falcons and Red Wings.

Despite never weighing more than 148 pounds during his NHL career, Aurie quickly became a fan favourite in Detroit due to the fearlessness he displayed while tangling on the ice against much larger opponents. Aurie's combination of skill and fiestiness is often compared to another Wings legend, Terrible Ted Lindsay.

"Pound for pound he was the most courageous player in hockey," Adams told *Canadian Press*.

Aurie's pugnacious style and his resemblance to heavyweight boxing champion Jack Dempsey earned him the nickname Little Dempsey, though he was also known as Rags due to his uncanny ability to rag the puck while killing penalties.

DETROIT HONOURS:

- Stanley Cup champion, 1935-36, 1936-37
- Named to NHL First All-Star Team, 1936-37
- Played in NHL All-Star Game, 1933-34
- Led NHL in goals, 1936-37
- Team captain, 1933-34; Led Detroit in scoring, 1933-34.

"He was one of hockey's all-time greats," New York Rangers manager Lester Patrick said in 1938.

Naturally, in blue-collar Detroit, Aurie's rambunctious style and fiery competitiveness made him a fan favourite, but he was much more than a mere agitator. He captained the team in 1932-33 and led the Wings in scoring in 1933-34, as Detroit reached the Stanley Cup final for the first time in franchise history. Aurie led all playoff scorers that spring.

In 1934, he and teammate Herbie Lewis represented the Wings in the First NHL All-Star Game, the Ace Bailey Benefit Game played at Toronto's Maple Leaf Gardens.

"Aurie has a remarkable shot, almost always on the net," wrote H.G. Salsinger in the *Detroit News*. "He is quick, exceptionally fast and usually aggressive. There are few flashier gentlemen in hockey."

Aurie's dedication to playing the game at both ends of the rink probably cost him more impressive offensive numbers, but it won him the respect of his peers.

"He's the hardest-checking right wing in the league," Toronto forward Harvey (Busher) Jackson told *Canadian Press.*

In 1935, Adams acquired centre Marty Barry from Boston, putting him between left wing Lewis and right wing Aurie and predicted that Detroit would win the Cup.

He proved a prophet. The unit quickly became one of the NHL's best and Detroit, which had missed the playoffs the year before, won the Stanley Cup the next two seasons.

During the 1935-36 season, Aurie suffered a chipped breastbone and two broken ribs, but he bounced back quickly and the 1936-37 campaign was Aurie's best. He was leading the NHL in scoring, netting his career-high 23rd goal of the year in the next-to-last game of the regular season.

Late in the game, Aurie collided with Rangers defenceman Art Coulter and fractured two bones just above his ankle, ending his season. He watched on crutches as the Wings successfully defended the Cup against those same Rangers.

He came back the following year, but wasn't the same player, scoring just 10 goals, and Aurie announced he would retire at the end of the season.

"A lot of big guys in the league will be glad to hear that," Toronto manager Conn Smythe said.

Aurie was to have played his final game as a Red Wing on March 21, 1938, at the Olympia against the New York Rangers. Adams started Aurie with his old linemates Barry and Lewis that night, but he was held pointless in a 4-3 Detroit win.

After the game, Adams announced no one would ever again wear No. 6.

"James Norris, owner of the Wings, has other plans for Larry," Adams told *Associated Press*. That's when Aurie was named player-coach at Pittsburgh, but it turned out he wasn't done performing in his No. 6 Red Wings sweater.

AURIE'S RED WINGS STATISTICS:									
	REGULAR SEASON					PLAYOFFS			
Season	GP	G	A	P	PIM	GP	G	A	P	PIM
1927-28	44	13	3	16	43	-	-	-	-	-
1928-29	35	1	1	2	26	2	1	0	1	2
1929-30	43	14	5	19	28	-	-	-	-	-
1930-31	41	12	6	18	23	-	-	-	-	-
1931-32	48	13	8	21	18	2	0	0	0	0
1932-33	45	12	11	23	25	4	1	0	1	4
1933-34	48	16	19	35	36	9	3	7	10	2
1934-35	48	17	29	46	24	-	-	-	-	-
1935-36	44	16	18	34	17	7	1	2	3	2
1936-37	45	23	20	43	20	-	-	-	-	-
1937-38	47	10	9	19	19	-	-	-	-	-
1938-39	1	1	0	1	0	-	-	-	-	-
Totals	489	148	129	277	279	24	6	9	15	10

With the injury-riddled Red Wings in need of help, Adams called his old compatriot back to the show. Aurie played one more game in a Detroit uniform on January 9, 1939, and scored a goal in a 3-0 win over Montreal.

Aurie left hockey in 1943 to take a job in Detroit as an investigator for the probate court, but returned to coach the Oshawa Generals from 1950-52.

"I learned a lot about stickwork and playmaking from him," said Red Wings Hall of Famer Alex Delvecchio, who was coached by Aurie in Oshawa.

Later, Aurie became an insurance salesman for the Auto Club of Detroit. Late in 1952, he suffered a stroke while at the wheel of his car. His vehicle went out of control and crashed into another car.

Aurie died in hospital a few hours later at the age of 47.

15 MARCEL PRONOVOST

Defence

Born: June 15, 1930, Lac-de- la-Tortue, Quebec
Died: April 26, 2015
Shot: Left **Height:** 6-0 **Weight:** 190 lbs.
Red Wing From: 1949-50 to 1964-65
Elected to Hockey Hall of Fame: 1978
Acquired: Signed by Detroit to a pro contract, September 9, 1949
Departed: Traded by Detroit to Toronto Maple Leafs with Lowell MacDonald, Larry Jeffrey, Ed Joyal and Autry Erickson for Andy Bathgate, Billy Harris and Gary Jarrett, May 20, 1965.

MARCEL PRONOVOST REMEMBERS IT WELL. HE WAS A rookie with the junior Windsor Spitfires, the Detroit Red Wings-sponsored club in the Ontario Hockey Association's junior A series. Pronovost and the Wilson brothers, Johnny and Larry, arrived in the fall of 1947 from their home in Shawinigan, Quebec, freshly signed to the standard C-form National Hockey League contract by the Wings.

They were armed with a dream of playing in the NHL for the Wings and the incentive of literally having the place where they'd play dangled right before their eyes.

"The three of us, we used to go sit on the benches in Windsor along the Detroit River and look across at Detroit," Pronovost recalled. "We'd say, 'Do you think any of us will make it there?'"

All of them did, and not only did they make it, but the three of them arrived together in Detroit at the most important time of the year, right as the 1950 Stanley Cup playoffs were getting under way.

In his first season of pro hockey, Pronovost had earned recognition as the top rookie in the United States Hockey League, then led all USHL playoff scorers with nine assists and 13 points.

He insists he wasn't the least bit surprised when at the age of 19 he was called to play in the big leagues during the biggest games of the season. "No, not really," Pronovost said. "But I was a cocky kid."

That 1950 post-season campaign was the spring when Detroit's Gordie Howe was lost to a near-fatal head injury suffered during the opening game of the playoffs. The Wings decided to shift defenceman Red Kelly to forward to fill Howe's spot, then threw their budding young defence prospect into the midst of the fire.

"I played the last nine games and that's how I got my name on the Cup the first time," Pronovost said, though the journey wasn't a smooth one. The Wings needed an overtime goal from Leo Reise, Pronovost's defence partner, to nip the Toronto Maple Leafs 1-0 in Game 7 of their semifinal series, then rallied from a 3-2 deficit to take the New York Rangers in the Cup final series, winning Game 7 on Pete Babando's goal in double overtime.

It was Pronovost's dump into the Rangers' zone that resulted in the attacking-zone faceoff which led to the Cup-winning goal. "I'd just come off the ice," Pronovost said. "I made the play to throw the puck in their end to freeze it for

---

DETROIT HONOURS:

- Stanley Cup champion, 1949-50, 1951-52, 1953-54, 1954-55
- Named to NHL First All-Star Team, 1959-60, 1960-61
- Named to NHL Second All-Star Team, 1957-58, 1958-59
- Played in NHL All-Star Game, 1950,1954,1955,1957,1958,1959,1960,1961,1963,1965
- Won Stanley Cup before ever playing an NHL regular-season game, 1949-50.

the faceoff. George Gee won the draw and Babando snapped it into the net past New York netminder Charlie Rayner."

Three more titles would follow by 1954-55. No player in Detroit history has won more Stanley Cups in a Red Wings uniform than the four earned by Pronovost, who played in eight Cup final series for the team.

Pronovost views his Stanley Cup wins the same way that proud parents speak of their children. Each one is wonderful in its own unique way. "There was something special in every Stanley Cup, really," Pronovost said.

The 1951-52 Red Wings swept to the title in a minimum eight games. In 1953-54, Detroit worked Game 7 OT again, this time against Montreal, Tony Leswick netting the Cup winner. The Wings remain the only team to win the Cup in a Game 7 overtime scenario. They did it twice and Pronovost was involved in both games, though with a little bit of luck, the second one might not have been necessary.

"I got in behind the Montreal defence twice in that game, but both times, Montreal goalie Gerry McNeil made fine saves to stop me," Pronovost said.

The 1954-55 triumph witnessed one of the greatest rallies to end a regular season in NHL history, as the Wings stormed back to capture their seventh successive first-overall finish at the expense of the rival Canadiens. "We were 10 points behind Montreal with 10 games to go," Pronovost recalled. "We were two points behind when we beat them 4-1 down there, then we beat them in our rink to clinch first place and home ice in the playoffs."

The home-ice advantage earned from that comeback turned out to be a huge development, because the Wings defeated Montreal in a seven-game final series in which the home team won every game. Pronovost earned an assist on Howe's Game 7 Cup winner.

"We definitely had the talent, but we also had a lot of heart," Pronovost said of that Detroit dynasty. "All the successful clubs have that element—character, camaraderie, chemistry—call it whatever you want, that team had it."

Though he often skated in the shadows of other Red Wings stars such as Howe, Ted Lindsay, Terry Sawchuk and Red Kelly, Pronovost steadily came to be recognized as being among the NHL's best players.

He was voted to the NHL's Second All-Star Team in 1957-58 and 1958-59, finishing third in Norris Trophy voting the latter season. Pronovost was a First All-Star Team selection in 1959-60 and 1960-61, and was runner-up to Montreal's Doug Harvey in the balloting for the 1960-61 Norris Trophy.

Pronovost was a quiet superstar. "I was more of a complete defenceman," Pronovost said. He could skate, puck handle, make plays and put it in the net when required. Pronovost was equally adept without the puck, armed with tremendous lateral movement that made him a devastating open-ice bodychecker.

PRONOVOSTS' RED WINGS STATISTICS:										
	Regular Season					Playoffs				
Season	GP	G	A	P	PIM	GP	G	A	P	PIM
1949-50	-	-	-	-	-	9	0	1	1	10
1950-51	37	1	6	7	20	6	0	0	0	0
1951-52	68	7	11	18	50	8	0	1	1	10
1952-53	68	8	19	27	72	6	0	0	0	6
1953-54	57	6	12	18	50	12	2	3	5	12
1954-55	70	9	25	34	90	11	1	2	3	6
1955-56	68	4	13	17	46	10	0	2	2	8
1956-57	70	7	9	16	38	5	0	0	0	6
1957-58	62	2	18	20	52	4	0	1	1	4
1958-59	69	11	21	32	44	-	-	-	-	-
1959-60	69	7	17	24	38	5	0	0	0	6
1960-61	70	6	11	17	44	9	2	3	5	0
1961-62	70	4	14	18	38	-	-	-	-	-
1962-63	69	4	9	13	48	11	1	4	5	8
1963-64	67	3	17	20	42	14	0	2	2	14
1964-65	68	1	15	16	45	7	0	3	3	4
Totals	983	80	217	297	717	118	7	23	30	90

"Marcel hit me once and it was the hardest I'd ever been hit in my life, other than the time I accidentally touched the electric fence on my farm with my elbow," Chicago Blackhawks superstar Bobby Hull said. "I wasn't going to let anyone know I was hurt, so right after the hit I just sauntered over to the bench, but I couldn't breathe for two minutes. He just knocked the wind right out of me."

Pronovost felt the same way the afternoon of May 20, 1965. Driving his car from Detroit to Windsor across the Ambassador Bridge, he heard on the radio that he'd been traded to the Leafs. "It was like being rejected by your mother," Pronovost said. "I'd spent 18 years in the Detroit organization."

In Toronto, Pronovost would win another Stanley Cup in 1966-67 and move into coaching after his playing days were done. He served as head coach of the Buffalo Sabres for two years and was an assistant coach with the Wings from 1980-81.

After coaching, Pronovost continued in the game as a scout, first with NHL Central Scouting and then with the New Jersey Devils, where he added three more Stanley Cups in 1995, 2000 and 2003, allowing him to set a record for the longest tenure between his first and last Stanley Cup inscription.

"It's provided me with a good living," Pronovost said modestly of the game of hockey. "Working with (Devils GM) Lou Lamoriello, it's so enjoyable. He's such a competent man and he's very loyal to his employees."

Based out of Windsor, which became his second home, Pronovost continued scouting for the Devils right up until his death in 2015.

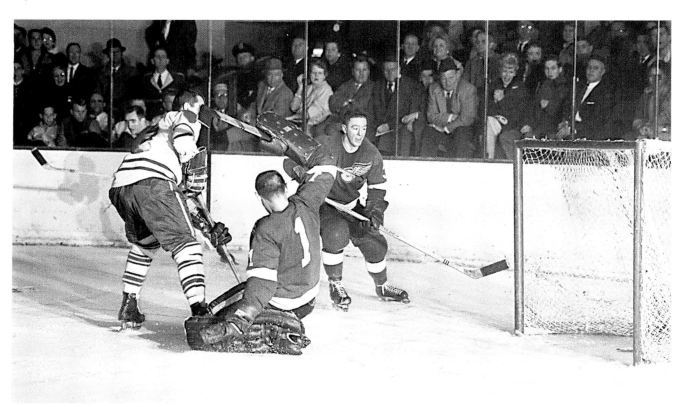

16 HENRIK ZETTERBERG
Left Wing

Born: October 9, 1980, Njurunda, Sweden
Shoots: Left **Height:** 5-11 **Weight:** 197 lbs.
Red Wing From: 2002-03 to present
Acquired: Selected 210th overall in June 26, 1999 NHL Entry Draft.

WHEN HENRIK ZETTERBERG ARRIVED IN DETROIT, HE'D already been recognized for his greatness back home in his native Sweden. Timra, the Swedish club for which Zetterberg starred prior to becoming a Red Wing, retired his No. 20 sweater, even though Zetterberg had yet to celebrate his 22nd birthday.

"I feel so good about that," Zetterberg said. "I was very happy when they put my number up. It was a great honour."

A decade later, the Wings recognized Zetterberg's penchant for leadership. In 2013, he was selected to follow fellow Swede Nicklas Lidstrom as captain of the team.

The choice was a popular decision inside and outside the Detroit dressing room. "If it had gone to a vote, it would have been unanimous," Wings forward Daniel Cleary said.

"I think with Hank, the biggest thing for me is that he's so unselfish. He's such a personable guy.

"He's a star, he's got great talent on the ice, but he's very respectful off the ice and he's vocal when he needs to be. He leads by example."

One of the game's most competitive all-around performers, in his decade in Detroit the Wings followed of the tempo established by their leader.

"He sets the tone," Detroit general manager Ken Holland said. "He plays hard every day in practice. He's a great two-way player."

Beyond the impressive skill set that has permitted Zetterberg to produce four 30-goal seasons and three 80-point seasons, former Detroit coach Mike Babcock admires the compete effort that Zetterberg brings to the ice on game night most.

DETROIT HONOURS:

- Stanley Cup champion, 2007-08
- Won Conn Smythe Trophy, 2007-08
- Named to NHL Second All-Star Team, 2007-08
- Named to NHL All-Rookie Team, 2002-03
- Selected to play in NHL All-Star Game, 2007, 2008, but missed both games due to injury
- Led Stanley Cup playoffs in goals and points, 2007-08
- Led Red Wings in goals, 2006-07, 2007-08
- Led Red Wings in assists and points, 2010-11, 2012-13, 2014-15
- Led Red Wings in points, 2011-12
- Set franchise record with points in first 15 games of 2007-08 season
- Team captain, 2013 to present
- Won gold medal with Sweden at 2006 Turin Winter Olympic Games
- Played for Sweden at 2010 and 2014 Winter Olympic Games
- Won World Championship with Sweden, 2005, 2006
- Won World Championship silver medal with Sweden, 2003
- Viking Award winner as best Swedish player playing North America, 2007, 2008
- Won King Clancy Memorial Trophy, 2014-15.

"I believe he has a will-tank deeper than anybody I've ever been associated with," Babcock said. "His drive-train is fantastic. When I watch Zetterberg he's the Energizer bunny. He just keeps coming. He doesn't care who it is or who he's playing.

"He's demanding of himself and he doesn't mind speaking his mind. He cares about his teammates. To me, that's pretty good leadership."

Like Zetterberg's game, the admiration society works both ways. "It's a challenge," Pittsburgh Penguins captain Sidney Crosby said of trying to get the better of Zetterberg in head-to-head meetings. "There's no surprise there. When I play against him, I expect to be tightly checked. These are the battles that you have to find ways to win."

Zetterberg won the battle with Crosby during the 2008 Stanley Cup final, which saw Detroit down the Penguins in six games. While holding Crosby, hockey's most dynamic player, in check, Zetterberg finished the post-season with leading 13-14-27 totals and was awarded the Conn Smythe Trophy as MVP of the playoffs.

Carolina Hurricanes centre Jordan Staal, another talented pivot who often is asked to fill a checking role, marvels at the work of Zetterberg.

"He's such a smart player on both sides of the puck," Staal said. "He doesn't make too many risky plays. It's tough to get chances on him when he's playing that way. And the offence is there as well, so it's a challenge."

Staal admitted he studies the way Zetterberg plays to gain an edge. "He's a remarkable player. He works hard at both ends of the ice. He takes care of his own end and he also knows how to score goals. His positioning is amazing—he's in the right spot at the right time. He's always on the right side of the puck and works hard on his defensive game.

"He's got a complete game. That's something I want to follow and learn from. It's kind of neat playing against a guy like that."

Selected 210th overall by the Red Wings in the 1999 NHL Entry Draft, Zetterberg arrived in Detroit with a solid resumé. He was named Swedish Elite League rookie of the year in 2000-01 and in the following year, was the only non-NHLer selected to play for Sweden's team at the 2002 Winter Olympic Games in Salt Lake City.

Though he only picked up one assist in four games, that Olympiad was the turning point which showed Zetterberg that he was ready to be a Red Wing. "All of the other players were NHLers and I knew that I could play with them," Zetterberg said. "I think that was a big reason I knew I was ready to take the step forward."

He scored 22 goals with Detroit in 2002-03 and was named to the NHL All-Rookie Team. Zetterberg's star blossomed even further in 2005-06, when he tallied 39 goals and 85 points. That summer, after a first-round playoff exit, captain Steve Yzerman hung up his skates, changing the dynamic of the franchise.

"Steve Yzerman retired and all of a sudden, up front it became Pav (Pavel Datsyuk) and Z's team," Holland said. "He's obviously a big reason we've been able to be competitive since '05."

| ZETTERBERG'S RED WINGS STATISTICS: | | | | | | | | | |
| Regular Season | | | | | Playoffs | | | | |
Season	GP	G	A	P	PIM	GP	G	A	P	PIM
2002-03	79	22	22	44	8	4	1	0	1	0
2003-04	61	15	28	43	14	12	2	2	4	4
2005-06	77	39	46	85	30	6	6	0	6	2
2006-07	63	33	35	68	36	18	6	8	14	12
2007-08	75	43	49	92	34	22	13	14	27	16
2008-09	77	31	42	73	36	23	11	13	24	13
2009-10	74	23	47	70	26	12	7	8	15	6
2010-11	80	24	56	80	40	7	3	5	8	2
2011-12	82	22	47	69	47	5	2	1	3	4
2012-13	46	11	37	48	18	14	4	8	12	8
2013-14	45	16	32	48	20	2	1	1	2	0
2014-15	77	17	49	66	32	7	0	3	3	8
Totals	836	296	490	786	341	132	56	63	119	75

Zetterberg began his career in Detroit seated next to Yzerman in the Wings' dressing room and recalled the lessons he learned from the man who was the team's longest-serving captain. "Just the way he handled himself on and off the ice, how he prepared for every practice and every game, how he led by example," Zetterberg said.

"When Nick was the captain as well, he did the same thing. Those are the things that I want to try to do."

Those are the things his teammates insist that Zetterberg does for them day in and day out.

Detroit defenceman Niklas Kronwall saw one common trait running through each of the captains he's played under as a Red Wing—Yzerman, Lidstrom and Zetterberg. "What makes them leaders is they're the hardest-working guys and they show up every night," Kronwall said.

Wings goaltender Jimmy Howard spotted one specific difference in Zetterberg's style compared to Lidstrom. "Z's definitely more vocal than Nick," Howard said. "Nick spoke when he needed to and led by example. Z is more vocal throughout the room."

Zetterberg's leadership style is substantive. "It's all about experience," Zetterberg said. "I feel comfortable for this task. I learned a lot throughout my years."

The Wings have learned a lot about Zetterberg throughout his years as well, and when they grade him out, they give the man known as Z all A's.

17 JACK STEWART

Defence

Born: May 6, 1917, Pilot Mound, Manitoba
Died: May 25, 1983
Shot: Left **Height:** 5-11 **Weight:** 190 lbs.
Red Wing From: 1938-39 to 1942-43; 1945-46 to 1949-50
Elected to Hockey Hall of Fame: 1964
Acquired: Signed to a pro contract Oct. 26, 1937.
Departed: Traded to Chicago Blackhawks with Pete Babando, Al Dewsbury, Harry Lumley and Don Morrison for Bob Goldham, Jim Henry, Metro Prystai and Gaye Stewart, July 13, 1950.

JACK STEWART NEVER CARED FOR HIS NICKNAME.

"Others called him Black Jack, but we on the team used to call him Silent Jack," former Wings captain Sid Abel recalled of the soft-spoken Stewart to the *Windsor Star* in 1983.

An opponent hung the former handle on the hard-hitting Stewart during his NHL days.

"I bodychecked some fellow one night and when he woke up the next day in the hospital, he asked who'd hit him with the blackjack?" Stewart explained to the *Montreal Gazette* in 1972.

Stewart felt the nickname portrayed him as a dirty player. A stay-at-home defender, there was no question that he played a hard, physical game, and didn't tolerate opposition players taking liberties with his teammates.

"I never argued with the referee," said Stewart, who led the NHL with 73 penalty minutes during the 1945-46 season. "I figured for every penalty I got, I used to get away with around 10.

"I thought I was more valuable on the ice than in the box."

For all of the toughness he brought to the ice, Stewart could never be labeled as someone who dished out cheap shots. He was respected throughout the league, even by those he'd pancaked with his punishing hits.

"He was one of the most easygoing guys off the ice, but one of the most strongest and intense on it," Abel said.

Not that he needed a lesson in Stewart's passion and desire, but Abel got one nonetheless as Detroit battled the New York Rangers in the 1950 Stanley Cup final.

Trailing the best-of-seven set 3-2 and facing elimination, Wings coach Tommy Ivan spirited the team away to Toledo on the off day prior to Game 6.

Centre Don Raleigh had given the Rangers their edge in the set by scoring overtime winners in Games 4 and 5, a fact that didn't sit well with Stewart, who knew that stopping Raleigh was Abel's assignment.

"Jack Stewart was one of our alternate captains," remembered Wings defenceman Marcel Pronovost. "Sid Abel was his roommate and Jack, he tore him a new one.

"Jack looked sternly at Sid and said, 'Don Raleigh is making a fool out of you.' I remember that Sid later told me. 'I was afraid to go to bed that night.'"

Abel scored twice to win Game 6, and Detroit captured the Cup with a seventh-game triumph, the second title that Stewart earned in a Red Wings uniform.

DETROIT HONOURS:

- Stanley Cup champion 1942-43, 1949-50
- Selected to NHL First All-Star Team 1942-43, 1947-38, 1948-49
- Selected to NHL Second All-Star Team 1945-46, 1946-47
- Played in NHL All-Star Game 1946, 1947, 1948, 1949
- Led NHL in penalty minutes, 1945-46

Paired with another tough customer in Jimmy Orlando, Stewart helped Detroit reach the Stanley Cup final for three straight seasons from 1941-43, finally tasting success when the Wings swept the Boston Bruins in the 1942-43 Cup final series.

Stewart was named to the NHL's First All-Star Team that season. There was no Conn Smythe Trophy in those days, but in 2001, *The Hockey News* commissioned a committee from the Society For International Hockey Research to select playoff MVPs from the pre-Conn Smythe era and Stewart was the choice for 1943.

Enlisting in the R.C.A.F. after that 1943 Cup triumph, Stewart returned to the Wings for the 1945-46 season following the conclusion of the Second World War and picked up right where he left off. He was named to the NHL's Second All-Star Team that season, becoming the first defenceman to be a league all-star both prior to and after the game-changing introduction of the centre red line for the 1943-44 season.

"He's a manager's dream," Adams explained to *Canadian Press*. "He's a very deceptive skater. He packs a terrific shot. He's an uncanny judge of a forward's play.

"He's one of the greatest in the game."

Stewart turned pro with the Wings in the fall of 1938. Detroit coach Jack Adams paired Stewart in training camp that spring with all-star Ebbie Goodfellow, and the youngster proved a quick study.

Off to a 4-11-1 start to the 1938-39 season, Adams opted to shuffle his lineup. He sold the contract of veteran defenceman Bucko McDonald, another legendary bodychecker, to the Toronto Maple Leafs for $10,000 and recalled Stewart, 21, from the American Hockey League's Pittsburgh Hornets.

The kid was an immediate hit, literally and figuratively.

"My first full season with the Wings was also his first full season," Abel recalled. "He was as tough as anyone's ever been.

"As a defenceman, he did everything on the ice that you're supposed to do. Stop the other people and knock them around."

STEWART'S RED WINGS STATISTICS:										
	Regular Season					Playoffs				
Season	GP	G	A	P	PIM	GP	G	A	P	PIM
1938-39	32	0	1	1	18	-	-	-	-	-
1939-40	48	1	0	1	40	5	0	0	0	4
1940-41	47	2	6	8	56	9	1	2	3	8
1941-42	44	4	7	11	93	12	0	1	1	12
1942-43	44	2	9	11	68	10	1	2	3	35
1945-46	47	4	11	15	73	5	0	0	0	14
1946-47	55	5	9	14	83	5	0	1	1	12
1947-48	60	5	14	19	91	9	1	3	4	6
1948-49	60	4	11	15	96	11	1	1	2	32
1949-50	65	3	11	14	86	14	1	4	5	20
Totals	678	39	122	161	955	98	6	16	22	157

In 1966, Adams picked Stewart and Boston legend Eddie Shore as the defencemen on his all-time NHL team.

Anyone who dared skate down Stewart's side of the ice paid a significant and painful price. He'd fix his piercing, dark eyes on them until they were within his bombsights, and then deliver his payload.

"He just looks at you coldly through those slits of eyes and then—whammo—he knocks you on your can," former NHL forward Bill Ezinicki told the *Calgary Herald*.

One night in Montreal, Canadiens star Maurice (Rocket) Richard tried to slip the puck through Stewart's legs, simultaneously coming up with his stick in a spearing motion, opening a five-stitch cut across the Detroit defenceman's forehead.

Stewart lifted Richard to shoulder height with his powerfully strong arms, and then angrily flung the Rocket. The Montreal star was airborne for six feet until he crashed into the boards.

Feats of Stewart's strength were legendary around the league.

"Once I lifted his stick and was shocked by how heavy it was," Red Wings legend Gordie Howe remembered. "I asked, 'How in the world do you shoot with this stick?'

"'I don't,'" Black Jack told me. "'I break arms with it.'"

Stewart's toughness wasn't limited to battles with opponents. He once took 33 stitches to the face after being clipped by an errant stick in a game versus Toronto.

Stewart was patched up and ordered to go to hospital for further observation. Instead, he returned to the ice minutes after being cut and took his regular shift for the remainder of the game.

After ten seasons as a Red Wing, Stewart was dealt to Chicago in 1950 in a seven-player deal, at the time the largest trade in NHL history.

He was elected to the Hockey Hall of Fame in 1964. "That was a great thrill, to have my name placed up there with all those great players," Stewart said.

After his playing days, Stewart dabbled in minor-league coaching and made a career as a harness-racing official in both Ontario and the United States.

Stewart died at the age of 66 after a battle with cancer.

18 SYD HOWE

Centre/Left Wing

Born: September 28, 1911, Ottawa, Ontario
Died: May 20, 1976
Shot: Left **Height:** 5-9 **Weight:** 165 lbs.
Red Wing From: 1934-35 to 1945-46
Elected to Hockey Hall of Fame: 1965
Acquired: Traded to Detroit by St. Louis Eagles with Ralph (Scotty) Bowman for Teddy Graham and $50,000, February 11, 1935.
Departed: Traded by Detroit to St. Louis (AHL), August 17, 1946.

A VISITOR TO MICHIGAN FROM THE SOUTHERN UNITED States opted to take in a Detroit Red Wings pre-season game at Olympia Stadium in the fall of 1944.

"Who's that kid out there?" the fellow asked, pointing toward the player wearing sweater No. 8 for the Wings. "He looks like a real comer."

You could say the Red Wings player he referenced had already arrived, since it was 33-year Syd Howe, a 15-season NHL veteran.

At that point in his career, Howe already was a 200-goal scorer, something only 10 players in NHL history had accomplished. He was coming off a career-high 32-goal season for the Wings. He'd also put a Detroit-record six goals past New York Rangers goalie Ken McAuley during a 12-2 rout of the Rangers on Feb. 3, 1944.

Serving as a machinist in a Detroit factory, his part of the wartime effort during World War II, Howe didn't let his hot night go to his head. "I'll be on the job at 7:10 a.m., just like I am six days a week," Howe explained. "I wonder what the boys in the shop will say?"

Howe scored his goals in bunches of pairs—two goals 18 seconds apart in the first period, a pair separated by 62 seconds in the second period, and another two 57 seconds from each other in the final frame.

In NHL history, only the Quebec Bulldog's Joe Malone had scored more, tallying seven against Toronto in a Jan. 31, 1920 game.

"They left me out there to try and get more goals," Howe told author Stan Fischler of his six-goal night. "I had a good chance to break the all-time record, but I couldn't do it."

The Rangers seemed to be Howe's personal property. On March 8, 1945, during a 7-3 win over them, Howe assisted on a goal by Joe Carveth to garner his 515th NHL point and move past Nels Stewart into the NHL's all-time scoring lead. Howe finished with 528 career points and would hold top spot until Feb. 12, 1947 when he was surpassed by Boston's Bill Cowley, like Howe a native of Ottawa, Ontario.

"Syd played almost 60 minutes a game, left wing, right wing, power play, killed penalties," Cowley told the *Ottawa Citizen* in 1991.

DETROIT HONOURS:

- Stanley Cup champion 1935-36, 1936-37, 1942-43
- Named to NHL Second All-Star Team, 1944-45
- Played in NHL All-Star Game, 1938-39
- Set club record, scoring six goals against New York Rangers on Feb. 3, 1944
- Team captain, 1941-42
- Led Detroit in scoring, 1934-35, 1939-40, 1940-41, 1942-43
- NHL All-Time scoring leader from March 8, 1945 to Feb. 12, 1947.

The Wings spent an astronomical amount of $50,000 to purchase the contracts of Howe and defenceman Ralph (Scotty) Bowman from the St. Louis Eagles, especially astonishing when you consider the transaction took place amidst the Great Depression.

"It was too attractive to pass up," Clare Brunton, managing director of the Eagles, told the *Associated Press*. "We had an opportunity to make a profitable trade and we accepted it."

Detroit coach-GM Jack Adams saw the additions setting up his team as a Stanley Cup contender for the 1935-36 campaign. Howe provided secondary scoring behind the top forward unit of Marty Barry, Larry Aurie and Herbie Lewis, while Bowman gave him a shutdown defender to deepen his blue-line corps.

Adams proved a genius when the Wings won back-to-back championships the next two seasons. Howe scored a career-high 16 goals for the 1935-36 Wings, and then tallied 17 times during the 1936-37 season.

He proved equally productive off the ice. Howe was Detroit's champion at dealing the cards.

"Rummy was the big game," recalled Mark Beltaire, who covered the Wings for the *Detroit News* from 1937-42 and shared train trips with the team. "The champion was Syd Howe. He was a hell of a card player."

Apparently, so was Mrs. Howe. "One trip, Jack Adams let the players' wives come along," Beltaire said. "Some of the guys wanted to play a little poker, and Syd Howe's wife (Frances) wanted in. They sneered at her, but she got in and cleaned them out.

"Boy, were they mad."

Howe displayed a knack for record-setting. In the opening game of the 1940 Stanley Cup quarter-finals, Howe tallied 25 seconds into overtime to give Detroit a 2-1 victory over the New York Americans. It was the fastest goal from the start of a playoff overtime game in NHL history and stood as the record until April 2, 1969, when Ted Irvine scored 19 seconds into the extra session to give the Los Angeles Kings a 5-4 decision over the Oakland Seals.

Howe classified his record overtime tally as his most memorable moment, ahead of his six-goal game.

	REGULAR SEASON					PLAYOFFS				
Season	GP	G	A	P	PIM	GP	G	A	P	PIM
1934-35	14	8	12	20	11	-	-	-	-	-
1935-36	48	16	14	30	26	7	3	3	6	2
1936-37	45	17	10	27	10	10	2	5	7	0
1937-38	48	8	19	27	14	-	-	-	-	-
1938-39	48	16	20	36	11	6	3	1	4	4
1939-40	46	14	23	37	17	5	2	2	4	2
1940-41	48	20	24	44	8	9	1	7	8	0
1941-42	48	16	19	35	6	12	3	5	8	0
1942-43	50	20	35	55	10	7	1	2	3	0
1943-44	46	32	28	60	6	5	2	2	4	0
1944-45	46	17	36	53	6	7	0	0	0	2
1945-46	26	4	7	11	9	-	-	-	-	-
Totals	513	188	247	435	134	68	17	27	44	10

HOWE'S RED WINGS STATISTICS:

"The other time I'll never forget is the night Detroit fans gave me toward the end of my career," Howe recalled of the Jan. 28, 1942 evening when the locals feted him prior to a game against Chicago. "I got a lot of gifts, including a piano."

To the delight of the Olympia crowd, Howe sat down at the piano and tickled the ivories with a couple of his favourite tunes. Among his other gifts were a desk set, a toaster, a tool box, a new suit, and a $100 cheque from Wings owner James Norris.

"They wanted him to know that they remembered what a grand fellow he had always been," wrote Doug Vaughan in the *Windsor Star*. "They wanted him to know that they would never forget the thrills he had given them, or the truly great hockey player he is."

Never a wordsmith, Silent Syd as he was known choked up as he tried to thank the fans. Once the game began, he would offer his appreciation to them in his usual fashion.

"You know how it is when they give you a night?" Howe said. "It usually turns out that team gets beat and you can't come close to scoring. I was a lot luckier. We beat the Black Hawks 2-0 and I scored both goals."

Like Gordie Howe—the two weren't related, by the way—Syd could play just about anywhere on the ice and filled in at every position except goal. And he seemed to get better with age, another trait he held in common with Gordie.

At the age of 33, Howe was an NHL Second All-Star in 1944-45, finished second in the Lady Byng Trophy voting and posted career bests with 32 goals and 60 points, joining Carl Liscombe (36) and Mud Bruneteau (35) to make Detroit the first team in NHL history to suit up a trio of 30-goal scorers.

Adams assigned Howe to Detroit's AHL farm club in Indianapolis midway through the 1945-46 season, bringing about an end to his NHL days.

Howe died in 1976 at the age of 64 following a lengthy illness.

19 MICKEY REDMOND

Right Wing

Born: December 27, 1947, Kirkland Lake, Ontario
Shot: Right **Height:** 5-11 **Weight:** 185 lbs.
Red Wing From: 1970-71 to 1975-76
Acquired: Traded to Detroit by Montreal Canadiens with Guy Charron and Bill Collins for Frank Mahovlich, January 13, 1971.
Departed: Announced retirement from hockey, September 13, 1976.

MICKEY REDMOND FIGURED HE WAS GIVEN A HARVARD education in hockey, followed by a Harvard education in broadcasting, and both led him to greatness in Detroit.

Redmond was born into a hockey family. His father Ed was a minor pro player and his younger brother Dick followed Mickey to the NHL. Mickey started in the Montreal Canadiens organization with the junior Peterborough Petes at the age of 14. He was named rookie of the year in the OHA Junior A series in 1963-64, and three years later won the Red Tilson Memorial Trophy as the league's MVP, finishing ahead of future NHLers Derek Sanderson and Walt Tkaczuk.

In 1967-68 he made the jump into the Canadiens lineup, winning Stanley Cups in each of his first two NHL seasons, even scoring an overtime winner in the 1969 semifinals against the Boston Bruins.

"I had the great chance to play with Jean Beliveau, Yvan Cournoyer, Henri Richard, John Ferguson, the whole crew in Montreal," Redmond said. "To win two Stanley Cups and to learn how it's done and what it's like to be in an organization like that, it was a great opportunity for me as a young 19 year old."

Nearly two decades earlier, the young Beliveau had learned the game with the minor-league Quebec Aces, where Redmond's father was one of his teammates. Mickey still remembers the night he brought his dad into the Montreal dressing room.

"Jean said to me, 'Mickey, I am getting old. First I play with the father, and now I play with the son.'"

Not for much longer, though. With the Habs loading up for another shot at the Stanley Cup in 1970-71, Redmond was included in part of a package that went to Detroit for future Hall of Fame left winger Frank Mahovlich.

"Talk about my good fortune again," Redmond said. "I come to Detroit and I had the good fortune to play with Gordie (Howe) and Alex (Delvecchio), and Bergy (Gary Bergman) and (Nick) Libett."

Even if originally, it didn't seem that way.

"Coming to Detroit was not a fun thing at first, because they were buried so far down they couldn't see up, but it

DETROIT HONOURS:

- Selected to NHL First All-Star Team, 1972-73
- Selected to NHL Second All-Star Team, 1973-74
- Played in NHL All-Star Game, 1974
- First player in franchise history to record a 50-goal season, 1972-73
- Set club record for power-play goals (21) in a season, 1973-74
- Played for Team Canada in 1972 Summit Series
- Led Red Wings in goals, 1971-72, 1972-73, 1973-74
- Led Red Wings in scoring, 1972-73
- Team captain, 1973-74.

gave me an opportunity to play full-time and to display my wares," Redmond said. "That's all a player can ask, is that you get a chance to play and show the team what you're made of and that you deserve to be in the lineup every day."

Redmond did much more than that. In fact, he did something that no Red Wing had ever done in franchise history. He produced a 50-goal season.

Redmond was on fire early in the season and had potted 37 goals through 54 games when he hit an eight-game goalless skid. "I was sitting there with 37 goals and people we're kind of saying, 'Well, you might have a chance to score 50 goals, but it's an outside chance,'" Redmond said of his mini-slump.

Just like that, he ignited again, scoring seven times in the next six games, including two-goal games versus the Philadelphia Flyers and St. Louis Blues. "The next thing you know, you wake up a week later and you're at 43 and you think, 'Wow, I do have a chance,'" Redmond said.

The milestone 50th came March 27 at Toronto's Maple Leaf Gardens. Redmond beat Toronto's Ron Low during an 8-1 rout of the Leafs and 18 seconds after netting No. 50 added No. 51 to his total.

"It's a wonderful memory to have," Redmond said, and yet, four decades later, it's still somewhat difficult to fathom.

"It's always been kind of strange, because Gordie (Howe) had 49 (goals in 1952-53) and the Big M (Mahovlich) had 49 (in 1968-69). I guess one of Gordie's goals (in 1952-53) was credited to the wrong guy (Red Kelly)."

In case anyone thought it was a fluke, Redmond—an NHL First All-Star Team selection who was tabbed to play for Team Canada in the 1972 Summit Series against the Soviet Union, followed his 52-goal 1972-73 campaign with a 51-goal season in 1973-74, including a club-record 21 power-play goals. Redmond and Steve Yzerman remain the only players in Red Wings history to post successive 50-goal seasons.

Then just like that, the explosion of goals came to a crashing halt. "I remember playing against St. Louis and Barclay Plager was on the defence on the other side,"

Redmond said of a play during the 1974-75 season. "In a normal situation, I could probably go down the outside and beat him and then cut to the net and get a scoring chance. This time, we ended up in the corner together and I thought, 'Something's drastically wrong here.'"

The problem originated in the fall of 1974, not long after Redmond had signed a five-year, $1 million contract with the Wings. He began experiencing intermittent back pain. It didn't seem serious at first, but grew to be so troublesome that trainers had to tie his skates because Redmond couldn't bend over.

"In those days, they didn't pay attention to us like they do today," Redmond said. "It was 'throw a Band-Aid on him and get back out there and go.'"

Redmond was diagnosed with a ruptured disc which was pressuring on a nerve controlling brain signals to his leg. He underwent surgery on Dec. 20, 1974 and returned to the lineup in March of 1975.

His back was okay but the numbness in the right leg remained. "It was the right side of my back and that affected all the strength in the leg," Redmond said. "The ability to be able to cut in was gone.

"I got to the Mayo Clinic and the doctors looked at me and said, 'If we saw you six months ago, we might have a chance to bring you back.' But it was almost too late then. A couple years later, I basically had to walk away."

REDMOND'S RED WINGS STATISTICS:

	Regular Season					Playoffs				
Season	GP	G	A	P	PIM	GP	G	A	P	PIM
1970-71	21	6	8	14	7	-	-	-	-	-
1971-72	78	42	29	71	34	-	-	-	-	-
1972-73	76	52	41	93	24	-	-	-	-	-
1973-74	76	51	26	77	14	-	-	-	-	-
1974-75	29	15	12	27	18	-	-	-	-	-
1975-76	37	11	17	28	10	-	-	-	-	-
Totals	317	177	133	310	107	-	-	-	-	-

Redmond played the last game of his NHL career on Jan. 18, 1976 at Olympia Stadium, an 8-3 loss to Kings. In September, he announced his retirement as a player.

"I tried to make a comeback in 1979 and it didn't work," Redmond said. "I only lasted two weeks in Glens Falls (Detroit's AHL farm club)."

Life in hockey was far from done for Redmond, though. He started working on Red Wings broadcasts and as an analyst for Hockey Night In Canada.

"Much like Montreal, I got to work with those stars like Danny Gallivan, Dick Irvin, Bob Cole, Jim Robson, Dave Hodge, all great guys and great broadcasters," Redmond said. "They were like the Canadiens in the broadcast field. For me to be there five years was really fortunate."

In 1985, he joined the Detroit crew for television broadcasts and has been in the booth for Wings games ever since. "When the Red Wings separated their television and radio was when I was asked to come here full-time, and of course it was an easy decision to make," Redmond said. "And here we are 29 years later."

In 2011, Redmond was presented the Foster Hewitt Memorial Award by the Hockey Hall of Fame. The honour recognizes those in the radio and television industry who have made outstanding contributions to their profession and the game of hockey.

"I always look at that situation as being blessed in two ways," Redmond said of his successful two-pronged hockey career. "I think having been part of two Original Six teams is the memory I'll always carry. And to still be a part of this one, with so much history, is as good as it gets.

"I never thought that one day I'd be behind the microphone for this length of time and having as much fun as I do."

20 CHRIS OSGOOD

Goal

Born: November 26, 1972, Peace River, Alberta
Shot: Left Height: 5-10 Weight: 180 lbs.
Red Wing From: 1993-94 to 2000-01; 2005-06 to 2010-11
Acquired: Selected 54th overall in June 22, 1991 NHL Entry Draft
Departed: Claimed by New York Islanders from Detroit in NHL Waiver Draft, September 28, 2001.
Reacquired: Signed as a free agent by Detroit, August 28, 2005.
Departed: Announced retirement from hockey, July 19, 2011.

THE WORLD OF OZ WAS A FUNNY, FUNNY PLACE.

Where the streets were paved with goals, and trashing Chris Osgood never grew old.

During his career with the Detroit Red Wings, Osgood was often a lightning rod for criticism, sometimes deservedly so, after his inability to handle long shots and his puck-handling gaffes put his club in dire straits.

Most of the time, though, as his resumé indicates, Osgood delivered the goods as well as almost anyone to ever strap on the goalie pads for Detroit. Only Terry Sawchuk (352, 85) posted more wins and shutouts in a Red Wings uniform. No netminder in franchise history earned more Stanley Cup rings than the man they call Ozzie.

He hopes he'll earn a spot in the Hockey Hall of Fame one day. "Hopefully, one day, it happens," Osgood said. "It means the world to me. I do believe I deserve to be there.

"I don't think I ever made it a secret that my goal was to someday rank among the legends."

Osgood jumped into the No. 1 role for Detroit in 1993 before he'd even reached his 21st birthday, when injuries scuttled the veterans on the depth chart ahead of him.

It seemed like the critics spent the remainder of Osgood's Detroit career trying to run him out of town. When the Wings won the Cup in 1997, Osgood took a back seat to Conn Smythe Trophy winner Mike Vernon. He took over for the traded Vernon the following spring and the Wings won again, but what's remembered more about Osgood's performance are the long-shot goals he surrendered to Jamie Langenbrunner and Al MacInnis.

Three years later, Osgood was finally exiled to the New York Islanders when the Wings acquired Dominik Hasek, who backstopped them to the 2002 Cup. In 2005, he returned to

DETROIT HONOURS:

- Stanley Cup champion 1996-97, 1997-98, 2007-08
- Shared William Jennings Trophy with Mike Vernon, 1995-96
- Shared William Jennings Trophy with Dominik Hasek, 2007-08
- Named to NHL Second All-Star Team, 1995-96
- Played in NHL All-Star Game, 1996, 1997, 1998
- Led NHL in wins, 1995-96
- Led NHL in goals-against average, 2007-08
- Led Stanley Cup playoffs in goals-against average, 2007-08
- Led Stanley Cup playoffs in wins, 1997-98, 2007-08
- Led Stanley Cup playoffs in shutouts, 2007-08, 2008-09
- Only Red Wings goalie to score a goal, March 6, 1996 versus Hartford Whalers
- With 4-0 victory over San Jose Sharks on April 20, 1994, joined John Ross Roach (1933) and Normie Smith (1936) as only Detroit goalies to post shutouts in their Stanley Cup debut as Wings
- Franchise career leader in Stanley Cup wins (67), shutouts (14) and games (110) by a goalie.

the Wings as a free agent, expected to serve as Hasek's back-up. But when Hasek struggled to start the 2008 playoffs, Osgood stepped in and backstopped the Wings to the Stanley Cup, his third title with the team, a total matched only by Sawchuk among Detroit's long history of puckstoppers.

"Ozzie played unbelievable for us," remembered Detroit centre Henrik Zetterberg, who won the Conn Smythe Trophy as playoff MVP that spring, though Osgood would have also been a worthy recipient. "He didn't let many goals in."

Osgood reflects back on that season, which saw the Wings down the Pittsburgh Penguins in the Cup final series, as one of his happiest moments in the game.

"It was one of those situations where you get into an unexplainable zone at the most important time of the year," Osgood said. "I'd always taken pride in playing well in the playoffs—even in junior and coming up (through the minors) in Adirondack.

"I enjoyed it. I thought it was a lot of fun. I loved stepping on the ice. In the playoffs, I couldn't wait to play the next game. I just enjoyed that time of year. I loved playing at that time."

It was scoring with a ball, not stopping a puck, that helped pave Osgood's path to the Red Wings net.

Ken Holland, then assistant GM of the Red Wings, was putting together a team to play in a summer ball hockey league in Medicine Hat, Alta. One of the players he recruited was Osgood, then goalie for the Western Hockey League's Medicine Hat Tigers.

"He was a forward," remembered Holland, now the GM of the Wings and the man who recommended the club draft Osgood in 1991. "He had great hands and could score and had great drive and competitiveness.

"I got to know him as a person, better than you usually get to know these kids heading into draft."

Holland felt that insight into Osgood's character helped make it easier for him to trade Vernon after Detroit's 1996-97 Stanley Cup win, placing the pressure to repeat on the shoulders of the boyish, frail-looking Osgood.

| OSGOOD'S RED WINGS STATISTICS: | | | | | | | | | | | |
| Regular Season | | | | | | Playoffs | | | | | |
Season	GPI	MIN	GA	SO	W-L-T	GAA	GPI	MIN	GA	SO	GAA	W-L
1993-94	41	2206	105	2	23-7-6	2.86	6	307	12	1	2.35	3-2
1994-95	19	1087	41	1	14-5-0	2.26	2	68	2	0	1.76	0-0
1995-96	50	2933	106	5	39-5-6	2.17	15	936	33	2	2.12	8-7
1996-97	47	2769	106	6	23-13-9	2.30	2	47	2	0	2.55	0-0
1997-98	64	3807	140	6	33-20-11	2.21	22	1361	48	2	2.12	16-6
1998-99	63	3691	149	3	34-24-5	2.42	6	358	14	1	2.35	4-2
1999-00	53	3148	126	6	30-13-9	2.40	9	547	18	2	1.97	5-4
2000-01	52	2837	127	1	25-16-7	2.69	6	365	15	1	2.47	2-4
2005-06	32	1846	85	2	20-6-5	2.76	-	-	-	-	-	-
2006-07	21	1161	46	0	11-3-6	2.38	-	-	-	-	-	-
2007-08	43	2409	84	4	27-9-4	2.09	19	1160	30	3	1.55	14-4
2008-09	46	2663	137	2	26-9-8	3.09	23	1406	47	2	2.01	15-8
2009-10	23	1252	63	1	7-9-4	3.02	-	-	-	-	-	-
2010-11	11	629	29	0	5-3-2	2.77	-	-	-	-	-	-
Totals	565	32438	1782	39	317-244-130	2.49	110	6555	221	14	2.02	67-37

"The day the playoffs started that spring, nobody in the league had any of the pressure or scrutiny that Chris Osgood had," Holland said. "He was replacing the Conn Smythe Trophy winner in the hockey-crazy city of the defending Stanley Cup champs."

When it was over and the Wings paraded around Washington's MCI Center with the Stanley Cup after sweeping the Capitals, Osgood could have chosen to have the last laugh, but instead opted not to chuckle.

"I don't look for vindication or revenge," Osgood said. "What I was looking for I got—ever since I was a little kid, I wanted to be the goalie on a team that won a Stanley Cup.

"It was very gratifying."

His teammates remembered the scrutiny and the pressure that Osgood endured as he backstopped Detroit to another title and admired the way he handled it all.

"He was under the gun all season," former Detroit defenceman Larry Murphy said of Osgood. "No matter what he did, it was always, 'Yeah, but can he do it in the playoffs?'"

"I was so happy for Ozzie," recalled Kevin Hodson, Detroit's back-up goalie in 1997-98. "He'd had to put up with so much (crap) that year. There were so many questions, and he answered them all."

Gone from Detroit from 2001-04, Osgood learned the hard way that there was a difference in the way the Wings operate, which is why he was thrilled to return and finish his career in Detroit.

"I know what it's like," he said. "The grass isn't greener. If anybody wants to ask me about it, I know what I'm going to tell them—don't leave."

Owner of three titles, over 400 NHL wins and a career winning percentage of .639, Osgood retired from the Wings in 2011 with little left to achieve as an NHL goalie.

"I just think it was the right time," said Osgood, limited to 11 games in 2010-11 due to a injury that required surgery.

He remains in the Red Wings' organization as the goalie development coach, working with goaltending prospects in the system as well as doing some amateur scouting of draft-eligible netminders and working on Wings telecasts.

21 HARRY LUMLEY

Goal

Born: November 11, 1936, Owen Sound, Ontario
Died: September 13, 1988
Shot: Left **Height:** 6-0 **Weight:** 195 lbs.
Red Wing From: 1943-44 to 1949-50
Elected to Hockey Hall of Fame: 1980
Acquired: Signed to a pro contract, October 13, 1943.
Departed: Traded by Detroit to Chicago Blackhawks with Jack Stewart, Al Dewsbury, Pete Babando and Don Morrison for Metro Prystai, Gaye Stewart, Bob Goldham and Jim Henry, July 13, 1950.

FEW PLAYERS CAN ATTEST THAT THEY MADE NHL HISTORY merely by stepping on the ice.

Harry Lumley was among this rare group.

When Lumley situated himself between the posts for the Detroit Red Wings at Madison Square Garden to start a 6-2 loss to the New York Rangers on Dec. 19, 1943, at 17 years and 38 days of age, he established a record that remains on the books today for the youngest goaltender in league history.

Unhappy with the work of Jimmy Franks, Detroit coach and general manager Jack Adams summoned the teenaged prodigy from the Wings' American League farm club in Indianapolis.

"He played a good game," Adams told *Associated Press* after Lumley turned aside 30 shots in his NHL debut. "Most of those goals weren't his fault at all. He didn't have a chance when those guys came in all alone."

He started the 1944-45 season back with Indianapolis, and was the leading netminder in the league when Adams summoned Lumley for what he termed would be a "two-week trial" with the Wings on Dec. 6, 1945.

Lumley never looked back, backstopping the Wings to the 1945 Stanley Cup final at the age of 18, another NHL record. Though Detroit lost in seven games to Toronto, Lumley posted two shutouts in the final series. His shutouts were the last by a rookie goalie in Stanley Cup play until Patrick Roy of the Montreal Canadiens blanked the Calgary Flames in Game 4 of the 1986 final.

Lumley, Roy, Carey Price and Semyon Varlamov are the only goalies in NHL history to post a Stanley Cup shutout prior to their 21st birthday.

"The kid is a real comer," Canadiens coach Dick Irvin told the *Windsor Star.*

Lumley led the NHL with seven shutouts in 1947-48, including a shutout sequence of 164 minutes and 54 seconds. The Wings were a rising power, reaching the Cup finals in 1948, 1949 and finally winning the elusive trophy after beating the New York Rangers in a seven-game final set.

Lumley posted back-to-back shutouts in Games 6 and 7 of Detroit's semifinal series win over the Leafs, and also blanked the Rangers in Game 3 of the final.

DETROIT HONOURS:

+ Stanley Cup champion 1949-50
+ Led NHL in shutouts, 1947-48
+ Led Stanley Cup playoffs in goals-against average, 1944-45
+ Led Stanley Cup playoffs in shutouts, 1945-46, 1949-50
+ Youngest goalie in NHL history (17 years, 38 days)
+ Youngest goalie in Stanley Cup final history (18 years, four months, 26 days)

"Those Rangers had me in a wee bit of a sweat," Lumley said.

Opponents would find themselves in a wee bit of trouble should they venture too close to Lumley's goal crease. "You are asking for a stiff body jolt or a rap on the noggin if you dare invade Mr. Lumley's home," noted *Windsor Star* columnist Doug Vaughan.

Lumley garnered 95 penalty minutes during his NHL career and wasn't averse to fisticuffs to protect his turf. In one game against the Leafs, he lumbered to centre ice to meet Toronto goalie Turk Broda, lunging at Broda in a swan dive that left both netminders rolling around the rink wrestling like a pair of grizzly bears.

"The defencemen and forwards have all the fun," Lumley explained. "They can hit and get hit, but us poor goalies are on the receiving end all the time."

Teammates learned quickly not to mess with the man they called "Apple Cheeks" due to his ruddy complexion. Lumley meticulously laid out his gear in front of his dressing room stall and anyone who disturbed his routine risked facing his wrath.

They were also astonished at how quickly Lumley could don his bulky goalie gear. "He could dress while I was still thinking about putting on my socks," former Detroit forward Joe Carveth said.

It was a bit of tomfoolery that would ultimately lead to Lumley's demise as Detroit's goalie. Participating as a forward as the Wings played a charity game against the International Hockey League All-Stars on Jan. 4, 1950, Lumley suffered a sprained ankle. He missed seven games due to the injury, giving the Wings a good long look at Terry Sawchuk, his heir apparent.

Even though he won the Cup in 1950 and had taken Detroit to four Cup final appearances in seven seasons, Lumley was shipped to Chicago as part of a seven-player trade in the summer of 1950.

He ended up playing for five of the six so-called Original Six teams before he was done, missing only the Canadiens. With Toronto Lumley set a club record by posting 13 shutouts in 1953-54. He won the Vezina Trophy by one vote over Sawchuk that spring, and in 1954-55 finished second in Hart Trophy voting for the NHL's MVP.

Finishing his career with Boston in 1959-60, Lumley's 803 games were an NHL record for a goaltender, a mark that would eventually be surpassed by Sawchuk.

"I enjoyed every team I played for," Lumley said. "Winning the Stanley Cup was the big thing, though."

Returning to his hometown of Owen Sound in retirement, Lumley was heavily involved with harness racing. He was a partner in ownership of Orangeville Raceway and also owned a car dealership. The arena in Owen Sound was named in his honour.

Lumley died of a heart attack at the age of 71.

| LUMLEY'S RED WINGS STATISTICS: | | | | | | | | | | | |
| Regular Season | | | | | | Playoffs | | | | | |
Season	GPI	MIN	GA	SO	W-L-T	GAA	GPI	MIN	GA	SO	GAA	W-L
1943-44	2	120	13	0	0-2-0	6.50	-	-	-	-	-	-
1944-45	37	2220	119	1	24-10-3	3.22	14	871	31	2	2.14	7-7
1945-46	50	3000	159	2	20-20-10	3.18	5	310	16	1	3.10	1-4
1946-47	52	3120	159	3	30-18-12	3.06		-	-	-	-	-
1947-48	60	3592	147	7	30-18-12	2.46	10	600	30	0	3.00	4-6
1948-49	60	3600	145	6	34-19-7	2.42	11	726	26	0	2.15	4-7
1949-50	63	3780	148	7	33-16-14	2.35	14	910	28	3	1.85	8-6
Totals	324	19432	890	26	171-103-58	2.74	54	3417	131	6	2.30	24-30

22 BILL QUACKENBUSH

Defence

HE WAS KNOWN AS HOCKEY'S OUTSTANDING GENTLEMAN, and when it came to playing fair, all took a back seat to Bill Quackenbush, who almost never took a seat in the penalty box.

His clean style of play earned Quackenbush accolades, awards and a ticket out of Detroit.

When Quackenbush patrolled the blue line for all 60 of the Red Wings' games during the 1948-49 NHL season without incurring a single penalty minute, it impressed the Lady Byng Trophy selection panel so much that they voted him the award, making Quackenbush the first defenceman to capture the trophy.

That performance and the outcome so appalled Detroit general manager Jack Adams that during the summer of 1949 he swapped Quackenbush, who had been an NHL First All-Star Team selection the previous two seasons, to the Boston Bruins for a package of players including forwards Pete Babando and Jimmy Peters Sr.

At first, Adams played off the trade merely as a hockey move, pointing out that with Quackenbush in the fold, Detroit had fallen in four straight games in successive Stanley Cup finals to the Toronto Maple Leafs.

"We want the Stanley Cup," Adams explained to the *Windsor Star*. "We have defencemen. We don't have forwards. You can be sure I hate to lose Quackenbush, but I have watched Peters and Babando since their junior days and they are two players I have always felt would be valuable assets to the Wings."

Quickly, though, the façade fell apart. "Quackenbush had tried too earnestly to become the Lady Byng Trophy winner as the game's most gentle player," reported the *Montreal Gazette*. "Adams doesn't like defencemen with such exemplary conduct."

As a player, Adams had led the NHL in penalty minutes with the Toronto St. Patricks in 1922-23, and ultimately, he left no doubt as to the way which he thought hockey was supposed to be played.

"They are substituting the Byng for bang in hockey," Adams told the *Montreal Gazette*. "The Lady Byng winners have taken over. Frankie Boucher and the other fellows have gained control of the rules and the game. It's all right for Boucher and the other Byng-ers to make them cut out interfering and holding, but to eliminate the other stuff is to take the fire out of hockey.

"Who made it the great game of the early days? Why the Ching Johnsons, the Eddie Shores, the Nels and Jack Stewarts and the Red Horners. Now they're making it a

115

DETROIT HONOURS:

+ Won Lady Byng Trophy, 1948-49
+ Named to NHL First All-Star Team, 1947-48, 1948-49
+ Named to NHL Second All-Star Team, 1946-47
+ Played in NHL All-Star Game, 1947, 1948

While Stewart was a punishing hitter, Quackenbush was a sensational skater and someone who relied on positioning and his poke-checking skills to slow and disarm the opposition. "I guess I just don't do the things you get put off for," Quackenbush told the *Boston Globe*.

His ability to perform as an all-star within the framework of the rules won him many admirers in the game. Montreal Canadiens superstar Maurice (Rocket) Richard selected Quackenbush to his all-time NHL team and Toronto GM Conn Smythe wondered aloud why anyone wouldn't want a player of Quackenbush's ilk in their lineup.

"It is supposedly awarded to the player combining effectiveness with gentlemanly conduct," Smythe told the *Windsor Star*. "If the award does not go to men like (Toronto captain Syl) Apps or Quackenbush, the trophy should be taken out of circulation."

Certainly, when he first arrived in Detroit, the Wings were excited by his potential, signing him to a pro contract at the age of 20 in the fall of 1942. "We may take a chance on him," said Adams, who inserted Quackenbush into his lineup for 15 games during the 1942-43 season.

He became an NHL regular the following campaign, and by the mid-1940s Quackenbush was Detroit's best all-around defender. Some nights, he'd log close to 40 minutes a game in ice time.

game for pantywaists. That's what's wrong with basketball. Too sissified. I don't want to see that happen to hockey."

The rugged Jack Stewart and Quackenbush actually paired on defence for the Red Wings early in Quackenbush's career, and both were named to the NHL First All-Star Team in 1947-48. While Stewart led the NHL in penalty minutes in 1945-46, Quackenbush was assessed just 95 PIM in 774 career NHL games, an average of seven seconds per game. He once went 131 consecutive games without sitting in the penalty box and fought only once during his career, a Dec. 17, 1947 tilt with Chicago Blackhawks forward Gaye Stewart.

"It was a sham," Quackenbush said of his lone fistic bout. "It was just two guys running into each other."

QUACKENBUSH'S RED WINGS STATISTICS:

	Regular Season					Playoffs				
Season	GP	G	A	P	PIM	GP	G	A	P	PIM
1942-43	10	1	1	2	4	-	-	-	-	-
1943-44	43	4	14	18	6	2	1	0	1	0
1944-45	50	7	14	21	10	14	0	2	2	2
1945-46	48	11	10	21	6	5	0	1	1	0
1946-47	44	5	17	22	6	5	0	0	0	2
1947-48	58	6	16	22	17	10	0	2	2	0
1948-49	60	6	17	23	0	11	1	1	2	0
Totals	313	40	89	129	49	47	2	6	8	4

When the Lady Byng ballots were tabulated in 1948-49, Quackenbush polled 52 of a possible 54 points. "When you think about what a defenceman does, that really was a remarkable achievement," remarked Toronto forward Harry Watson, who finished second in the voting.

After the deal with Boston was completed, the Bruins were certainly excited to add such an experienced all-star as Quackenbush to their fold. "He'll be a big factor in our rebuilding plans," Bruins owner Weston Adams told the *Montreal Gazette*.

Quackenbush played in four Stanley Cup finals—three with the Wings and one in Boston—but never lifted Lord Stanley's mug as champion. He retired following the 1955-56 season.

After he finished playing hockey, Quackenbush remained in Boston, fashioning a career in the construction supply business during the day and attending Northeastern University at night, working toward an engineering degree.

While at Northeastern, Quackenbush helped coach the hockey team. In 1967, he was hired as the hockey and golf coach at Princeton and also started a women's hockey program. The women's team won three Ivy League titles, while his men's golf team won five. Quackenbush himself was an excellent golfer who recorded six holes in one.

Elected to the Hockey Hall of Fame in 1976, Quackenbush was 77 when he died of pneumonia and complications from Alzheimer's disease in Newtown, Pa. in 1999.

23 VLADIMIR KONSTANTINOV
Defence

Born: March 19, 1967, Murmansk, Russia
Shot: Left **Height:** 5-11 **Weight:** 190 lbs.
Red Wing From: 1991-92 to 1996-97
Acquired: Selected 221st overall in June 17, 1989 NHL Entry Draft
Departed: Career ended by closed-head injury suffered in June 13, 1997 limousine accident.

To the denizens of red-and-white clad Detroit fans who'd pack Joe Louis Arena on game night, he was The Vladinator—protector and defender of the Red Wings.

To everyone else, he was Vlad the Impaler, among the NHL's most reviled stick-men.

There was no middle ground where Vladimir Konstantinov was concerned.

Konstantinov liked the sound of that. "For my game, I don't need to score the goal," he once said. "I need someone to start thinking about me and to forget about scoring goals."

If Konstantinov is on your team, you loved him. If he wasn't…

"You always had to have your head up," former Detroit winger Brendan Shanahan said.

Konstantinov's irritating, agitating, irascible style sometimes led opponents to lose complete control of their senses. Former NHL sniper Keith Tkachuk was driven into an obscenity-laced tirade when confronted by Konstantinov during the 1996 playoffs, questioning the parentage and reproductive capabilities of the Detroit defenceman.

"He never hits you clean," Tkachuk said at the time. "It's all elbows and stick."

As deft with the verbal jab as he was with his hockey stick, Konstantinov thrived on drawing reactions from opponents. "He's just a selfish player who takes dumb penalties," Konstantinov said when taunted by Tkachuk.

Konstantinov was never surprised by the reaction he got and even wondered what it would be like to play against himself. "Would I like me?" he'd ask rhetorically. "I don't think so."

The Konstantinov who patrolled the blue line for Detroit was a contradiction in terms. On the ice, he was unyielding, a warrior, a man who asked no quarter and gave none.

"I have known Vladimir for years," former Detroit teammate Igor Larionov said. "As a young boy, he played centre. So what you had was a player with great skill who was also the toughest defenceman in the NHL. That is the kind of chemistry which produces a lethal formula."

Beyond his rugged exterior, Konstantinov contributed in many other ways. In 1993-94, his three shorthanded goals led NHL defenders. He led the NHL with a plus-minus rating of plus-60 in 1995-96, the highest rating the league had seen since Wayne Gretzky's plus-70 in 1986-87.

Away from the rink, Konstantinov was as warm and as friendly as a man could be. "Vladdy liked everybody," Detroit senior vice-president Jimmy Devellano said. "And he had time for everyone."

"Great guy," former teammate Slava Fetisov said, recalling his friend and teammate. "Big heart. Easy going."

DETROIT HONOURS:

+ Stanley Cup champion 1996-97, 1997-98
+ Named to NHL Second All-Star Team, 1995-96
+ Named to NHL All-Rookie Team, 1991-92
+ Won Alka Seltzer Plus Award, 1995-96.

Konstantinov and Mnatsakanov were both comatose after suffering closed head injuries. Konstantinov also suffered severe nerve and muscle damage to one arm. Mnatsakanov, 44, suffered brain damage and was left paralyzed in both legs and one arm. Konstantinov also suffered permanent brain damage from the crash and today still gets around with the aid of a walker.

Undoubtedly the most touching moment among all four of the team's Stanley Cup wins since 1997 came the night the Wings clinched back-to-back titles in 1998 at Washington's MCI Center.

Amidst the celebration, Konstantinov, wearing his No. 16 Red Wings sweater, was wheeled out on the ice to join the party, the first time he'd been between the boards since the previous spring's Cup clincher against the Philadelphia Flyers. Fetisov and Larionov, his Russian countrymen, toured him around the rink in a victory celebration and helped him carry the Stanley Cup.

"Win No. 16 is for No. 16," Fetisov said, his voice cracking with emotion. "Vladdy's spirit was with us in the room all season."

"This is so emotional, it's great," Larionov said. "This is for Vladdy and Sergei."

The Wings arranged for Konstantinov's name to be listed on the Stanley Cup for the 1997-98 triumph and even those he terrorized around the NHL now tip their cap in

As much as he grated on the opposition, their memories of Konstantinov forever changed the night of June 13, 1997—Friday the 13th of all days. Less than a week after the Wings won their first Stanley Cup since 1955, the players organized a golf outing, one final day together before heading their separate ways for the summer.

Konstantinov left early in a limo with Fetisov and team masseur Sergei Mnatsakanov. The call came a couple of hours later. There had been an accident. "Fender bender," Shanahan recalled thinking. "Do we have to go pick them up?" he asked someone.

When they arrived at the hospital, it was the other players who needed to be picked up after learning the severity of their teammates' injuries. The limousine had veered off Woodward Avenue in Birmingham, Mich. and slammed into a tree at an estimated 50 mph.

KONSTANTINOV'S RED WINGS STATISTICS:									
	REGULAR SEASON					PLAYOFFS			
Season	GP	G	A	P	PIM	GP	G	A	P	PIM
1991-92	79	8	26	34	172	11	0	1	1	16
1992-93	82	5	17	22	137	7	0	1	1	8
1993-94	80	12	21	33	138	7	0	2	2	4
1994-95	47	3	11	14	101	18	1	1	2	22
1995-96	81	14	20	34	139	19	4	5	9	28
1996-97	77	5	33	38	151	20	0	4	4	29
Totals	446	47	128	175	838	82	5	14	19	107

admiration. "If you had 20 guys like him in your lineup, you'd win the Stanley Cup every year," Tkachuk said of Konstantinov. "He was just a great competitor. He never let up. He was always looking to hit you.

"I can't say that I looked forward to our meetings, but I always relished the challenge."

Konstantinov remains a regular visitor to Joe Louis Arena and each appearance is greeted with a standing ovation out of respect for the unique element he brought to the Wings. "Vladdy's game never changed," former Detroit coach Dave Lewis said. "He forced the other team to change their game in order to deal with him."

Dealing with Konstantinov was an assignment no one on an opposing team relished. "On the ice, he was as tough as they came and probably the most competitive player in the league," former Detroit centre Kris Draper said of Konstantinov. "Off the ice, he was a tremendous leader and a huge influence in our dressing room."

To this day, Konstantinov remains an inspiration to the Red Wings. "Everyone in our dressing room and everyone in the city know what Vladdy means to our hockey team," Draper said.

"How could you ever forget a guy like Vladdy?" asked former Detroit goalie Chris Osgood.

Years after the crash, no one has.

24 REED LARSON

Defence

REED LARSON SET THE TONE FOR WHAT WAS TO COME WITH the first goal of his NHL career. It was a power-play goal and a game winner in a 4-3 decision over the Pittsburgh Penguins on Oct. 26, 1977, but that wasn't what made the tally so impressive or memorable.

Fed the puck at the point by Paul Woods, Larson hammered a drive into the glove of Penguins goalie Denis Herron, but the force of the shot snapped back Herron's arm and the puck sailed loose from his grasp and into the net.

Overpowering goaltenders would become Larson's trademark. "I don't care what anyone says, Bobby Hull never shot the puck as hard as Reed Larson," claimed former Red Wings goalie Ron Low.

Until Larson came along, no American-born NHLer had scored 200 career goals. And amazingly, if Larson had come to pass a football, all of it might have never happened.

When he arrived at a sporting crossroads in his young life, Larson opted for the path less travelled at the time by an American athlete. A two-sport star in football and hockey at Roosevelt High School in Minneapolis, Larson opted to take to the ice and accept an NCAA hockey scholarship with the powerhouse Minnesota Golden Gophers.

Larson was named to the NCAA All-Tournament team in 1975 and the Wings selected him in the 1976 NHL amateur draft after he'd helped Minnesota to the NCAA title. He moved to Detroit late in the 1976-77 season and blossomed quickly during his first full NHL campaign. His 60 points in 1977-78 was an NHL record for a rookie defenceman and he finished second to New York Islanders forward Mike Bossy in Calder Trophy voting for the NHL's rookie of the year.

"He's a good skater, moves the puck well and has quite a shot," was Hall of Fame coach Scotty Bowman's scouting report on Larson.

Almost as quickly, Larson moved among the NHL elite. He's one of just four Red Wings defencemen to register a hat trick in a game, and Larson is the only among the group to do it twice. He was the third defenceman in NHL history to record four consecutive 20-goal seasons, joining Bobby Orr

DETROIT HONOURS:

- Played in NHL All-Star Game, 1978
- First U.S.-born NHLer to score 200 goals
- Played for United States, 1981 World Championship
- Played for United States, 1981 Canada Cup
- Led Red Wings in assists, 1977-78, 1978-79, 1979-80
- Led Red Wings in penalty minutes, 1981-82
- Elected to U.S. Hockey Hall of Fame, 1996
- Won Lester Patrick Trophy, 2006
- Team captain, 1980-82
- One of four Detroit defencemen to record a hat trick (Nicklas Lidstrom, Red Kelly, Mathieu Schneider).

and Denis Potvin. And on Feb. 18, 1984, Larson turned in a three-assist performance to become the highest-scoring U.S.-born player in NHL history.

"The shot was the thing," said former Islanders defenseman Ken Morrow, who faced Larson in college and the pros. "He terrorized goalies with it." In 1985, Larson's shot was clocked at 136 mph by a radar gun at Joe Louis Arena.

Larson told the *Montreal Gazette* that he started developing his powerful and punishing shot as far back as when he played peewee hockey. "I worked on it because as a defenceman I knew I'd be shooting from far out," Larson said. "I also played with kids two and three years older than me and that helped.

"Actually, I guess I got my shot because of a lot of different things. Like working on my sticks, things like that. I liked my stick to have a stiff shaft. That's why the forwards on the team wouldn't use it. They'd say there's no feel to it."

Like many who played for the Wings in the 1970s, the only thing missing from Larson's resumé was team success. In 10 seasons with Detroit, he reached the playoffs just three times and enjoyed a series win only once, in 1978, his second season with the team.

At the 1986 NHL trade deadline and as Detroit stumbled along with the league's worst record, the Wings dealt Larson to the Boston Bruins for the more defensive-minded Mike O'Connell.

Larson scratched "adios" on the chalkboard in the Detroit dressing room and left for Beantown. "I never came right out and asked to be traded," Larson said. "But it was clear I was coming to a turning point in my career. All the losing was draining mentally. The timing for a move was right."

Larson also played for the Minnesota North Stars, Islanders, Edmonton Oilers and Buffalo Sabres before leaving the NHL for good in 1990. Elected to the United States Hockey Hall of Fame in 1996, Larson won the Lester Patrick Trophy for service to hockey in the United States in 2006.

The Reed Larson Award is presented annually to the top senior boys' high-school hockey defenceman in Minnesota.

| | LARSON'S RED WINGS STATISTICS: | | | | | | | | | |
| | Regular Season | | | | | Playoffs | | | | |
Season	GP	G	A	P	PIM	GP	G	A	P	PIM
1976-77	14	0	1	1	23	-	-	-	-	-
1977-78	75	19	41	60	95	7	0	2	2	4
1978-79	79	18	49	67	169	-	-	-	-	-
1979-80	80	22	44	66	101	-	-	-	-	-
1980-81	78	27	31	58	153	-	-	-	-	-
1981-82	80	21	39	60	112	-	-	-	-	-
1982-83	80	22	52	74	104	-	-	-	-	-
1983-84	78	23	39	62	122	4	2	0	2	21
1984-85	77	17	45	62	139	3	1	2	3	20
1985-86	67	19	41	60	109	-	-	-	-	-
Totals	708	188	382	570	1127	14	3	4	7	45

25 HERBIE LEWIS

Left Wing

Born: April 17, 1906, Calgary, Alberta
Died: January 20, 1991
Shot: Left Height: 5-9 Weight: 163 lbs.
Red Wing From: 1928-29 to 1938-39
Elected to Hockey Hall of Fame: 1989
Acquired: Claimed by Detroit from Duluth (AHA) in NHL Inter-League Draft, May 14, 1928.
Departed: Named player-coach of Indianapolis (IAHL), September 21, 1939.

THE LONGEST GAME IN STANLEY CUP HISTORY WAS about to enter its sixth overtime period. A contest that began on March 24, 1936 had continued well into the next day without a goal being scored by either the Montreal Maroons or the visiting Detroit Red Wings, and many among the crowd at the Montreal Forum had either given up and headed home or nodded off in their seats.

Detroit left winger Herbie Lewis was still full of vigour as the teams took the ice for their ninth period of play.

"We aren't keeping you boys up, are we?" Lewis playfully asked journalists covering the game as he whizzed past the ice-level press box.

Had things gone the other way in January of 1927, Lewis might have easily been wearing a Maroons sweater during that fateful game.

A decade earlier, Lewis was the star of the minor pro American Hockey Association's Duluth Hornets, leading the league in scoring and earning First All-Star team status during the 1925-26 campaign, as well as the catchy nickname "The Duke of Duluth."

A report in the January 28, 1927 edition of the *Montreal Gazette* claimed that Lewis had jumped his Duluth contract and signed with the Maroons for $8,000. Lewis was in the midst of a three-year pact with the Hornets, and William Grant, the man who ran the AHA, acquired a court injunction to prevent the move. The two sides eventually reached an out-of-court settlement and Lewis returned to Duluth.

A year later, the Wings claimed Lewis from Duluth in the inter-league draft, and this time he went to the NHL.

The speedy forward quickly made his mark. In just his third NHL game, Lewis burst through the Boston Bruins defence tandem of Eddie Shore and Lionel Hitchman and into the clear. Bruins goalie Tiny Thompson parried his first drive, but Lewis followed in to bury his rebound for the winner in a 2-0 victory over the team that would win the Stanley Cup that spring.

By the 1929-30 campaign, Lewis, who many considered the fastest skater in the NHL, was a 20-goal scorer.

He potted 20 goals again in 1932-33, and the next season was named captain as he led the Wings to the first Stanley Cup final appearance in franchise history. Though Detroit

127

DETROIT HONOURS:

- Stanley Cup champion 1935-36, 1936-37
- Played in NHL All-Star Game, 1934
- Captain, 1933-34
- Retired as club's all-time goal-scoring leader with 148
- Led Stanley Cup playoffs in goals, 1933-34, 1936-37
- Played for all three Detroit teams—Cougars, Falcons and Red Wings
- Team captain, 1933-34

"That's the way it was for us from 1935-37 when we had Marty Barry, Larry Aurie, Johnny Sorrell, Lewis and (Ebbie) Goodfellow to throw in whenever the opposition was penalized. They scored 35 times on that play in 1935-36, an average of three goals every two games. Next season, it worked almost as well."

Considered among best thinkers of the game, Lewis was known as much for his skill without the puck as he was for his work with the disk. The key to Detroit's 1936 Cup final triumph over Toronto was that the Lewis-Barry-Aurie trio were able to control the Leafs powerful Kid Line of Joe Primeau, Charlie Conacher and Busher Jackson, especially the work Lewis turned in controlling right winger Conacher, the NHL's top goal scorer in five of the previous six seasons.

"Herbie did a grand job of checking Charlie," Adams told the *Border Cities Star*, a joy that was shared by Lewis.

"What pleases me more than anything else is that we kept Jackson and Conacher, the two best players in the league, from dangerous shots," Lewis said.

In 1935, Lewis signed a new contract worth $8,000 per season, making him the league's highest-paid player. "Lewis lost the final series to Chicago, Lewis led all playoff scorers with five goals.

Detroit's top forward unit of Cooney Weiland, between Lewis and Larry Aurie, was known around the league as the "Tricky Trio," but it was the deal that sent Weiland to Boston for Marty Barry, who replaced him as centre of the Wings top forward unit, that turned the club into a championship-calibre squad.

The Barry-Lewis-Aurie combination quickly became the NHL's most feared forward line and Detroit's power play was lethal. "When you have a set of men who can apply the pressure, the other team doesn't play quite so hard," Detroit coach Jack Adams explained to the *Vancouver Sun*. "They want to avoid penalties. They know that losing a man is almost like giving a team a goal.

	LEWIS'S RED WINGS STATISTICS:								
	REGULAR SEASON					PLAYOFFS			
Season	GP	G	A	P	PIM	GP	G	A	P	PIM
1928-29	36	9	5	14	33	-	-	-	-	-
1929-30	44	20	11	31	36	-	-	-	-	-
1930-31	43	15	6	21	38	-	-	-	-	-
1931-32	48	5	14	19	21	2	0	0	0	0
1932-33	48	20	14	34	20	4	1	0	1	0
1933-34	43	16	15	31	15	9	5	2	7	2
1934-35	47	16	27	43	26	-	-	-	-	-
1935-36	45	14	23	37	25	7	2	3	5	0
1936-37	45	14	18	32	14	10	4	3	7	4
1937-38	42	13	18	31	12	-	-	-	-	-
1938-39	42	6	10	16	8	6	1	2	3	0
Totals	483	148	161	309	248	38	13	10	23	6

is a sportsman of the highest type," Adams said at the time. "I defy baseball, football, or boxing to produce an individual who can eclipse Herbie Lewis as a perfect role model for what an athlete should stand for."

Lewis also was a player who stood up for his teammates. During a 1936 game with the Montreal Canadiens, Montreal forward Toe Blake elbowed Detroit defenceman Ebbie Goodfellow, who retaliated by cross-checking Blake. As both players were headed for the sin bin, Blake charged up from behind, and swung his stick at Goodfellow's head.

Lewis raised his stick to parry the blow, saving Goodfellow from serious injury and immediately tore into Blake. A brawl ensued and police were called onto the Olympia Stadium ice to stop the fight, as virtually every Detroit player went after Blake.

By the late 1930s, Detroit was in a rebuilding mode and even Lewis acknowledged that the end of his career was near. "I'm getting to be an old guy," he told the *Calgary Herald*. "The old legs can't hold out forever, you know."

In the fall of 1939, Adams named Lewis player-coach of Detroit's International American Hockey League farm club in Indianapolis, and Lewis, who left Detroit as the club's all-time goal-scoring leader with 148, was impressed with the hockey talent he saw on the American side of the border.

"Yes the United States is producing good hockey players and I look forward to the time when it will give to professional hockey the majority of players," he proclaimed to the *Windsor Star*.

In December of 1940, with the Wings roster riddled by injury, Adams called out to Lewis for reinforcements. Lewis offered to play himself. "He's a pretty good hockey player, that Lewis," Lewis said. He came up to Detroit, but did not play.

Inducted into the Hockey Hall of Fame in 1989, Lewis died of heart failure at the age of 85 in 1991.

Born: December 3, 1960, Voskresensk, Russia
Shot: Left **Height:** 5-9 **Weight:** 170 lbs.
Red Wing From: 1995-96 to 1999-2000; 2000-01 to 2002-03
Elected to Hockey Hall of Fame: 2008
Acquired: Traded to Detroit by San Jose Sharks for Ray Sheppard, October 24, 1995.
Departed: Signed as a free agent by Florida Panthers, July 1, 2001.
Reacquired: Traded to Detroit by Florida Panthers for Yan Golubovsky, December 28, 2000.
Departed: Signed as a free agent by New Jersey Devils, September 10, 2003.

DETROIT'S FIRST STANLEY CUP TITLE IN 42 YEARS SECURED, the Cup was passed to Red Wings captain Steve Yzerman by NHL commissioner Gary Bettman, and Yzerman knew who exactly among his teammates he wanted to get the second touch of Lord Stanley's mug.

He called upon Slava Fetisov and Igor Larionov to take the Cup from him in unison.

As much as Yzerman had laboured for years to get a title to Detroit, he realized his battle paled in comparison to the one waged by Larionov and Fetisov. These men had tangled with the political system in their native Russia and pinned the mighty Soviet bear, freeing Russians to play in the NHL.

"I wanted Igor and I to carry the Cup together," Fetisov explained. "All of the Olympics and World Championships we shared together. We fought the Soviet system to get here. It was right that we should carry it together."

Larionov described the moment as "a big honour, a great feeling, an unbelievable feeling.

"Myself and Slava, we went through tough times together," Larionov said. "This is the only trophy that was missing from our collection."

In Detroit's search for a championship, Larionov was one of the final pieces missing from their collection of superstars. Acquired from the San Jose Sharks early in the 1995-96 season, he joined Fetisov, Sergei Fedorov, Vladimir Konstantinov and Slava Kozlov in forming an all-Russian unit for Red Wings coach Scotty Bowman to send over the boards.

The Russian Five confounded the opposition and Larionov was their spiritual and on-ice inspiration. "There were many great players who wanted the chance that we have, but none were willing to go against the Soviet system, because they didn't have what Igor has here," Fetisov said, gently tapping his heart. "Igor Larionov is a very brave man. And he is my good friend."

Besides the three Stanley Cups, Larionov was a two-time Olympic gold medalist, a four-time world champion and a Canada Cup winner. "His character is so strong," Dave King, former coach of the Canadian Olympic team, said of Larionov. "He went against the Soviet system in the days when you couldn't step out of line, because he wanted time for his family. He was principled. We should all be so strong."

Often called the Russian Wayne Gretzky, Larionov's strength came not from his 5-9, 170-pound body, considered small by NHL standards, but from his fertile mind. "He

DETROIT HONOURS:

* Stanley Cup champion 1996-97, 1997-98, 2001-02
* Became oldest player to score a goal in a Stanley Cup final game (41 years, six months, five days) when he tallied after 54:47 of overtime in Game 3 against the Carolina Hurricanes on June 8, 2002
* Won bronze medal with Russia at 2002 Salt Lake City Winter Olympic Games.

made great passes but he was so good defensively," King said. "He didn't get beat even with his size because he was so smart. He was always on the defensive side of the man he was covering."

This combination of responsibility and creativity freed Larionov's wingers to focus on putting the puck in the net. "Pavel Bure cried for a year when Vancouver let Igor go," remembered Geoff Courtnall, Larionov's teammate with the Canucks.

Coming to the NHL at the age of 29, Larionov's commitment to nutrition and conditioning permitted him to play 14 seasons in the league.

Larionov's secret to eternal youth? "Two glasses of wine every day," suggested the man former teammate Brendan Shanahan called "the Dick Clark of hockey."

"Summer whites, winter reds," Larionov said, further explaining the secret to longevity. "In the summer, you're eating more fresh fruits and vegetables, so white wine is best. During hockey season, I would enjoy a nice Cabernet or Piat d'Or."

This sampling of the grape was combined with a diet and exercise regimen which made some of the younger players shudder with the demands it placed upon Larionov's body.

The man his Detroit compatriots called the Professor is also a chess master, so skilled that none of his teammates would challenge him. "In chess, you're always in an attacking mode, thinking two or three steps ahead," Larionov said. "That's the way hockey should be played. Of course, you can take 20 minutes to two hours between moves. And no one is throwing elbows and stuff at you. That's the biggest difference."

There was no NHLer who saw the ice better than Larionov. Such vision got him to the NHL and kept him going long after the other original Russians left. "Larionov

viewed this as a great adventure," said former coach Pat Quinn, Larionov's first NHL bench boss.

Larionov's theory of hockey was one he shared with each member of Detroit's Russian five. "If you have the puck, the other team cannot score," Larionov explained. "When we were on the ice together, we tried to create. We all came from the same Russian hockey schools, so our play was very similar."

The Red Wings also developed a theory during Larionov's time in Detroit—if you had him in the lineup, chances are you would succeed.

Larionov retired from the NHL in 2004 and held a testimonial match to say farewell on Dec. 13, 2004 at Moscow's Luzhniki Palace of Sports, Soviet site of the 1972 Summit Series. Larionov chose the cozy, 12,000-seat rink over more modern facilities because, as he said at the time, "I played there and I wanted it to be where I played my last game."

Today, Larionov markets his own line of wines and works as a player agent.

LARIONOV'S RED WINGS STATISTICS:										
	REGULAR SEASON					PLAYOFFS				
Season	GP	G	A	P	PIM	GP	G	A	P	PIM
1995-96	69	21	50	71	34	19	6	7	13	6
1996-97	64	12	42	54	26	20	4	8	12	8
1997-98	69	8	39	47	40	22	3	10	13	12
1998-99	75	14	49	63	48	7	0	2	2	0
1999-00	79	9	38	47	28	9	1	2	3	6
2000-01	39	4	25	29	28	6	1	3	4	2
2001-02	70	11	32	43	50	18	5	6	11	4
2002-03	74	10	33	43	48	4	0	1	1	0
Totals	539	89	308	397	302	105	20	39	59	38

27 VYACHESLAV KOZLOV
Centre/Left Wing

Born: May 3, 1972, Voskresensk, Russia
Shoots: Left **Height:** 5-10 **Weight:** 180 lbs.
Red Wing From: 1991-92 to 2000-01
Acquired: Selected 45th overall in June 16, 1990 NHL Entry Draft
Departed: Traded by Detroit to Buffalo Sabres with a 2002 first round draft choice (the choice was later traded to Columbus, and then Atlanta, who selected Jim Slater) and future considerations for Dominik Hasek, July 1, 2001.

AS FRAGILE AS THE FINE ENGLISH BONE CHINA HE COLLECTS. As distant as the Russian television programs he so enjoys.

Slava Kozlov was the mystery man of the Detroit Red Wings, the unknown factor amidst their fabled Russian Unit. Beyond the legends (Slava Fetisov and Igor Larionov), the superstar (Sergei Fedorov) and the Vladinator (Vladimir Konstantinov), there was Kozlov.

Quiet? Yes. But also quietly efficient. There was definitely a Kozzy effect for Detroit in the Stanley Cup playoffs. "It's a different game in the playoffs than in the regular season," said Kozlov, who took pride in coming up big in the biggest games of the season.

Between 1995-99, Kozlov scored 30 goals in post-season play as Detroit won two Stanley Cups and reached three finals. In that span, only Joe Sakic (38) Claude Lemieux (37), Steve Yzerman (34) and Jaromir Jagr (34) scored more often.

"That was Kozzy's time of year," former Detroit coach Dave Lewis said of the playoffs.

In 1995, Kozlov led the playoffs with four game-winning goals as Detroit reached the Cup final series for the first time since 1966. In fact, it was his overtime winner—one of two he scored during his NHL career—in a 2-1 win over Chicago at Joe Louis Arena that clinched the Western Conference title for the Wings and moved them into the final round.

In 1998, he again topped all shooters with four game-winners as Detroit won the Cup for the second successive spring. "He loved to play at that time of year," Lewis said. "He'd find a way to find open ice."

Away from the rink, Kozlov also sought out ways to disappear, to blend into the scenery.

He didn't get major endorsement deals like Fedorov. He never drew the respect of the hockey world the way Larionov and Fetisov did, or the ire of its players, the way Konstantinov did.

And that was just fine with him.

"I'm a quiet guy," Kozlov said. "I don't like to get a lot of attention. I don't like being in big crowds.

"I'm not comfortable in those situations. Sometimes, I just like to be by myself."

Not that Kozlov was afraid to speak his mind when he felt wronged by someone. He was outspoken in his criticism of Russia's performance at the 1996 World Cup of Hockey, his first chance to play alongside all the best players from his country.

"I was looking forward to the World Cup, thinking this would be a great experience," Kozlov recalled. "Getting the chance to play with so many great players, I thought would be very good, but the (Russian Ice Hockey) Federation ruined everything because they would not listen to the players."

135

DETROIT HONOURS:

• Stanley Cup champion 1996-97, 1997-98
• Played for Russia in 1994 World Championship
• Played for Russia in 1996 World Cup of Hockey.

"They gave us a coach, (Boris) Mikhailov that no one wanted to play for. He had never coached the game in a North American rink and did not understand the difference from the European game. He tried to make us play a European style, instead of an NHL style of game."

Kozlov indicated that morale quickly disintegrated as the tournament grew closer. "I thought in the games we would be okay, because we had so many great players—(Sergei) Fedorov, (Alexander) Mogilny, (Alexei) Yashin—but everybody wanted only to score goals. Many players were selfish. Nobody wanted to play defence. We had no system and this is because we had a coach who knew nothing."

Kozlov never again played for Russia after that experience.

During his years in Detroit, Kozlov maximized his down time. He'd relax by viewing his china collection, inside cabinets at his home in Bloomfield Hills, Mich. Very well-read, he acknowledged a passion for historical works. "I like to read Russian newspapers," Kozlov said. "Igor calls them the yellow press."

Adapting to the North American lifestyle was arduous for Kozlov, a task he admits he had no desire to undertake when he arrived in Detroit in the midst of the 1991-92 season. "I spent 2-3 months here and (Wings coach) Bryan Murray, he wanted me to stay for the summer," Kozlov remembered.

"I said 'No, I have to go home, I must see my family,' and I went back to Russia."

The Wings were afraid Kozlov might not return and they had cause for concern. "My first two years here, I was very homesick," Kozlov said. "A couple of times, I nearly went home."

Over the years, he grew to love the Motor City and credited this turnaround to Larionov, his roommate with the Wings. "Igor is a very intelligent man," Kozlov said.

"He knew the American system very well and he taught me what I should do."

On the ice, Kozlov never needed much help. He was a key contributor to Detroit's back-to-back Stanley Cup wins in 1996-97 and 1997-98, but in a room full of superstars, the soft-spoken, effective performer continued to go mostly unnoticed.

Kozlov never minded that one bit.

Just as quietly, he left town, but even in his departure, Kozlov contributed to another Detroit Cup win. Dealt to Buffalo in the summer of 2001, the Wings acquired six-time Vezina Trophy winner Dominik Hasek for Kozlov.

A year later, Hasek posted a playoff-leading six shutouts as the Wings rolled to the title. Meanwhile, Kozlov later played with the Atlanta Thrashers, and then returned home to play in Russia's Kontinental Hockey League, where his playoff touch remains intact.

Kozlov has been part of two Gagarin Cup championship teams in the KHL.

KOZLOV'S RED WINGS STATISTICS:									
	REGULAR SEASON					PLAYOFFS			
Season	GP	G	A	P	PIM	GP	G	A	P	PIM
1991-92	7	0	2	2	2	-	-	-	-	-
1992-93	17	4	1	5	14	4	0	2	2	2
1993-94	77	34	39	73	50	7	2	5	7	12
1994-95	46	13	20	33	45	18	9	7	16	10
1995-96	82	36	37	73	70	19	5	7	12	10
1996-97	75	23	22	45	46	20	8	5	13	14
1997-98	80	25	27	52	46	22	6	8	14	10
1998-99	79	29	29	58	45	10	6	1	7	4
1999-00	72	18	18	36	28	8	2	1	3	12
2000-01	72	20	18	38	30	6	4	1	5	2
Totals	607	202	213	415	376	114	42	37	79	76

28 JOHN OGRODNICK

Left Wing

Born: June 20, 1959, Ottawa, Ontario
Shot: Left **Height:** 6-0 **Weight:** 204 lbs.
Red Wing From: 1979-80 to 1986-87; 1992-93
Acquired: Selected 66th overall by Detroit in August 9, 1979 NHL Entry Draft.
Departed: Traded by Detroit to Quebec Nordiques with Basil McRae and Doug Shedden for Brent Ashton, Gilbert Delorme and Mark Kumpel, January 17, 1987.
Reacquired: Signed by Detroit as a free agent, September 29, 1992.
Departed: Released by Detroit, June 19, 1993.

AT FIRST, JOHN OGRODNICK ADMITTED, THE NEWS THAT he was to become a Detroit Red Wing was greeted with shudders of concern.

Years later, when he was told that he'd no longer be a Red Wing, Ogrodnick was so heartbroken he could not speak.

In between, he scored goals at a pace never before seen in franchise history.

A two-time Memorial Cup winner with the New Westminster Bruins, Ogrodnick tallied a combined total of 107 goals over those two championship seasons, so when he slid all the way to the fourth round of the 1979 NHL entry draft, the Wings were delighted to call his name.

Ogrodnick did not share their excitement.

"I was really upset at the time, not just because of the fourth-round thing, but because it was Detroit," Ogrodnick told the *Edmonton Journal*. "A lot of New Westminster players had been drafted late by Detroit and they all ended up in Kalamazoo (of the International League) and they were never heard from again.

"I didn't want to be like that."

Detroit wouldn't bury Ogrodnick in the minor leagues, and the only things he buried were plenty of goals.

He split the 1979-80 season between the Wings and Detroit's Adirondack American League farm club, then made the NHL grade for good the following year, potting 35 goals and 80 points in 70 games, the first of six consecutive seasons in which he'd lead the team in goals.

"It was all a matter of confidence," said Ogrodnick, who admitted he fretted early in his career about whether he'd be good enough to make the grade as an NHLer.

He scored 138 goals between 1982-85, posting successive 40-goal seasons in 1982-83 and 1983-84, netting 19 power-play goals in the latter campaign, two shy of Mickey Redmond's club record. But Ogrodnick's best was yet to come.

He peaked with a career-best 55 goals and 50 assists in 1984-85, making Ogrodnick, Sergei Fedorov and Steve Yzerman the only players in club history to garner 50 goals and 100 points in the same season.

DETROIT HONOURS:

- Named to NHL First All-Star team, 1984-85
- Played in NHL All-Star Game, 1981, 1982, 1984, 1985, 1986
- Set Detroit record with 55 goals, 1984-85 (since broken by Steve Yzerman)
- One of only five players in franchise history to record a 100-point season
- Played for Canada in 1981 World Championship
- Led Detroit in goals, 1980-81, 1981-82, 1982-83, 1983-84, 1984-85, 1985-86
- Led Detroit in points, 1982-83, 1984-85.

"If you look at my career, you can't say that I had a fluke season," Ogrodnick said. "I had four seasons where I averaged 40 goals per season."

The big winger's patented scoring style was to blow down the wing at top speed and hammer a low slapshot past the goaltender just inside the far goalpost. It was exactly how he tallied his 53rd goal during the 1984-85 season to shatter Redmond's previous single-season mark for goal-scoring by a Red Wing.

He bore in down the wing and rifled a low slapper past Minnesota North Stars goalie Roland Melanson for the record goal. "That's how I scored 90 percent of the time," Ogrodnick said.

Almost as quickly, it was all over in Detroit for Ogrodnick. Midway through the 1986-87 season, he was shipped to the Quebec Nordiques as part of a six-player trade.

When the news was broken to him, Ogrodnick broke down. He couldn't speak to reporters.

"John had a hard time leaving," remembered teammate Gerard Gallant. "He'd been here so long and had been a heckuva hockey player."

While the hockey came naturally, Ogrodnick admitted the adjustment to living in Quebec was a culture shock to his family.

"In Detroit we had a lot of friends and lot of activities outside of hockey," Ogrodnick said. "There it was just hockey, hockey, hockey.

"Don't get me wrong, Quebec is a great and beautiful city. But if you don't speak French, it's much tougher, much slower in the adjustment."

After a half-season with the Nordiques, Ogrodnick was dealt to the New York Rangers, where he spent the next five campaigns. But when the Rangers let him go, Ogrodnick, just 33, shockingly found out there were no takers for his services.

"I was really surprised by the lack of interest," Ogrodnick recalled. "At the time, when I was going through the termination of my contract (with the Rangers), Tampa

OGRODNICK'S RED WINGS STATISTICS:									
	REGULAR SEASON					PLAYOFFS			
Season	GP	G	A	P	PIM	GP	G	A	P	PIM
1979-80	41	8	24	32	8	-	-	-	-	-
1980-81	80	35	35	70	14	-	-	-	-	-
1981-82	80	28	26	54	28	-	-	-	-	-
1982-83	80	41	44	85	30	-	-	-	-	-
1983-84	64	42	36	78	14	4	0	0	0	0
1984-85	79	55	50	105	30	3	1	1	2	0
1985-86	76	38	32	70	18	-	-	-	-	-
1986-87	39	12	28	40	6	-	-	-	-	-
1992-93	19	6	6	12	2	1	0	0	0	0
Totals	558	265	281	546	150	8	1	1	2	0

showed a lot of interest. When I received my buyout, the interest wasn't there anymore."

When he became a free agent, there was interest in Ogrodnick from an old friend. He'd get himself a reunion in Detroit, but he'd have to earn it the hard way. The Wings invited Ogrodnick to their training camp in Flint, Mich. and he won himself a contract for the 1992-93 season.

"We knew pretty well what John was all about," remembered Bryan Murray, Detroit's coach-GM at the time. "He was a veteran guy, who was strong offensively and had really become a decent defensive player over the years.

"The thing you worry about most with a veteran player is his hands. That's the first thing to go. But what I found out was that John still had the touch, he still had the quick release."

The chance to be a Red Wing again motivated Ogrodnick. "It was a strange feeling coming in here," Ogrodnick recalled. "I tried to approach it as just coming to training camp, like any other year."

On a deep, talented Red Wings team, playing opportunities were rare for Ogrodnick. He appeared in just 19 games in what would be his final NHL season, but skated enough to reach the 400-goal plateau.

Ogrodnick still lives in the Detroit area, where he works as an investment counselor, and is regularly seen during Wings games at Joe Louis Arena.

29 GARY BERGMAN

Defence

Born: October 7, 1938, Kenora, Ontario
Died: December 8, 2000
Shot: Left Height: 5-11 Weight: 188 lbs.
Red Wing From: 1964-65 to 1973-74; 1974-75
Acquired: Claimed by Detroit from Montreal Canadiens in NHL Intra-League Draft, June 10, 1964.
Departed: Traded by Detroit to Minnesota North Stars for Ted Harris, November 7, 1973.
Reacquired: Traded to Detroit by Minnesota North Stars for a 1975 third round draft choice (Alex Pirus), October 1, 1974.
Departed: Traded by Detroit to Kansas City Scouts with Bill McKenzie for Peter McDuffe and Glen Burdon, August 22, 1975.

GARY BERGMAN'S DETROIT RED WINGS CAREER HAD BARELY begun when it was nearly terminated by a traffic mishap on an off-day during the 1966 Stanley Cup playoffs.

The Wings had sequestered their team in Toledo, which was the habit in those days, and Bergman was walking to his car in the rain, headed to the theatre with teammates to take in a movie, when he slipped while crossing the road, falling into the path of an oncoming car.

By the time the car came to a stop, one tire was resting against Bergman's legs and the entire front bumper of the vehicle hovered perilously over his prone body.

"I tried to scramble up, but I couldn't," Bergman explained to the *Windsor Star*. "When the car stopped, the tire was against my leg.

"It was a devil of an experience."

Funny, but that's how opponents generally viewed the experience of bringing the puck down Bergman's side of the ice.

No shrinking violet, you didn't dare skate toward Bergman with your head down, because if you did, the rest of your body would soon join it in the down and out position.

Fighting Bergman also wasn't a good idea. Chicago Blackhawks star Bobby Hull tried it once and the only damage he inflicted was to the ligaments of the knuckles of his right hand.

"He was a rock," Hall of Fame defenceman Bobby Orr recalled of Bergman.

That was the thing about Bergman's steady, reliable game. It wasn't flashy, it didn't make headlines, but the Wings knew that with him in the lineup, they could make headway.

"He has speed, is offensive-minded and has a good shot," Detroit coach-GM Sid Abel said after grabbing Bergman from the Montreal Canadiens farm system in the 1964 NHL Intra-League draft.

Bergman, a Memorial Cup winner with the 1958-59 Winnipeg Braves, admitted the move to Detroit likely saved his hockey career. "I was ready to quit hockey," he said after spending his first five pro seasons bouncing around Montreal's farm system.

The chance with Detroit paid dividends for both parties. In Bergman's rookie season, the Wings finished first in the NHL standings. As a sophomore he helped them reach the Stanley Cup final, and was front and centre in the key play of the Cup final series against Montreal, the Cup-winning goal scored in overtime of Game 6 by Habs centre Henri Richard.

DETROIT HONOURS:

- Played in NHL All-Star Game, 1973
- Selected to Team Canada for 1972 Summit Series.

In the summer of 1972, he was a surprise selection to play for Team Canada in the upcoming Summit Series with the Soviet national team.

"We chose our squad very carefully," Team Canada coach Harry Sinden explained to writer Jim Coleman. "Bergman was chosen for his versatility. He moves around well defensively. He can skate and he is strong. Also, he is a competent point-man on power plays. Furthermore, all the reports which I received on Gary's personality, his attitude and his character were exceptionally positive."

Bergman later admitted the call was as much a surprise to him as it was to most hockey fans. "I thought idly that it would be nice to play for Canada," he said. "But really, it never occurred to me that I'd be selected.

"There were so many good defencemen in the league, and after all, the Red Wings had been in the Stanley Cup final only once in the previous six years."

Paired with Brad Park, Bergman provided a steadying influence as Canada rallied from a 3-1-1 series deficit to win the eight-game set. Bergman was one of just seven Canadian players to suit up for all eight games.

Bergman and Richard both went to the ice as Richard drove to the net and somehow, the puck found its way past Detroit goalie Roger Crozier. To this day, Wings players from that team insist Richard pushed the puck in with his hand and the goal should have been disallowed.

The closest to the play, Bergman was adamant that it couldn't possibly have been a legal goal. "There was no way he was going to shoot it because I spun him around and dragged him down and I had his stick right in my hand," Bergman related years later.

While Detroit's fortunes took a downturn after the spring of 1966, Bergman's stock in hockey circles only continued to rise. He collected a career-high 41 points in 1967-68 and was an impressive plus-45 the following season for a Wings team that missed the playoffs.

	BERGMAN'S RED WINGS STATISTICS:									
	REGULAR SEASON					PLAYOFFS				
Season	GP	G	A	P	PIM	GP	G	A	P	PIM
1964-65	58	4	7	11	85	5	0	1	1	4
1965-66	61	3	16	19	96	12	0	3	3	14
1966-67	70	5	30	35	129	-	-	-	-	-
1967-68	74	13	28	41	109	-	-	-	-	-
1968-69	76	7	30	37	80	-	-	-	-	-
1969-70	69	6	17	23	122	4	0	1	1	2
1970-71	68	8	25	33	149	-	-	-	-	-
1971-72	75	6	31	37	138	-	-	-	-	-
1972-73	68	3	28	31	71	-	-	-	-	-
1973-74	11	0	6	6	18	-	-	-	-	-
1974-75	76	5	25	30	104	-	-	-	-	-
Totals	706	60	243	303	1101	21	0	5	5	20

"He just played incredible hockey," remembered Summit Series hero Paul Henderson to the *Canadian Press*. "He was one of the great unsung heroes of that series."

In Game 7 in Moscow, Russian forward Boris Mikhailov kicked Bergman with his skates so hard that Bergman's leg was cut through his shin pad. Bergman responded by drilling Mikhailov to the ice. Years later, during a Russian oldtimers' tour of Canada, Mikhailov suggested that it was the hardest he'd ever been hit.

"He was a big part of that team," Team Canada forward Rod Gilbert said of Bergman. "He was a tremendous teammate. The type of defenceman he was, he played the body extremely well, and he was a smart player.

"You felt secure when he was on the ice."

Bergman's other enduring memory of the series was the impressive physical conditioning of the Russian players. "I nailed one of them in the ribs," Bergman recalled. "It felt as if I had bounced my stick off a parking meter."

Returning to the NHL, Bergman's ability seemed to be more recognized by his peers. In 1973, he was selected to the NHL All-Star Game for the first time. "He's got plenty of poise and experience," Detroit GM Ned Harkness said at the time.

A year later, with the Wings rebuilding, Bergman was dealt to the Minnesota North Stars for veteran defenceman Ted Harris, but Detroit moved to reacquire him in the off-season. He played the 1974-75 season with the Wings, then finished his NHL career with the Kansas City Scouts in 1975-76.

Cancer claimed Bergman's life in 2000 at the age of 62. Perhaps the most appropriate eulogy came from one of the Soviet players he'd tormented back in 1972.

When a commemorative set of 1972 Summit Series hockey cards was printed, Russian forward Alexander Volchkov admitted he couldn't get the image of Bergman bearing down on him out of his mind.

"Every time I was on the ice, I'd be hit by Gary Bergman," Volchkov noted. "I don't remember any free time with the puck."

30 MARTY BARRY

Centre

Born: December 8, 1905, Quebec City, Quebec
Died: August 20, 1969
Shot: Left **Height:** 5-11 **Weight:** 175 lbs.
Red Wing From: 1935-36 to 1938-39
Elected to Hockey Hall of Fame: 1965
Acquired: Traded by Boston Bruins to Detroit with Art Giroux for Ralph (Cooney) Weiland and Walt Buswell, June 30, 1935.
Departed: Released by Detroit, October 19, 1939.

IN THE SPRING OF 1935, DETROIT RED WINGS COACH AND general manager Jack Adams found himself attending the Stanley Cup final between the Toronto Maple Leafs and Montreal Maroons as a spectator. It had been a tough winter for Adams, whose team missed the playoffs one season after playing Chicago in the 1934 Cup final series.

He was looking to make changes, and happened upon Boston Bruins GM Frank Patrick, who after watching his own team exit the playoffs early following a first-place finish, was also seeking to shake things up.

The object of Patrick's affection was a former Bruin now with Detroit, forward Cooney Weiland. "If I had Weiland," Patrick reasoned, "I would win the Stanley Cup."

The two got to talking trade and after a couple of months of back-and-forth negotiating, ultimately Adams got the guy who'd win his team the Stanley Cup when he pried centre Marty Barry out of Boston.

With "Goal-A-Game-Barry," as he was known, playing between right winger Larry Aurie and left winger Herbie Lewis, they became the NHL's most dangerous forward line. Detroit finished first overall in 1935-36 and the Wings captured the first Stanley Cup in franchise history, and Adams couldn't have been happier with his new acquisition.

"To my way of thinking, Marty is the smartest centre in the league today," Adams told the *Vancouver Sun*. "He thinks up a lot of the scoring plays we use and with wings like Larry Aurie and Herbie Lewis, it is only a matter of minutes before they have them down pat."

Others shared Adams' vision. "He's the finest forward in the NHL," Toronto Maple Leafs forward Ace Bailey said of Barry. The durable Barry missed just two games during his first 10 NHL seasons.

Perhaps the happiest person to see Barry in a Detroit uniform was Red Wings goalie Normie Smith. "Not so much this season, because Barry's let up, but last season he delighted in making all sorts of fancy shots during practice," Smith said during the 1936-37 season. "The other fellows used to stop play to watch him beat me time after time.

DETROIT HONOURS:

- Stanley Cup champion 1935-36, 1936-37
- Won Lady Byng Trophy, 1936-37
- NHL First All-Star Team 1936-37
- Played in NHL All-Star Game 1937
- Scored Stanley Cup-winning goal 1937
- Led Stanley Cup playoffs in scoring 1937
- Led Detroit in scoring 1935-36, 1936-37, 1938-39.

"Of all the centres I've ever faced, not one compared to Marty. I'd say to myself, 'Smith, you don't know how lucky you are to be on the same team with Barry.'"

That 1936-37 campaign proved to be Barry's best. He finished second in NHL scoring with 40 points, was runner-up to Babe Siebert of the Montreal Canadiens in Hart Trophy voting and was awarded the Lady Byng Trophy.

Then he took his game to an even higher level in the playoffs, leading all scorers with 4-7-11 totals.

Trailing the New York Rangers 2-1 in the best-of-five Stanley Cup final series, the defending champion Red Wings were deadlocked in a scoreless battle that appeared headed to overtime when Barry took charge late in the third period.

Barry cut loose with a burst of speed through the centre of the rink, split the New York defence of Art Coulter and Ott Heller, cut to the left and snapped a wrist shot past Rangers goalie Dave Kerr and into the net just inside the far post.

In the decisive fifth game, Barry netted a pair of goals, including the Cup-winner, as Detroit blanked the Rangers 3-0. "Boy it's great," Barry told *Canadian Press*. "First they award me the Lady Byng Trophy and then I score two goals tonight.

"I guess I was celebrating."

The celebration didn't last much longer. The Wings missed the playoffs in 1937-38 and following the 1938-39 season, even though he'd finished fourth in NHL scoring, the Wings opted to release Barry as part of a youth movement.

"We want a young club and that is why Barry is leaving," Red Wings owner James Norris told the *Pittsburgh Post-Gazette*. "We decided that rather than sell or trade Marty, he should be given a chance to make his own bargain.

"We owe him that."

Barry played one more NHL season with the Montreal Canadiens and then entered into coaching. He was inducted into the Hockey Hall of Fame in 1965.

In later life, Barry managed a grocery store in Dartmouth, N.S. He died of a heart attack at the age of 64.

BARRY'S RED WINGS STATISTICS:

	Regular Season					Playoffs				
Season	GP	G	A	P	PIM	GP	G	A	P	PIM
1935-36	48	21	19	40	16	7	2	4	6	6
1936-37	47	17	27	44	6	10	4	7	11	2
1937-38	48	9	20	29	34	-	-	-	-	-
1938-39	48	13	28	41	4	6	3	1	4	0
Totals	191	60	94	154	60	23	9	12	21	8

31 GERARD GALLANT

Left Wing

Born: September 2, 1963, Summerside, P.E.I.
Shot: Left **Height:** 5-10 **Weight:** 190 lbs.
Red Wing From: 1984-85 to 1992-93.
Acquired: Selected 107th overall in 1981 NHL entry draft.
Departed: Signed as a free agent by Tampa Bay Lightning, July 21, 1993.

GERARD GALLANT WASTED LITTLE TIME IN MAKING A NAME for himself as a Detroit Red Wing.

The club was mired in 12-game winless skid when Gallant was summoned from Adirondack of the American Hockey League for a Jan. 22, 1985 game against the New York Islanders. The Wings were 5-4 winners that night, thanks in part to Gallant, who counted his first NHL goal in his NHL debut.

"It felt super getting my first goal," Gallant told *Canadian Press*. "It made it all the nicer, winning."

Gallant also remembered the jitters he felt taking the ice against some of his boyhood idols from the Islanders teams that won four Stanley Cups between 1980-83.

"Seeing guys like (Bryan) Trottier and (John) Tonelli playing against you, all your favourite players from when you were a kid, it was a little scary, really."

It didn't take long before the tough, competitive Gallant was putting the fear into opposing players. "He was a feisty player, a rugged winger," Detroit senior vice-president Jim Devellano remembered.

Gallant's leadership qualities soon emerged and he became a key character player for the Detroit teams that made successive Western Conference final appearances during the 1986-87 and 1987-88 seasons, the furthest the Wings had gone in the playoffs since their 1965-66 Stanley Cup final appearance.

"He's the kind of player who inspires others," said former Wings captain Steve Yzerman, often Gallant's linemate.

"And the more he scores, the better he plays and the more inspirational he gets."

Jacques Demers, who coached those Detroit conference final clubs, compared Gallant to Brian Sutter, one of the game's most determined competitors and captain for Demers when he coached in St. Louis.

"Gerard Gallant is a carbon copy of Brian Sutter," Demers said. "He was not gifted talent-wise, but gifted with great heart, great determination and great pride in wearing the uniform.

"He's a tremendously gifted person—gifted with character. That's a positive because Gerard is what hockey's all about. He was dedicated and came to play every night and don't think the other team didn't know it when he wasn't playing."

On the ice, Gallant was all business, but away from the rink, his practical jokes were the stuff that kept the Wings loose. "I've always been a practical joker," Gallant said. "It's just a part of me. You've got to have a sense of humour in this game. I mean, you're around 20 guys all the time."

His favourite prank was a night in Washington early in his career when Gallant altered the footwear of several of his veteran teammates.

"All the guys sat down with me to eat and I put sour cream on every one of their shoes," Gallant explained. "I did it not knowing who they were. It turned out to be all the big guys. It was guys like Danny Gare, John

DETROIT HONOURS:

+ Selected to NHL Second All-Star Team, 1988-89
+ Led team in penalty minutes, 1988-89
+ Played for Canada at 1989 World Championship.

a spot on the NHL's Second All-Star Team. But Gallant never forgot the other side of his game, garnering over 200 penalty minutes in each of those four 30-goal campaigns.

In 1993, with the Wings revamping their lineup, Gallant left via free agency for Tampa Bay, and still remembers his emotional return to Detroit during the 1993-94 season as an opponent for the first time.

A fan bellowed "Gerard, we miss you," upon Gallant's arrival for his first shift. Former teammates whispered, "How ya doing?" as they lined up for faceoffs.

"It was a weird feeling, skating out on the ice for the warm-up," Gallant admitted. "Looking at that crest at centre ice, looking down at those shirts, the shirt I'd worn for so many years, it just felt so unusual.

"I was looking down the ice at the guys—Yzerman, (Bob) Probert, (Steve) Chiasson—it just felt so unusual to see them on the other team."

Gallant's playing days concluded in 1995 and he entered the coaching ranks, serving as head coach of the Columbus Blue Jackets and guiding the St. John Sea Dogs to the 2011 Memorial Cup title.

Today, Gallant works as head coach of the Florida Panthers.

Ogrodnick and Reed Larson. Here I was, 21 years old, under the table.

"Then I snuck out from under the table and those guys didn't have a clue who it was until about a month later."

The Wings of Gallant's early years needed those laughs in order to get through some long nights. "My first two years were really tough," Gallant said. "You never want to be a part of losing. I think that made me a better person. You know what it's like to lose and you just don't want it to happen again.

"We were losing big time and it was no fun."

Gallant was a big part of the turnaround. He posted four straight 30-goal seasons starting with 1986-87, including career-high 39-54-93 totals in 1988-89 that earned him

GALLANT'S RED WINGS STATISTICS:										
	REGULAR SEASON					PLAYOFFS				
Season	GP	G	A	P	PIM	GP	G	A	P	PIM
1984-85	32	6	12	18	66	3	0	0	0	11
1985-86	52	20	19	39	106	-	-	-	-	-
1986-87	80	38	34	72	216	16	8	6	14	43
1987-88	73	34	39	73	242	16	6	9	15	55
1988-89	76	39	54	93	230	6	1	2	3	40
1989-90	69	36	44	80	254	-	-	-	-	-
1990-91	45	10	16	26	111	-	-	-	-	-
1991-92	69	14	22	36	187	11	2	2	4	25
1992-93	67	10	20	30	188	6	1	2	3	4-
Totals	563	207	260	467	1600	58	18	21	39	178

32 KRIS DRAPER

Centre

Born: May 24, 1971, Toronto, Ont.
Shot: Left **Height:** 5-11 **Weight:** 185 lbs.
Red Wing From: 1993-94 to 2010-11
Acquired: Traded to Detroit by Winnipeg Jets for future considerations (one dollar), June 30, 1993.
Departed: Annouced his retirement as a player, July 26, 2011.

AMONG THE VAST ARRAY OF MULTIMILLION DOLLAR TALENT that populated the Detroit Red Wings dressing room, he was the team's bargain-basement banger.

Their dollar-store special.

The wisest buck the Wings ever parted with.

"I never dreamt I'd get a player for the price of a smoothie at McDonald's," Red Wings owner Mike Ilitch said.

You spend more on your cup of coffee or that pack of gum you grab at the corner store than the Wings gave the Winnipeg Jets to acquire Kris Draper's services on June 30, 1993.

They purchased his contract for one dollar.

"I think it was even a Canadian dollar," Draper said.

"A dollar, that's pretty much giving a guy away," said Darren McCarty, Draper's Grind Linemate. "You give a guy away who wins four Stanley Cups, and you wonder why some people don't have jobs."

Draper and Kirk Maltby, teamed first with Joe Kocur and later with McCarty, formed a relentless checking unit with a knack for driving the opposition to distraction.

"There was always something going on when they were out there, and usually it was their mouths," Kocur recalled.

Opponents resented them with a passion equal to the effort Draper and Maltby put into getting under their skins.

"They were always at you and they'd never stop talking," Phoenix Coyotes forward Shane Doan said, explaining what made him despise them so much.

"They'd always give you a little extra shot when you're not expecting it—rubbing guys in the face, slashing guys across the backs of the legs, everything they could do to make it not an enjoyable game for you."

Their on-ice work forged a bond between the two that carried over off the ice.

"A brother from another mother," is how Draper describes his relationship with Maltby.

In the spring of 2004, when Draper and Maltby joined Canada's world championship bid after Detroit was eliminated from the Stanley Cup playoffs, their first order of business was to set out to mend some fences.

"As soon as we got there, we went around the dressing room and apologized to every guy," Draper said. "We cleared the air right off the top."

They also helped Canada win the gold medal, earning Draper a spot on Canada's team for the 2006 Turin Winter Olympics.

Draper played 1,137 of his 1,157 games with the Red Wings over 17 seasons, which is fifth on the team's all-time list behind Gordie Howe, Steve Yzerman, Alex Delvecchio

---

DETROIT HONOURS:

- Stanley Cup champion 1996-97, 1997-98, 2001-02, 2007-08
- Won Selke Trophy, 2003-04
- Played for Canada at 2006 Winter Olympics
- Won 2005 World Cup with Canada
- Played for Canada at 2000, 2001, 2003 and 2005 World Championship, winning gold medal in 2003 and silver medal in 2005.

"He just did everything right," Wings coach Mike Babcock said. "He was allowed to hold everyone accountable because he did it right."

McCarty, who arrived in Detroit the same season as Draper, puts it into simpler terms.

"Drapes, he was the heartbeat of the team," McCarty said. "He was the pulse in the dressing room.

"We always knew his value."

The best dollar the team ever spent.

After retirement, Draper took a position as a special assistant to Detroit general manager Ken Holland. "All the intangibles he stands for, he's brought to the front office," Holland said.

and Nicklas Lidstrom. Draper's 222 playoff games place him among the NHL's all-time top 10.

He won four Stanley Cups (in 1997, 1998, 2002 and 2008), and the Selke Trophy as the NHL's top defensive forward in 2003-04.

"I consider myself one of the luckiest athletes of all time to be able to play with this organization for 17 years," Draper said. "To be able to play over 1,000 games with the Red Wings is probably what I'm most proud of."

Draper's tremendous skating ability and tenacious forechecking made him into an asset that the Wings couldn't afford to lose. "If you can skate and you work, you can wear people down," teammate and regular penalty-killing partner Dan Cleary said of Draper. "The one thing about him was he was so competitive.

"He had a hate on for everybody he played against."

So dedicated to the game was Draper that he actually built a workout regimen into his Hawaiian honeymoon.

DRAPER'S RED WINGS STATISTICS:									
	Regular Season				Playoffs				
Season	GP	G	A	P	PIM	GP	G	A	P	PIM
1993-94	39	5	8	13	31	7	2	2	4	4
1994-95	36	2	6	8	22	18	4	1	5	12
1995-96	52	7	9	16	32	18	4	1	5	12
1996-97	76	8	5	13	73	20	2	4	6	12
1997-98	64	13	10	23	45	19	1	3	4	12
1998-99	80	4	14	18	79	10	0	1	1	6
1999-00	51	5	7	12	28	9	2	0	2	6
2000-01	75	8	17	25	38	6	0	1	1	2
2001-02	82	15	15	30	56	23	2	3	5	20
2002-03	82	14	21	35	82	4	0	0	0	4
2003-04	67	24	16	40	31	12	1	3	4	6
2005-06	80	10	22	32	58	6	0	0	0	6
2006-07	81	14	15	29	58	18	2	0	2	24
2007-08	65	9	8	17	68	22	3	1	4	10
2008-09	79	7	10	17	40	8	1	0	1	0
2009-10	81	7	15	22	28	12	0	0	0	16
2010-11	47	6	5	11	12	8	0	1	1	2
Totals	1137	158	203	361	781	220	24	22	46	160

33 MARTY PAVELICH

Left Wing

Born: November 6, 1927, Sault Ste. Marie, Ontario
Shot: Left **Height:** 5-11 **Weight:** 168 lbs.
Red Wing From: 1947-48 to 1956-57
Acquired: Signed by Detroit to pro contract March 30, 1947.
Departed: Annouced his retirement as a player, August 30, 1957.

FOUR PLAYERS WERE EVER-PRESENT WHEN THE DETROIT Red Wings finished first overall in the NHL regular-season standings for a record seven consecutive seasons between 1948-49 and 1954-55.

Three of them were Gordie Howe, Ted Lindsay and Red Kelly, and the fourth was a fellow described by Wings GM Jack Adams as "one of the four players around whom we built our hockey team."

That player was left winger Marty Pavelich.

Pavelich changed his game from junior scorer to defensive dynamo at the NHL level and was rewarded with a long career as one of the best checking forwards of his era. Teamed with Tony Leswick and Glen Skov, they were Detroit's 1950s version of the Grind Line.

"Our checkers weren't worried as much about scoring as players are today," former Wings coach Jimmy Skinner once explained. "They would come back to our bench after a shift and say, 'Ha, those bastards didn't score on us this time.'

"Marty always had the desire. He was out there checking all of the time."

As a junior with the Galt Red Wings, Pavelich averaged nearly a goal and two points per game, but changed his game dramatically as an NHLer, earning him recognition as one of the league's elite defensive forwards.

"Guys like Skov and Pavelich and Leswick were great checkers," recalled former Wings forward Bill Dineen. Had there been a Selke Trophy in his day, Pavelich would have been a multiple winner of the award.

"I was a pretty consistent goal scorer in Galt, but when I arrived in the NHL with the Red Wings, I was told from Day 1 to concentrate on the defensive side of the game," Pavelich explained. "Myself and my linemates were sent out to face the offensive threats of the opposition, and it was our job to stop them.

"Our goals came from others on the team."

Not always, however. Often—as was the case in the 1990s with the likes of Kris Draper and Kirk Maltby—Detroit's grinders often delivered fine offensive performances in key games. Leswick netted the Stanley Cup-winner in 1954. The following spring, in Game 1 of the final series between the Wings and Montreal, Pavelich broke a 2-2 tie while Detroit was shorthanded, when he jumped in the passing lane to deflect a pass by Canadiens defenceman Doug Harvey, chased down the loose puck, broke in alone and snapped a high shot for the game winner.

Detroit would win that series in seven games. Pavelich scored four of his 13 career playoff games in Stanley Cup final play. He's one of 10 players in Red Wings history to earn four Stanley Cup inscriptions, and it's those that he treasures most about his Detroit days.

"It was just great fun," Pavelich said. "You have to have that chemistry and we did."

His best season was in 1951-52, when Pavelich garnered 17-19-36 totals. Detroit won the Cup in the minimum eight games that spring and like most, he feels that was the best club in franchise history.

DETROIT HONOURS:

- Detroit Honours: Stanley Cup champion 1949-50, 1951-52, 1953-54, 1954-55
- Played in NHL All-Star Game, 1949, 1951, 1953, 1954.

"I used to feel sorry for the teams we played the night after we'd lost, because we'd just kick the crap out of them," Pavelich recalled. "That team could have kept playing all summer long and would have never stopped winning."

As the Wings readied for training camp in the summer of 1957, Adams offered Pavelich a two-way contract with a minor-league option, a commonplace occurrence with veteran players in those days.

Pavelich and teammate Ted Lindsay were co-owners of a successful car parts company, and he retired to run the company, which the two men eventually sold 23 years later. "It turned out to be the smartest thing I ever did, walking out of Adams's office," Pavelich said.

Lindsay and Pavelich also operated a hockey school in Port Huron, Mich., one of the first major hockey schools opened in the United States. In 1975 Pavelich and Lindsay headed a group that unsuccessfully sought to buy the Red Wings for $10 million from Bruce Norris and move to a new rink to be built in Pontiac.

The brother of Hockey Hall of Fame linesman Matt Pavelich, Marty became a referee in retirement and worked NCAA games. More recently, Pavelich served a tour on the Hall's selection committee.

An avid skier, Pavelich eventually relocated to Big Sky, Montana, where he still resides today.

PAVELICH'S RED WINGS STATISTICS:										
	Regular Season					Playoffs				
Season	GP	G	A	P	PIM	GP	G	A	P	PIM
1947-48	41	4	8	12	10	10	2	2	4	6
1948-49	60	10	16	26	40	9	0	1	1	8
1949-50	65	8	15	23	58	14	4	2	6	13
1950-51	67	9	20	29	41	6	0	1	1	2
1951-52	68	17	19	36	54	8	2	2	4	2
1952-53	64	13	20	33	49	6	2	1	3	7
1953-54	65	9	20	29	57	12	2	2	4	4
1954-55	70	15	15	30	59	11	1	3	4	12
1955-56	70	5	13	18	38	10	0	1	1	14
1956-57	64	3	13	16	48	5	0	0	0	6
Totals	634	93	159	252	454	91	13	15	28	74

34 MIKE VERNON

Goal

1-800-459-2266

Born: February 24, 1963, Calgary, Alberta
Shot: Left Height: 5-9 Weight: 180 lbs.
Red Wing From: 1994-95 to 1996-97
Acquired: Traded to Detroit by Calgary Flames for Steve Chiasson, June 29, 1994.
Departed: Traded by Detroit to San Jose with Detroit's fifth-round choice (Andrei Maximenko in 1999
Entry Draft for San Jose's second-round choice—later traded to St Louis Blues (St Louis selected
Maxim Linnik) in 1998 NHL Entry Draft and San Jose's second-round choice—later traded to Tampa
Bay Lightning (Tampa Bay selected Sheldon Keefe) in 1999 NHL Entry Draft, Aug 18, 1997.

THE GRAVEYARD THAT WAS THE DETROIT RED WINGS' GOAL crease during the early 1990s was the perfect place for Mike Vernon to take up residence.

The little fellow with a big chip on his shoulder, equipped with a caustic wise-guy persona, he was as effective at deflecting any abuse that would be aimed his way as he was at parrying pucks. "I've been booed by fans and cheered by them," Vernon explained. "I've been praised and crapped on in the papers. You have to learn to live with it, because it's all part of the game."

He would also succeed where the likes of Glen Hanlon, Greg Stefan, Tim Cheveldae and Bob Essensa failed, twice taking Detroit to the promised land, and once all the way to nirvana.

With Vernon between the pipes, the Wings reached the Stanley Cup final in 1995 for the first time since the spring of 1966. Two years later, he backstopped them all the way to a Stanley Cup championship, Detroit's first since 1954-55.

"Mike Vernon was always such a difficult playoff opponent," former NHL forward Geoff Courtnall said. "That was exactly why the Wings went after Vernon's services, trading veteran defenceman Steve Chiasson to the Calgary Flames in the summer of 1994.

When then Detroit coach Scotty Bowman set out to find a goalie, he consulted his first NHL netminder. "When Mike Vernon was available, I talked to Glenn Hall, who was the goalie coach in Calgary," Bowman said. Hall was Bowman's goaltender in St. Louis, where Bowman earned his first NHL coaching assignment in 1967.

"He told me, 'You'll like him. He plays big in big games. He's a winner.' That was good enough for me."

Vernon, a Calgary native, had taken his hometown Flames to the 1986 final and to the only title in franchise history when Calgary upended the Montreal Canadiens in the 1989 Stanley Cup final.

"He literally won us the Stanley Cup (in 1989)," former Flames GM Cliff Fletcher recalled. "In the first series that year, we played Vancouver and ended up in overtime in Game 7. Mike made three saves in overtime that were just miraculous. A few years earlier (in 1986), he was just tremendous when we eliminated a superb Edmonton team.

"When you look at the goaltenders who entered the league in the 1980s, he belongs every bit as much in that top category as any of the others. I consider him one of the

---

DETROIT HONOURS:

+ Stanley Cup champion, 1996-97
+ Shared William Jennings Trophy with Chris Osgood, 1995-96
+ Won Conn Smythe Trophy, 1996-97
+ Led Stanley Cup playoffs in wins, 1996-97.

best money goaltenders of all time. The bigger the game, the more you could count on Mike."

In his first season with Detroit, Vernon took the Wings to the Cup final, but took much of the heat when Detroit was swept by New Jersey. "A lot of people gave up on him after that, but I never did," Bowman said.

Nonetheless, Chris Osgood usurped Vernon's No. 1 job in 1995-96 and when he played 30 of Detroit's first 41 games during the 1996-97 campaign, Vernon was ready to give up on himself as a Red Wing.

"If you had asked me at Christmas that year, I would have thought for sure that I'd be traded by the deadline," Vernon said. "Towards the end of February, Scotty called me into his office and said he was going to get me some chances to play, that he was going to go with me."

Vernon caught fire in the playoffs that spring, allowing two goals or less in 17 of 20 games as the Wings rolled to a Cup final sweep of the Philadelphia Flyers and Vernon was awarded the Conn Smythe Trophy as Stanley Cup MVP.

Just like that, he was gone. With Osgood waiting in the Wings, Vernon was dealt in the summer to the San Jose Sharks, joining Earl Robertson (1938, New York Americans), Harry Lumley (1950, Chicago Blackhawks) and Terry Sawchuk (1955, Boston Bruins) as Detroit goalies traded away immediately after backstopping the Wings to a Stanley Cup.

"He did everything we expected him to do," Red Wings senior vice-president Jimmy Devellano said. "We were very happy with Mike Vernon."

Vernon also felt a sense of satisfaction over what he accomplished during his brief tenure in Detroit. "I was brought here for a couple of things—to win a Stanley Cup and to help Chris Osgood develop into a front-line NHL goalie," Vernon said. "I think I did my job in those respects."

| VERNON'S RED WINGS STATISTICS: | | | | | | | | | | | |
| REGULAR SEASON | | | | | | PLAYOFFS | | | | | |
Season	GPI	MIN	GA	SO	W-L-T	GAA	GPI	MIN	GA	SO	GAA	W-L
1994-95	30	1807	76	1	19-6-4	2.52	18	1063	41	1	2.31	12-6
1995-96	32	1855	70	3	21-7-2	2.26	4	243	11	0	2.72	2-2
1996-97	33	1952	79	0	13-9-10	2.43	20	1229	36	1	1.76	16-4
Totals	95	5614	225	4	53-22-16	2.40	42	2535	88	2	2.08	30-12

35 ROGER CROZIER

Goal

Born: March 16, 1942, Bracebridge, Ontario
Died: January 11, 1996
Shot: Left Height: 5-8 Weight: 165 lbs.
Red Wing From: 1963-64 to 1969-70
Acquired: Traded to Detroit by Chicago Blackhawks with Ron Ingram for Howie Young, June 5, 1963.
Departed: Traded to Buffalo Sabres by Detroit for Tom Webster, June 10, 1970.

ROGER CROZIER ARRIVED IN TRAINING CAMP FOR THE 1964-65 season, just one of many question marks facing the Detroit Red Wings during a season of transition for the team.

He'd won a Memorial Cup with St. Catharines in 1959-60 and was named AHL rookie of the year in 1963-64, but even Crozier wondered if he'd be able to carry on the legacy of sensational puckstopping that Wings fans had grown accustomed to witnessing on a game-in, game-out basis.

"Detroit have had such great goalies as Terry Sawchuk, Glenn Hall and Harry Lumley," Crozier said. "And now they're stuck with a little runt like me."

After watching Crozier in action for just 15 NHL games during the 1963-64 campaign, Detroit coach-GM Sid Abel opted to let veteran Sawchuk go for nothing to the Toronto Maple Leafs in the NHL Intra-League Draft, handing the keys to the crease to the unproven Crozier, who was just 22.

"If he doesn't do the job, I'll be sitting out there in the stands like everyone else, wondering what the devil went wrong," Abel admitted during training camp.

His decision was met with criticism from around the league. New York Rangers netminder Jacques Plante predicted Detroit would miss playoffs with Crozier between the pipes. Leafs coach-GM Punch Imlach felt Crozier was too frail to last the season.

Crozier heard their words, and admitted that it hurt. "It's hard for goaltenders to come into the league," Crozier told the *Pittsburgh Press*. "Right away they think you're not good enough."

Then he set out and proved them all wrong.

Crozier played in all 70 of Detroit's regular season games—the last time a goaltender has done that in NHL history—and was awarded the Calder Trophy as the NHL's top rookie when he backstopped the Wings to a first-place finish for the first time since the 1956-57 campaign.

"You can credit it to defence, desire and a little bundle of dynamite named Roger Crozier," former Red Wing Vic Stasiuk, who coached Crozier in the AHL with the Pittsburgh Hornets, told the *Pittsburgh Post-Gazette*. "That Crozier is something. This boy could turn out to be one of the all-time greats."

The tone of the reviews of Crozier's work quickly changed. "He has the best reflexes of anyone in hockey," Montreal Hall of Famer Maurice (Rocket) Richard expressed.

An acrobatic goalie who was willing to do whatever it took to stop the puck, Crozier once took a Frank Mahovlich shot square in the cheekbone, fracturing it in two places. After 10 minutes of medical treatment, he returned to finish the game.

He led all NHL goalies with 40 wins as a rookie, and Crozier backstopped Detroit to the Stanley Cup final

DETROIT HONOURS:

- Won Calder Trophy, 1964-65
- NHL First All-Star Team, 1964-65
- Led NHL with 40 wins, 1964-65
- Led NHL in shutouts, 1964-65, 1965-66
- Led NHL goalies with 70 games, 1964-65
- Won Conn Smythe Trophy, 1965-66
- Led Stanley Cup playoffs in shutouts, 1965-66.

in 1965-66. Even though the Wings lost in six games to Montreal, the Detroit netminder was awarded the Conn Smythe Trophy as playoff MVP, the first time a player from the losing side was honoured.

Then, almost as rapidly as his rise, things went south for Detroit's spectacular little netminder. Crozier, who developed an ulcer when he was 17, was diagnosed with pancreatitis in 1965 and he admitted the pressure of being an NHL puckstopper was wearing on his psyche.

"A few summers ago, I worked for a warehousing company in Bracebridge and found it so relaxing to do an honest day's work and then go home and forget about it," Crozier told *Canadian Press*.

"When I'm playing hockey, I'm worried all the time that someone is going to get my job. The only time I really forget about my problems is after a game when we've won. But by the next morning, I'd be worrying again.

"I like everything about hockey—the travelling, the friends I've made, the interviews. Everything but the games. They're pure torture."

Detroit missed the playoffs in 1966-67 and when the Wings slumped badly to start the 1967-68 season, Crozier, after allowing 18 goals in a three-game span, announced in early November of 1967 that he was retiring from hockey.

"I'd be a nut within three weeks if I continued," Crozier said.

Abel had planned to give Crozier a minor-league stint with Fort Worth of the Central League to find his game. "Roger has

CROZIER'S RED WINGS STATISTICS:											
REGULAR SEASON						PLAYOFFS					
Season	GPI	MIN	GA	SO	W-L-T	GAA	GPI	MIN	GA	SO	GAA	W-L
1963-64	17	900	51	1	5-6-4	3.40	3	126	5	0	2.38	0-2
1964-65	70	4168	168	6	40-22-7	2.42	7	420	23	0	3.29	3-4
1965-66	64	3734	173	7	27-24-12	2.78	12	668	26	1	2.34	6-5
1966-67	58	3256	182	4	22-29-4	3.35	-	-	-	-	-	-
1967-68	34	1729	95	1	9-18-2	3.30	-	-	-	-	-	-
1968-69	38	1820	101	0	12-16-3	3.33	-	-	-	-	-	-
1969-70	34	1877	83	0	16-6-9	2.65	1	34	3	0	5.29	0-1
Totals	313	17484	853	20	131-121-41	2.92	23	1248	57	1	2.74	9-12

taken this slump worse than anyone," Abel told the *Windsor Star*. "He told me he'd lost his confidence and forgot how to play goal. He felt he was headed for a nervous breakdown.

"I think he'll reconsider after a few weeks at home. At least I hope he will."

Crozier's teammates were also hopeful that they hadn't seen the last of him between the pipes. "I sure hope he doesn't stick to his retirement," Wings captain Alex Delvecchio said. "He's too valuable."

Crozier did return to action in late January of 1968. "My nerves are in much better shape than when I left," he told the *Montreal Gazette*. "I think I just needed a rest to relieve the pressure."

Two years later, Crozier helped the Wings return to the playoffs for the first time in four years. But that summer, Detroit traded him to the expansion Buffalo Sabres, who were seeking an experienced goalie to build their new team around.

Crozier made it back to the Stanley Cup final with the Sabres in 1975 and finished his playing career with the Washington Capitals in 1977, later serving as coach and GM of that team.

After hockey, Crozier worked as senior vice-president of the MBNA credit card company from 1983 until his 1996 death from cancer. The annual NHL award for the goaltender with the best save percentage is named in his honour.

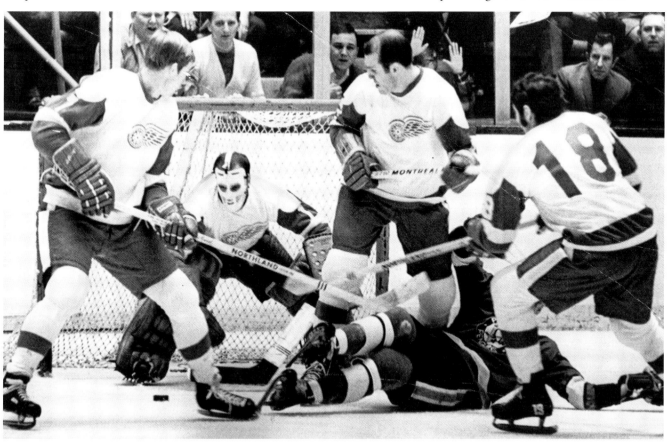

Born: January 23, 1973, Pitea, Sweden
Shot: Left Height: 6-0 Weight: 200 lbs.
Red Wing From: 1996-97 to 2011-12
Acquired: Selected 257th overall by Detroit June 29, 1994 NHL Entry Draft.
Departed: Announced retirement from hockey, January 22, 2013.

As a youngster growing up in Pitea, Sweden, not far from the Arctic Circle, Tomas Holmstrom saw nothing but bleak darkness 23 hours a day for much of the winter. No wonder the Detroit Red Wings forward found the black hole in front of the other team's net to be such an inviting location.

"Nobody wanted to go in front of the net when I started playing hockey," Holmstrom recalled. "I was smaller than everybody else, and I played with guys who were three years older, but I didn't mind to go in front of the net even then."

Most of Holmstrom's 243 NHL goals were earned the hard way, and in the slot he paid the price for tipping in pucks and banging home rebounds, and he wears many scars from those net-front battles. "That was my area, around the net," Holmstrom said. "That's where I scored my goals, in the blue paint. I take a lot of pride in that for sure. I wouldn't change that for anything."

In Sweden, they called Holmstrom "Demolition Man," after the Sylvester Stallone film role, but at least one NHL goalie saw Holmstrom as a much different fictional character. Former Boston Bruins goaltender Tim Thomas compared Holmstrom to Neo, the character portrayed by Canadian actor (and former goalie) Keanu Reeves in the film trilogy *The Matrix*.

"Tomas Holmstrom, he was very good at actually getting out of the way of the puck," Thomas explained. "He'd get right in that lane. If you watched him, he was like the guy in *The Matrix*. If it was a high shot, he'd roll out of the way. That's one of the talents that he had, is getting out of the way. That's what made him so good. And he was willing to just stand there and take any punishment whatsoever that you were willing to dish out."

Holmstrom played on the edge and lived on the edge. Watching Holmstrom in action on any given night it was easy to think, 'This must be what it's like to earn a living as a crash-test dummy.'

"It's got to be a little bit tearing on the body to play the way he did," Wings defenceman Jonathan Ericsson said. "It's pretty amazing that he could play as many games as he has."

Two hernia surgeries and countless knee operations were the prices Holmstrom's career choice exacted upon his person. "He had bad knees when he first joined the league," said former Wings captain Nicklas Lidstrom, Holmstrom's best friend. "Seeing him battling through those things, and knowing he was in pain, just his determination and his willingness to battle through it to be on the ice, it showed a lot about his character."

DETROIT HONOURS:

- Stanley Cup champion, 1996-97, 1997-98, 2001-02, 2007-08
- Played 1,000th NHL game Feb. 10, 2012 vs. Anaheim Ducks, becoming one of six players to play 1,000 games in a Red Wings uniform (Gordie Howe, Alex Delvecchio, Steve Yzerman, Nicklas Lidstrom, Kris Draper)
- Won gold medal with Sweden at 2006 Turin Winter Olympic Games
- Won silver medal with Sweden at 2007 World Championship
- Played for Sweden in 2002 Winter Olympics and 2005 World Cup of Hockey.

Holmstrom cited Rob Blake as the defenceman who punished him the most, crediting the former Los Angeles Kings blue liner for providing three of his career concussions.

"What a true warrior," former NHL forward Ryan Smyth said of Holmstrom. "He's one of the best, if not the best, in my opinion. I watched him over the years, and I picked up a few things.

"I have tremendous respect for him."

Selected 257th overall by the Wings in the 1994 NHL entry draft, scouts said Holmstrom was too slow and too skinny to make it in the show. "Even over in Sweden, I remember some people said, 'Why would they bring him over?'" Lidstrom recalled.

No one wondered that once they saw Holmstrom at work. They merely looked at the punishment dished out Holmstrom's way, and gazed upon him with wonder.

"A lot of guys can stand there and deflect the puck in the net when no one's cross-checking you," former Wings coach Mike Babcock said. "But most guys are trying to find out who's cross-checking them, and not worried about the puck.

"The good guys don't worry about getting cross-checked, they can always find the puck. That's what he was real good at. He had great hockey sense, he knew how to play, he knew to protect the puck, knew how to get it back, he knew where to stand. He wasn't an elite skater, and yet he was an elite competitor.

"It just goes to show you players come in all different sizes, shapes and abilities, and Homer managed to have a good enough package to play a long time."

In the end, as much as it hurt him to walk away from hockey, it was how much it hurt him to play hockey that made Holmstrom's mind up that it was time to hang up his skates in 2013. "After a while, it wears on you," he said. "Getting out of bed in the morning and stumbling to make it to the bathroom. And all of the medication they give you for the pain, it can't be good for you."

These days, Holmstrom is feeling like a new man.

"I feel that I'm walking better," he said. "I sleep way better at night. I don't have the pain and the aches when I get up in the morning. It's nice. I fall asleep right away, I sleep through the night and wake up rested. Little things like that, you never think about them."

Holmstrom left the game third all-time in Red Wings history in power-play goals (122), sixth in regular-season games played (1,026) and fourth in playoff games played (180).

"It's not easy," Holmstrom said of retirement. "For sure, I'm going to miss the game and the boys. Sooner or later, we all have to go. It doesn't matter how good you are."

HOLMSTROM'S RED WINGS STATISTICS:

	Regular Season					Playoffs				
Season	GP	G	A	P	PIM	GP	G	A	P	PIM
1996-97	47	6	3	9	33	1	0	0	0	0
1997-98	57	5	12	17	44	22	7	12	19	16
1998-99	82	13	21	34	69	10	4	3	7	4
1999-00	72	13	22	35	43	9	3	1	4	16
2000-01	73	16	24	40	40	6	1	3	4	8
2001-02	69	8	18	26	58	23	8	3	11	8
2002-03	74	20	20	40	62	4	1	1	2	4
2003-04	67	15	15	30	38	12	2	2	4	10
2005-06	81	29	30	59	66	6	1	2	3	12
2006-07	77	30	22	52	58	15	5	3	8	14
2007-08	59	20	20	40	58	21	4	8	12	26
2008-09	53	14	23	37	38	23	2	5	7	22
2009-10	68	25	20	45	60	12	4	3	7	12
2010-11	73	18	19	37	62	11	3	4	7	8
2011-12	74	11	13	24	40	5	1	1	2	2
Totals	1026	243	287	530	769	180	46	51	97	162

37 MARCEL DIONNE

Centre

Born: August 3, 1951, Drummondville, Quebec
Shot: Right **Height:** 5-9 **Weight:** 190 lbs.
Red Wing From: 1971-72 to 1974-75
Acquired: Selected 2nd overall by Detroit in June 10, 1971 NHL Amateur Draft.
Departed: Signed as a free agent by Los Angeles Kings, June 17, 1975. As compensation to Detroit, NHL orchestrated trade of Dionne's rights to Los Angeles with Bart Crashley for Terry Harper, Dan Maloney and Los Angeles' second round choice (later traded to Minnesota North Stars—Minnesota selected Jim Roberts) in 1976 NHL amateur draft.

REGRETS? NOT IN MARCEL DIONNE'S CASE. Disappointments? Just one, that he never won a Stanley Cup during a Hall of Fame career in which he scored over 700 goals.

His was an NHL career that first blossomed in Detroit.

"The game rewards you with all kinds of things," Dionne said. "Not only financially, but people never forget you."

While disappointed he never got a chance to win a championship, Dionne is secure in knowing that he competed hard every night and that he respected the fans that paid his wages. "My biggest goal when I was in Detroit was to never embarrass my mom and dad," Dionne said. "Today's athletes, not a lot really care about that.

"You're a role model whether you want to be or not. I didn't want to disappoint the people that looked up at me."

Dionne could be looked upon as a role model for his brethren. In the summer of 1975, he shook the very foundation of the NHL when after four productive seasons with the Red Wings, he signed as a free agent with the Los Angeles Kings.

"It was an era when players were just starting to stand up for themselves," Dionne said. "I was one of the early ones to do that. It was all about the management.

"If I ran my business like that, I'd be broke."

Mickey Redmond remembers the day well. Still a close friend of Dionne's to this day, he billeted Dionne in his home during the stocky centre's rookie NHL season of 1971-72.

When the Kings made their offer to Dionne, he sought out the counsel of his friend and Detroit teammate. "He came to me and said, 'What do you think?'" Redmond recalled. "I said, 'You know what? You're going to have to go.'

"As much as I hated to say it—he was a good friend, a great teammate and a heck of a hockey player—but it was the best thing for him, as it turned out, and it might have changed the industry."

175

DETROIT HONOURS:

♦ Won Lady Byng Trophy, 1974-75
♦ Played in NHL All-Star Game, 1975
♦ Set NHL rookie record with 77 points, 1971-72
♦ Led NHL with 10 shorthanded goals, 1974-75
♦ Selected to Team Canada for 1972 Summit Series
♦ Team captain, 1974-75
♦ Led Red Wings in assists and points, 1971-72, 1973-74, 1974-75
♦ Won Lester Patrick Trophy, 2006.

It certainly changed the view of Detroit in NHL circles. Change was coming to the Wings. The end of the era of ownership of the Norris family was coming to a close, but not soon enough for Dionne.

"Now you see it's Hockeytown," Dionne said. "I was caught in the middle then."

Dionne was supposed to be the linchpin to a Detroit renaissance when they selected him second overall from the junior St. Catharines Black Hawks in the 1971 NHL amateur draft.

"He was an incredible talent," Redmond said. "He had an incredible will to play and to win and was such a very, very strong guy.

"I wish we never would have lost him. It was unfortunate at the time that the organization was messed up and they pretty much forced him out of town."

Former Detroit coach Jimmy Skinner, a long-time member of the Detroit front office, was convinced that Dionne never wanted to leave the Red Wings. "He told me that the very next year," Skinner said. "He liked it in Detroit. He said his leaving was all caused by a misunderstanding. For some reason, nobody sat down with him to straighten it out."

The Wings also claimed to be worried at the draft table in the spring of 1971 that the Montreal Canadiens, with the first pick, wouldn't take Quebec star Guy Lafleur and leave Dionne for them. "We didn't want Montreal to do a flip-flop and take Dionne," Wings GM Ned Harkness told the *Windsor Star*. "I would have picked Dionne over Lafleur."

Dionne wasted little time living up to that billing, setting an NHL rookie record with 77 points in 1971-72. "I

wouldn't trade Dionne for any other rookie in the league," Detroit coach Johnny Wilson told the *Vancouver Sun*.

"He has stardom written all over his forehead," added Red Wings legend Gordie Howe.

While Dionne seemed to get better every year, the Wings only got worse. By the time he was winning the Lady Byng Trophy and earning his first NHL All-Star Game selection in 1974-75, the Wings were nearing the bottom of the league.

When the opportunity came to leave, Dionne—who became an NHL superstar with the Kings, winning two Lester Pearson Awards and the NHLPA's top player and one NHL scoring title—felt he had no other choice.

"There was chaos in Detroit," Dionne said. "I'm sorry it happened."

He's never forgotten what the city meant to him, or how it launched him toward NHL stardom.

"Detroit is still close to my heart," Dionne said. "That's a great hockey town."

Today, Dionne lives in Niagara Falls, Ont., where he operates a sports memorabilia business and a restaurant.

DIONNE'S RED WINGS STATISTICS:										
	Regular Season					Playoffs				
Season	GP	G	A	P	PIM	GP	G	A	P	PIM
1971-72	78	28	49	77	14	-	-	-	-	-
1972-73	77	40	50	90	21	-	-	-	-	-
1973-74	74	24	54	78	10	-	-	-	-	-
1974-75	80	47	74	121	14	-	-	-	-	-
Totals	309	139	217	356	59	-	-	-	-	-

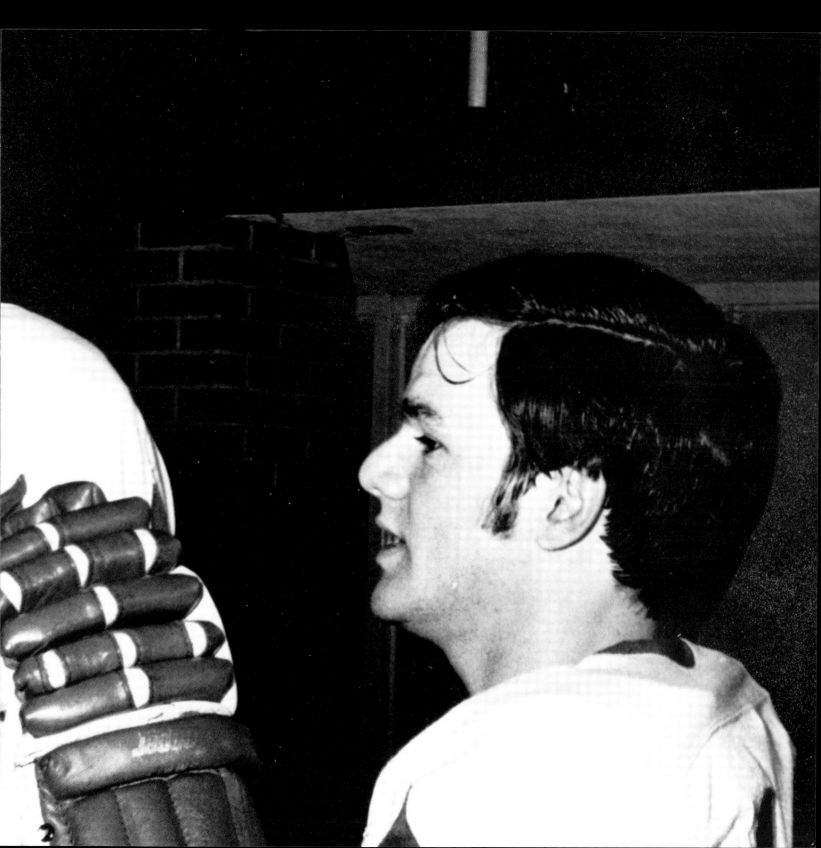

38 BILL GADSBY

Defence

Born: Calgary, Alberta, August 8, 1927
Shot: Left **Height:** 6-0 **Weight:** 180 lbs.
Red Wing From: 1961-62 to 1965-66
Elected to Hockey Hall of Fame: 1970
Acquired: Traded to Detroit by New York Rangers for Les Hunt, June 13, 1961.
Departed: Announced retirement, May 8, 1966.

THE DETROIT RED WINGS WERE TANGLING WITH THE NEW York Rangers during the dog days of the 1959-60 NHL season when Detroit star Gordie Howe found himself being taken hard into the boards by rugged Rangers defenceman Bill Gadsby.

"Take it easy Gads," Howe said under his breath. "I hear we're getting you tomorrow."

Howe was partially right. The Wings would eventually get Gadsby, but not until the conclusion of the following season. A February 5, 1960 deal that was to send Red Kelly and Billy McNeill to the Rangers for Gadsby and Eddie Shack was scuttled when Kelly and McNeill refused to report to New York.

In June of 1961, the Wings finally got their man, shipping prospect Les Hunt to the Rangers for Gadsby. It was a steal of a deal. While Gadsby was a future Hall of Famer, Hunt would never play in the NHL.

Decades later, Gadsby remains amazed by the hockey public's complete association of him with the Red Wings.

"It is astonishing," Gadsby said of his link with the Wings, a team he was with for only one-quarter of his 20-season NHL career. "But what I'm finding from the people that I meet, unless they are over 70 like me, they don't remember me as anything but a Red Wing."

A seven-time NHL All-Star during his first 15 NHL campaigns with the Rangers and the equally-woeful Chicago Blackhawks, Gadsby had never won a Stanley Cup series, but thought his arrival in Detroit would prove to be his ticket to Cup glory.

"Coming to Detroit, I thought it was going to be a chance to win it all," Gadsby said. "We had some tremendous teams."

The Red Wings lost the 1963 final to Toronto in five games, then dropped a heartbreaking seven-game decision against the Leafs the following spring, squandering a 3-2 series lead. In overtime of Game 6 that spring, Bob Baun's game-winner banked over the shoulder of Wings goalie Terry Sawchuk off Gadsby's stick.

"I didn't see the puck until the last second and it was too late to get the stick out of the way," Gadsby recalled. "I thought we were going to win the Cup that night."

The 1964-65 season was another strong one for Gadsby. He finished third in the Norris Trophy as the NHL's top defenceman behind winner Pierre Pilote of Chicago and Montreal's Jacques Laperriere.

When Gadsby and Howe took the ice for Detroit's season opener of the 1965-66 season, they joined former Boston star Dit Clapper as the only 20-year players in the NHL history. Gadsby was the first defenceman in NHL history to record 500 career points and held league marks for assists in a season (46) and games played (1,248) by a rearguard.

That spring, the Wings were back in the Stanley Cup final. Up 2-0 on the Montreal Canadiens, they lost the

DETROIT HONOURS:

- Selected to NHL Second All-Star Team, 1964-65
- Played in NHL All-Star Game, 1964-65
- Elected to Hockey Hall of Fame, 1970.

series in six games on a controversial overtime goal by Habs centre Henri Richard, which the Wings were convinced was illegally pushed into the net by Richard's gloved hand.

"Richard crashed into (goalie) Roger Crozier and pushed the puck into the net with his glove," Gadsby said. "If they'd had replay back then, it could have changed the outcome."

Leaving the ice following the 1966 setback, Gadsby told his wife Edna that he was done playing.

"That's what she tells me, although I can't remember saying it," Gadsby said. "It had been a goal of mine to play 20 seasons and I thought I'd had enough."

Gadsby estimates that he took 650 stitches from the neck up, had his nose broken 11 times, suffered two shoulder separations and a broken leg, and had seven teeth knocked out.

A few weeks later, Gadsby officially hung up his skates for good.

"I've played my last game," Gadsby announced, and he held firm to that statement. Midway through the 1966-67 season, the Wings called, seeking to convince Gadsby, now coach of the junior Edmonton Oil Kings, to return to active duty. He declined the offer.

On June 2, 1968, Gadsby was hired as the sixth coach in Red Wings history, but just three games into the 1969-70 season, he was shockingly dismissed.

Even though he never got to sip from Lord Stanley's mug, you'll never find Gadsby complaining about what hockey didn't provide him.

"I had a wonderful career and got to play with some great players," he said. "You can't dwell on the disappointments.

"In the end, the positives far outweigh the negatives. I've been blessed."

GADSBY'S RED WINGS STATISTICS:										
	Regular Season					Playoffs				
Season	GP	G	A	P	PIM	GP	G	A	P	PIM
1961-62	70	7	30	37	88	-	-	-	-	-
1962-63	70	4	24	28	116	11	1	4	5	36
1963-64	64	2	16	18	80	14	0	4	4	22
1964-65	61	0	12	12	122	7	0	3	3	8
1965-66	58	5	12	17	72	12	1	3	4	12
Totals	323	18	94	112	478	44	2	14	16	78

39 PAUL COFFEY
Defence

Born: June 1, 1961, Weston, Ontario
Shot: Left Height: 6-0 Weight: 185 lbs.
Red Wing From: 1992-93 to 1995-96
Elected to Hockey Hall of Fame: 2004
Acquired: Traded to Detroit by Los Angeles Kings with Sylvain Couturier and Jim Hiller for Jimmy Carson, Marc Potvin and Gary Shuchuk, January 29, 1993.
Departed: Traded by Detroit to Hartford Whalers with Keith Primeau and a 1997 first round draft choice (Nikos Tselios) for Brendan Shanahan and Brian Glynn, October 9, 1996.

WHEN MARC BERGEVIN WAS ACQUIRED BY THE DETROIT Red Wings and paired with Paul Coffey, the most prolific defenceman in the history of the NHL, he figured it was best to discuss his on-ice role with him.

Coffey's advice to his new partner? "Always give me the puck," Coffey said. "And then, get out of the way."

The Detroit Red Wings had gone nearly 38 years without a Cup when they reached out for some Coffey.

Having played in five Stanley Cup finals, winning on four occasions, Coffey could think of nothing he'd have enjoyed more than helping Detroit return to glory. "This is such a great hockey town," Coffey said of the place called Hockeytown. "You could feel the tradition when you stepped out on the ice."

In the history of the game, no other defenceman accomplished what Coffey achieved. When he arrived in Detroit, Coffey held or shared 10 NHL records for defencemen, including the single-season mark for goals by a defenceman, scoring 48 times for Edmonton in 1985-86.

While Coffey was with Edmonton, he collected eight points in a 12-3 win over Detroit, a single-game NHL record for defencemen he shares with Tom Bladon. "It was much nicer watching him wind it up and head away from my net," former Detroit goalie Tim Cheveldae said. "He did things on the ice that were just unbelievable. He was such a fabulous passer."

Breaking in with the Edmonton Oilers as a teenager, Coffey was part of three Stanley Cup winners there. "They probably had the six best players in the world, all in the same lineup," former Detroit captain Steve Yzerman said, referring to those Edmonton clubs and the likes of Wayne Gretzky, Mark Messier, Coffey, Jari Kurri, Glenn Anderson and Grant Fuhr.

They were hockey's answer to the Brat Pack, those Oiler teams of the 1980s. A, young, brash, cocky and successful bunch. "We all came up together around the same time and most of us were 18 or 19 when we broke in," Coffey said. "We learned together. We lived through the ups and downs together and we had a great leader in (Glen) Sather."

With Edmonton, Coffey set Stanley Cup marks for goals (12), assists (25), and points (37) by a defenceman in one

183

DETROIT HONOURS:

- Won Norris Trophy, 1994-95
- Named to NHL First All-Star Team, 1994-95
- Played in NHL All-Star Game, 1993, 1994, 1996
- Holds Red Wings club records for assists (63) and points (77) by a defenceman in a single season
- Led Red Wings in assists and points, 1994-95
- Became first defenceman in NHL history to register 1,000 career assists, December 13, 1995.

playoff year, and by the time he arrived in Detroit, getting another Stanley Cup ring was all that mattered to him.

"I used to think about points, but by then, just winning was the most important thing," Coffey said. "I loved the playoffs.

"I just got more excited. That's a poor excuse, because we got paid a lot of money to play every day. But in the playoffs, everything was more important.

"Everybody is watching. All of the TVs are on. All of the other teams are watching. It's exciting. It's what the game is all about."

Unfortunately for Coffey, individual honours would be all that he'd accomplish with the Wings. He skated in the 1993 NHL All-Star Game, the first time in a decade that Detroit had sent a rearguard to the mid-season classic. He set club records for a defenceman with 63 assists and 77 points in 1993-94 and won the Norris Trophy as the NHL's top defender in 1994-95.

"Coffey, he was such a great skater," former Detroit captain Nicklas Lidstrom said. "You go D to D with him and he could carry it up through the neutral zone. With his great speed, he was good at jumping up and becoming part of the offence."

On December 8, 1995, with a helper on an Igor Larionov goal during a 3-1 win over the Chicago Blackhawks, Coffey became the first defenceman in NHL history to collect 1,000 career assists. "One thousand assists in this league is unbelievable," said Columbus Blue Jackets associate coach Craig Hartsburg, himself a former NHL All-Star defenceman. "He's probably the best all-time offensive defenceman ever."

Detroit reached the Stanley Cup final in 1995, but were swept by the New Jersey Devils. They won an NHL-record 61 games in 1995-96, but after falling to the Colorado Avalanche in the Western Conference final, the Wings opted to take another direction, including Coffey in a deal with the Hartford Whalers that brought power forward Brendan Shanahan to Detroit.

Coffey's only regret about his time in Detroit was that he never got to pour anything into a Cup. "There are some things in this game that you can't measure with goals and assists," Coffey said.

COFFEY'S RED WINGS STATISTICS:

Season	REGULAR SEASON					PLAYOFFS				
	GP	G	A	P	PIM	GP	G	A	P	PIM
1992-93	30	4	26	30	27	7	2	9	11	2
1993-94	80	14	63	77	106	7	1	6	7	8
1994-95	45	14	44	58	72	18	6	12	18	10
1995-96	76	14	60	74	90	17	5	9	14	30
Totals	231	46	193	239	295	49	14	36	50	50

40 LARRY MURPHY

Defence

Born: March 8, 1961, Scarborough, Ontario
Shot: Right **Height:** 6-2 **Weight:** 210 lbs.
Red Wing From: 1996-97 to 2000-01
Elected to Hockey Hall of Fame: 2004
Acquired: Traded to Detroit by Toronto Maple Leafs for future considerations (Red Wings picked up a portion of Murphy's contract with Toronto), March 18, 1997.
Departed: Released by Detroit, May 22, 2001.

ONCE HE GOT A SAMPLE OF WHAT IT WAS LIKE TO BE A Stanley Cup winner, Larry Murphy discovered it was a taste he could not live without.

"I found it tougher not to win it once I'd won a Cup," Murphy said. "After that, every year I didn't win, I knew exactly what I was missing out on. Before, it didn't hurt as much, because I had no idea what it felt like to win the Cup."

When Toronto Maple Leafs GM Cliff Fletcher called to ask Murphy if he'd waive the no-trade clause in his contract to go to the Detroit Red Wings at the 1997 NHL trade deadline, Murphy asked for some time to think about it.

He put down the phone and told his wife Nancy the news. They took one look at each other and Murphy immediately called Fletcher back.

"I wasn't going to pass it up," Murphy said. "The Stanley Cup is what it's all about."

It turned out to be a great move for both sides. Murphy, a two-time Stanley Cup champion with the Pittsburgh Penguins, fit in seamlessly next to Nicklas Lidstrom as the Wings captured back-to-back Stanley Cups in 1996-97 and 1997-98, Detroit's first titles since 1955.

Detroit coach Scotty Bowman used Murphy and Lidstrom, another thinking man's defenceman, to put the Philadelphia Flyers' Legion Of Doom unit of Eric Lindros, John LeClair and Mikael Renberg out of commission during the 1997 Cup final.

"We looked at the pairings, looked at what (Murphy) could and couldn't do and thought we had an advantage," former Flyers forward John LeClair recalled. "But it turned out very bad for us."

The strategy, clearly a victory of brains over brawn, led to a Detroit sweep. "Murphy and Lidstrom made a joke out of that forward line," remembered Hall of Fame defenceman Denis Potvin. "They were three steps ahead of them, four games in a row."

The end result turned LeClair into a Murphy believer. "He was incredibly smart and very gifted with the puck," LeClair said. "That made it extremely hard to play against him."

Lidstrom, a seven-time Norris Trophy winner, marvelled at Murphy's consistency. "Murph was very smart with the puck," Lidstrom said. "He knew when to get rid of it, when to hang on and make plays. He was great at hanging on at the blue line and keeping pucks in. He was always an out for me."

It wasn't always so smooth. Murphy was such a poor skater as a youngster, he was the last player picked in the draft for

DETROIT HONOURS:

+ Stanley Cup champion 1996-97, 1997-98
+ Played in NHL All-Star Game, 1999
+ Surpassed Tim Horton (1,446) to become the NHL defenceman with the most career games played, Feb. 5, 1999
+ One of only six players in NHL history to win two or more Stanley Cups with two different teams.

his house league in the Toronto suburb of Scarborough. His coach wouldn't let him skate out past his own blue line, because Murphy wouldn't be able to get back to his defence position if the puck was turned over.

By the time he was a midget, Murphy was helping the Don Mills Flyers to the Canadian title and a trip to Russia. Two years later, he was part of a Peterborough team which won the Memorial Cup.

As a rookie with Los Angeles, Murphy set NHL records for a first-year defenceman with 60 assists and 76 points.

"He reinvented excellence," suggested Bill Clement, who played in the NHL against Murphy. "He's the perfect example that you don't have to follow a prototype to be successful, but it took him years to get everybody else to believe it."

Underestimated and undervalued during his career, Murphy was living proof that to the steady goes the race. The solid, reliable, rearguard played his 1,447th National Hockey League game Feb. 5, 1999 against the Colorado Avalanche, moving past Tim Horton for the most games played by a defenceman in league history.

"It's something I don't think about a lot, but it is something I take pride in," Murphy said of his place in history. "Being able to last a lot longer than a number of other players, I take pride in that accomplishment."

His lack of speed has made Murphy an easy target for fans. They mocked him in Toronto and Washington, two of his previous NHL stops. But those inside the game insisted it was Murphy's sharp hockey mind which made him such a valuable part of four Stanley Cup championships squads.

"He's the smartest player I've ever seen," said New Jersey Devils right winger Jaromir Jagr, a teammate of Murphy's on the Penguins' title-winning teams of 1990-91 and 1991-92.

Murphy simply found a way to succeed and it earned him a place in the Hockey Hall of Fame in 2004.

"We can't all skate like Howie Morenz," said Hall Of Fame defenceman Harry Howell, who played 1,411 NHL games. "Some of us had to find other methods to be successful. And Larry Murphy is a perfect example of someone who found those methods."

After hockey, Murphy worked for a time on Red Wings television broadcasts. An avid auto racing fan, he operated his own race team that competed in the American Le Mans Series.

| MURPHY'S RED WINGS STATISTICS: | | | | | | | | | |
| Regular Season | | | | | Playoffs | | | | |
Season	GP	G	A	P	PIM	GP	G	A	P	PIM
1996-97	12	2	4	6	0	20	2	9	11	8
1997-98	82	11	41	52	37	22	3	12	15	2
1998-99	80	10	42	52	42	10	0	2	2	8
1999-00	80	10	30	40	45	9	2	3	5	2
2000-01	57	2	19	21	12	6	0	1	1	0
Totals	311	35	136	171	136	67	7	27	34	20

41 DINO CICCARELLI

Right Wing

Born: February 8, 1960, Sarnia, Ontario
Shot: Right **Height:** 5-10 **Weight:** 185 lbs.
Red Wing From: 1992-93 to 1995-96
Elected to Hockey Hall of Fame: 2010
Acquired: Traded to Detroit by Washington Capitals for Kevin Miller, June 20, 1992.
Departed: Traded by Detroit to Tampa Bay Lightning for Tampa Bay's fourth-round choice (later traded to Toronto Maple Leafs—Toronto selected Alexei Ponikarovsky) in the 1998 Entry Draft, August 27, 1996.

DINO CICCARELLI FIGURED THAT IF YOU DREW A CIRCLE around the area from where he registered the majority of his 608 career goals, it would pale in comparsion to the 200x85-foot circumference of an NHL ice surface.

"My goals all came from about 10-15 feet in front of the net," Ciccarelli said.

If Wayne Gretzky's office was behind the net, Ciccarelli set up shop night after night in the slot area in front of the goal, paying a terrible price in terms of physical punishment in order to put the puck into the other team's net.

"That was my game," said Ciccarelli, who accepted the lacerations and contusions as part of his day's work. "If I was a little better skater or a little bigger player, I probably wouldn't have had to go through some of the things I did. That wasn't the case, so you have to make do with what you've got. I knew I had to play hockey a certain way to be successful."

Making himself a nuisance in front of the other team's net wasn't always Ciccarelli's game plan. Coming up to the NHL with the Minnesota North Stars during the 1980-81 season, Ciccarelli was a sensation in that spring's playoffs, setting Stanley Cup rookie records with 14 goals and 21 points. He produced a pair of 50-goal seasons as a North Star.

"My role changed," Ciccarelli said. "Earlier in my career, I was more of a set-up guy along the boards. In Detroit, we had so many talented players, if I wanted to be successful on that team I had to get in the way of the goaltender.

"My aim was to screen the goalie, to get in front of the net and clutch and distract them."

Former Detroit goalie Mike Vernon, often a Ciccarelli opponent, figured Dino was a great success at this.

"His game gave goaltenders fits," Vernon said. "I know he gave me fits. He got in your face and always got to the rebound."

Ciccarelli's style was especially valuable in the playoffs, where the so-called dirty goals came to even more prominence. He potted six hat tricks in Stanley Cup play, two of them as a Red Wing. In NHL playoff history, only Wayne Gretzky (10), and Maurice (Rocket) Richard and Jari Kurri, with seven apiece, collected more three-goal games.

Ciccarelli achieved several NHL milestones while wearing the winged wheel. He recorded his 1,000th point March 9, 1994 with a goal in a 5-1 win over the Calgary Flames. Earlier that season, Ciccarelli potted his 500th NHL goal when he beat Los Angeles Kings goalie Kelly Hrudey on January 8, 1994. Ciccarelli joined Gordie Howe as the only players to score their 500th NHL goal in a Detroit uniform.

Two years later, when Red Wings captain Steve Yzerman joined the 500-goal club, as he returned to the bench

---

DETROIT HONOURS:

- Scored 500th NHL goal Jan. 8, 1994 versus Los Angeles Kings goalie Kelly Hrudey
- Collected 1,000th NHL point March 9, 1994 with a goal against Calgary Flames
- Played 1,000th NHL game March 29, 1995 vs. Anaheim Mighty Ducks
- Elected to the National Italian American Sports Hall of Fame in 2000.

with the milestone puck, he found himself seated next to Ciccarelli and a victim of Ciccarelli's biting sense of humour.

"I told him, 'Welcome aboard,'" Ciccarelli said. "'And oh, by the way, I've got some stuff for you to sign. 500-goal-scorers' signatures are worth a lot of money.'"

On March 28, 1995, Ciccarelli played his 1,000th NHL game as the Wings dumped the Mighty Ducks of Anaheim 6-4.

All this from a guy who suffered a badly broken leg while playing with London of the OHL in 1979, requiring the insertion of an 18-inch metal rod into his right leg, where it remains today.

"Given the fact I broke my leg and I was overlooked in my draft year, I was just hoping to make it to the NHL, never mind play 1,000 games," Ciccarelli said. "And if someone had told me my 1,000th game would come against the Mighty Ducks, I really would have laughed."

The Wings reached the Stanley Cup final in 1995 before losing to the New Jersey Devils and when they were upset by the eventual Stanley Cup champion Colorado Avalanche in the 1996 Western Conference final, management opted to reshape the team and dealt Ciccarelli, then 36, to the Tampa Bay Lightning.

"We didn't win the Stanley Cup with Dino, so we had to go in a different direction," then Wings coach Scotty Bowman said of the deal which sent Ciccarelli to Tampa Bay for a conditional 1998 draft pick. "We can lose the Stanley Cup just as well with younger players."

As is his nature, Ciccarelli didn't take the criticism lying down and fought back just as viciously. "It was hard for me to keep my mouth shut when he puts me down," Ciccarelli said at the time of Bowman, who cited Ciccarelli as a selfish player, especially in the 1996 playoffs, when he victimized Detroit with some retaliatory penalties.

"It's a team game and it was his team," Ciccarelli said of Bowman. "It was team success and he got credit for it. But when things went wrong, people got singled out. It was me taking a (bad) penalty. It was Ozzie (goalie Chris Osgood) coming up with a bad game. It was Paul (Coffey) giving the puck away. Never once did he accept criticism for being out-coached."

Ciccarelli even went as far as to suggest that there might have been a conspiracy against outspoken players in the Detroit dressing room, all of whom were traded away by the start of the 1996-97 season. "Look at the guys who spoke up," he said. "I spoke up. Coff spoke up. Burrsie (Shawn Burr) spoke up. Prims (Keith Primeau) spoke up. You need guys like that.

"Do you want a bunch of robots? Maybe he (Bowman) does."

After Bowman's "robots" won back-to-back Stanley Cups in the first two seasons without Ciccarelli in the lineup, Ciccarelli admitted he was rooting for them from afar.

"I went through it all with them," Ciccarelli said. "I was home when they won it and I watched the whole thing on TV."

When Ciccarelli retired in 1999, the Stanley Cup was still missing from his resumé. "You always wonder about what might have been. There were mixed emotions, but having played there for a few years and gotten to know the Detroit fans, I was happy for them."

Ciccarelli has even found it in his heart to forgive Bowman, the man he felt had run him out of town.

"I realize that it was just part of the business," Ciccarelli said. "They had a lot of depth at right wing and they had to do something."

In retirement, Ciccarelli bought into ownership of the OHL Sarnia Sting, his hometown junior team, opened a bar in downtown Detroit and a nightclub in the Detroit suburbs, where he lives.

In 2010, he was inducted into the Hockey Hall of Fame.

| CICCARELLI'S RED WINGS STATISTICS: | | | | | | | | | | |
| Regular Season | | | | | Playoffs | | | | | |
Season	GP	G	A	P	PIM	GP	G	A	P	PIM
1992-93	82	41	56	97	81	7	4	2	6	16
1993-94	66	28	29	57	73	7	5	2	7	14
1994-95	42	16	27	43	39	16	9	2	11	22
1995-96	64	22	21	43	99	17	6	2	8	26
Totals	254	107	133	240	292	47	24	8	32	78

42 NORMIE SMITH

Goal

Born: Toronto, Ontario, March 18, 1908
Died: February 2, 1988
Shot: Left **Height:** 5-7 **Weight:** 165 lbs.
Red Wing From: 1934-35 to 1938-39; 1943-44 to 1944-45
Acquired: Traded to Detroit by St. Louis Eagles for Burr Williams, October 21, 1934.
Departed: Traded to Boston Bruins with $10,000 for Cecil (Tiny) Thompson, November 26, 1939.
Suspended by Detroit when he refused to report.
Reacquired: Signed as a free agent by Detroit, December 15, 1943.

NORMIE SMITH'S ARRIVAL IN DETROIT WAS MET WITH groans and uncertainty. His departure was equally controversial, but in between, he did what no goaltender in franchise history had ever done before.

Smith led the Wings to the Stanley Cup title.

Coming off their 1933-34 Cup final series loss to the Chicago Blackhawks, the Wings were suddenly without a netminder after Wilf Cude, who'd led them to their best season ever, was recalled from loan by the Montreal Canadiens.

The Wings reached out to acquire Smith, a 26-year-old journeyman pro whose only NHL experience was a forgettable 21-game stint with the 1931-32 Montreal Maroons in which he went 5-12-4.

In fact, he wasn't their first choice. Originally, Detroit coach-GM Jack Adams sought to lure Charlie Teno, goalie for the senior Hamilton Tigers, to turn pro, but when Teno resisted, he traded with the St. Louis Eagles for Smith.

At the outset, it wasn't a marriage made in heaven. Sharing time with veteran John Ross Roach, Smith turned in a pair of shutouts and an impressive 2.01 goals-against average, posting a 12-11-1 slate for a team that missed the playoffs, but that didn't stop the persistent "We want Cude" chants from the Olympia Stadium faithful.

Reluctantly, Smith won the No. 1 job the following season, but behind the scenes, amidst the continued fan unrest, Adams worked to pry a veteran goalie out of another club. Instead, Smith convinced his doubters that he was the man for the job. He topped the NHL with 24 wins and led Detroit to the NHL's best record, posting a .918 save percentage.

If there were any doubters left, Smith silenced them as he silenced the Maroons in his Stanley Cup debut, blocking 90 shots for a shutout in the NHL's longest game, which ended when Detroit's Modere (Mud) Bruneteau scored after 176:30 of play.

"I went to a pub and had a couple beers (after the game)," Smith told author Brian McFarlane in his book *Legendary Stanley Cup Stories*. "Then I staggered and almost fell down. People thought I was drunk, but I was simply too exhausted to stand up."

DETROIT HONOURS:

- Stanley Cup champion 1935-36, 1936-37
- Won Vezina Trophy, 1936-37
- NHL First All-Star Team, 1936-37
- Led NHL in wins, 1935-36, 1936-37
- Led NHL in shutouts and goals-against average, 1936-37
- With 1-0 victory over Montreal Maroons on March 24, 1936, joined John Ross Roach (1933) and Chris Osgood (1994) as only Detroit goalies to post shutouts in their Stanley Cup debut as Wings.

If anyone thought the performance was a fluke, Smith followed up by blanking the Maroons 3-0 in Game 2 of the series, becoming the first goalie to post shutouts in each of his first two Stanley Cup games. He assembled a shutout sequence of 248:32 to launch his NHL playoff career.

Smith returned to Detroit a conquering hero. As Detroit's train arrived in Windsor, fans packed the station. "Where's Smith?" the crowd shouted. "We want Smith."

He carried the Wings all the way to their first Cup that spring, but the best was ahead for Smith. He again led the NHL in wins (25) and shutouts (six), winning the Vezina Trophy and earning First All-Star Team status as Detroit repeated as regular-season champions.

The Wings would once more win the Stanley Cup, but they'd do so minus Smith, out for the season after tearing an elbow ligament in the opening playoff round versus the Canadiens. Minor-leaguer Earl Robertson stepped in to fill the void.

Nonetheless, Adams showed his faith in Smith that summer, dealing Robertson to the New York Americans and top prospect Turk Broda to the Toronto Maple Leafs, but almost as suddenly as Smith's star illuminated, it would flame out.

The Wings missed the playoffs in 1937-38 and Smith was 0-4 to open the 1938-39 season when he missed the team train from New York to a game in Montreal and was banished to Pittsburgh of the AHL as punishment.

Curiously, Charlie Teno's brother Harvey replaced Smith in Detroit's goal. "If Teno lives up to expectations, it may be tough for Smith to get back with our club," Adams suggested.

Smith, who had a solid job in Detroit as assistant to Harry Bennett, personnel director for the Ford Motor Company, wasn't about to take that lying down. He announced his retirement from hockey.

"One night in Pittsburgh was enough for me," Smith explained to *Associated Press*. "I won't play minor-league hockey. I am either good enough to play for the Red Wings or not at all.

"I told Adams at the start of the season that when I had to play minor-league hockey, I was through. And I am. Detroit is my home and my living is there and I intend to stay."

Adams shipped Smith's rights to the Boston Bruins along with $10,000 for four-time Vezina winner Tiny Thompson, though Smith wasn't about to play minor-pro hockey for the Bruins either. But his NHL days—and his Detroit days—weren't done yet.

| | | | | SMITH'S RED WINGS STATISTICS: | | | | | | | |
| | REGULAR SEASON | | | | | | PLAYOFFS | | | | |
Season	GPI	MIN	GA	SO	W-L-T	GAA	GPI	MIN	GA	SO	GAA	W-L
1934-35	25	1550	52	2	12-11-2	2.01	-	-	-	-	-	-
1935-36	48	3030	103	6	24-16-8	2.04	7	538	12	2	1.00	6-1
1936-37	48	2980	102	6	25-14-9	2.05	5	282	6	1	1.28	3-1
1937-38	47	2930	130	3	11-25-11	2.66	-	-	-	-	-	-
1938-39	4	240	12	0	0-4-0	3.00	-	-	-	-	-	-
1943-44	5	300	15	0	3-1-1	3.00	-	-	-	-	-	-
1944-45	1	60	3	0	1-0-0	3.00	-	-	-	-	-	-
Totals	178	11090	417	17	76-71-31	2.26	12	820	18	3	1.31	9-2

With so many NHLers gone as part of the war effort during the Second World War, Adams reached out to his old goalie and Smith ended his five-year retirement in December of 1943, opting to play home games for Detroit.

There was just one problem—Boston still claimed Smith's NHL rights, albeit briefly. In the spirit of the holiday season, Bruins GM Art Ross relinquished all ties to Smith.

"Stop worrying, Jack," Ross told the *Edmonton Journal*. "The Boston Bruins take great pleasure in presenting Smith to your club as a New Year's gift.

"I realize he would never play for any other club."

Smith played six games over two seasons for the Wings, posting a 4-1-1 record, and then left the game for good.

43 BOB GOLDHAM

Defence

Born: Georgetown, Ontario, May 12, 1922
Died: November 6, 1991
Shot: Right **Height:** 6-2 **Weight:** 195 lbs.
Red Wing From: 1950-51 to 1955-56
Acquired: Traded to Detroit by Chicago Blackhawks with (Sugar) Jim Henry, Gaye Stewart and Metro Prystai for Al Dewsbury, Harry Lumley, (Black) Jack Stewart, Don Morrison and Pete Babando, July 13, 1950.
Departed: Announced retirement from hockey April 11, 1956.

EARLY IN HIS NHL CAREER, BOB GOLDHAM HELPED BREAK the hearts of the Detroit Red Wings. As his career wound down, he played a key role in the greatest dynasty in Red Wings history.

You could say that Goldham was a defenceman who threw himself into his work. Many in the game consider him to have been the finest shot blocker in NHL history.

"Blocking shots is an art and he was the best practitioner," explained former Detroit defenceman Al Arbour, himself an outstanding shot blocker, an element of his game he credits solely to Goldham's tutelage.

"I learned the right way to do it from Bob Goldham."

Some in hockey called him the second goalie and it's clear that next to the goal posts, Goldham was a netminder's best friend.

"Arbour and Bob Goldham were the two best defencemen I ever played behind," Hall of Fame goalie and former Wing Glenn Hall expressed to the *Edmonton Journal*. "Arbour, he was great at blocking the shots. He got that from Bob Goldham, who was the first to do that."

A rookie with the Toronto Maple Leafs in 1941-42, Goldham saw little ice time through the first three games of the Stanley Cup final as the underdog Red Wings raced to a 3-0 series lead.

Shaking up his dormant team, Toronto coach Hap Day moved Goldham into a more prominent role in place of veteran Bucko McDonald and the Leafs rallied to win the series in seven games, the first time in NHL history that a team had come back to win a seven-game set after trailing 3-0. Goldham played a major role. He scored a goal in Game 6 and drew an assist on Pete Langelle's Cup-winning tally, finishing the series with 2-2-4 totals.

"Detroit had developed what was a completely new wrinkle at the time—shooting the puck in from centre and sending people in deep to forecheck," Goldham explained to the *Toronto Star*. "We found it confusing."

Injecting more youth and speed into his lineup, Day eliminated Detroit's advantage. "The bottom line was Day outcoached Jack Adams of Detroit," Goldham said.

In 1947, Goldham moved to Chicago as part of a blockbuster deal that brought NHL scoring champ Max Bentley to Toronto, but life with the lowly Blackhawks was difficult.

"(Emile) Cat Francis was the goalie and he probably wished he had a mask," Goldham once explained. "He didn't get much help from us. The only time we saw a lot of the forwards was in the dressing room between periods."

DETROIT HONOURS:

- Stanley Cup champion 1951-52, 1953-54, 1954-55
- Played in NHL All-Star Game (1952, 1954, 1955).

leader, a calming influence, and became a mentor to some of the club's up-and-coming defenders such as Arbour and future Hall of Famer Marcel Pronovost.

"I guess they all can't be as lucky as I was," Pronovost said. "For five years, I played alongside Bob Goldham. Goldie was tops. He went out of his way to help me over the rough spots."

He played in four Stanley Cup finals in six seasons as a Red Wing, winning three times to go with the two Cups he'd garnered as a Maple Leaf.

When the Wings took the ice for overtime in Game 3 of their 1956 semifinal series against the Leafs, Goldham predicted the outcome. "Take pity on an old man's creaking joints, and let's get this over in a hurry," Goldham asked of his teammates as they exited the dressing room. "If you don't, I will." The teams weren't four minutes into the extra session when Goldham set up Ted Lindsay for the winner in a 5-4 triumph.

After Detroit's loss to Montreal in the 1956 final, Goldham announced his retirement.

"It's quit being fun to play," he said. "It's just work."

Offered a position as coach of Detroit's junior club

Goldham's hockey fates took a turn for the better when he was involved in another blockbuster trade during the summer of 1950—a then NHL-record seven-player deal that brought him from the Blackhawks to the reigning Stanley Cup champion Red Wings.

Goldham's first season in Detroit was his best as an NHLer, as he produced career highs in goals (five), assists (18) and points (23). With the Wings, Goldham was a

GOLDHAM'S RED WINGS STATISTICS:

Season	REGULAR SEASON					PLAYOFFS				
	GP	G	A	P	PIM	GP	G	A	P	PIM
1950-51	61	5	18	23	31	6	0	1	1	2
1951-52	69	0	14	14	24	8	0	1	1	8
1952-53	70	1	13	14	32	6	1	1	2	2
1953-54	69	1	15	16	50	12	0	2	2	2
1954-55	69	1	16	17	14	11	0	4	4	4
1955-56	68	3	16	19	32	10	0	3	3	4
Totals	406	11	92	103	183	53	1	12	13	22

in Hamilton, Goldham declined. He later coached the Toronto St. Michael's juniors, but made a name for himself as an insightful analyst on Hockey Night In Canada.

Even in retirement, Goldham never lost his competitive edge. Playing for the NHL oldtimers, they were dominating their much weaker opponents one night when someone suggested that perhaps it would be sporting to allow the amateurs to pot a goal.

"I'll let them score—if they can go around me," Goldham growled.

The veteran defenceman died of a stroke in 1991 at the age of 69.

On and off the ice, Goldham was universally respected as someone who was without flaws.

In 2010, the Georgetown Minor Hockey Association in Goldham's hometown renamed its annual Christmas house league tournament the Bob Goldham Memorial. He was inducted into Halton Hills Hall of Fame in 2011, but many veterans of the game insist Goldham belongs in the Hockey Hall of Fame.

"To this day, I can't understand why he's not in the Hall of Fame," former Detroit coach Jimmy Skinner once expressed. "He was one of the best stay-at-home defencemen the game has ever seen."

44 BOB PROBERT

Left Wing

Born: June 5, 1965, Windsor, Ontario
Died: July 5, 2010
Shot: Left Height: 6-3 Weight: 255 lbs.
Red Wing From: 1985-86 to 1993-94
Acquired: Selected 46th overall in June 8, 1983 NHL Entry Draft
Departed: Signed as a free agent by Chicago Blackhawks, July 23, 1994.

THE WIDE, GAP-TOOTHED SMILE. THE WARM EMBRACE. The welcoming sense he left everyone feeling after they'd met him.

Those are the moments that Jacques Demers recalls most fondly about Bob Probert.

Probert was someone who was never involved in assessing his self-importance, but Demers believes everyone in the Red Wings organization owes Probert a debt of gratitude. The turnaround that saw Detroit evolve from the Dead Things era into the NHL's model franchise was a process that began at Joe Louis Arena during Demers' watch in the mid-1980s.

As far as Demers is concerned, Probert was a significant catalyst in that evolution.

"I think he did a lot for the franchise," Demers said. "Bob Probert changed the dynamic of the building. If you want to come play in Detroit, there's (Bruise Brothers) Probert and (Joe) Kocur. That won us a lot of games.

"(Steve) Yzerman was great, no question, but those two guys, they helped us a lot."

The NHL's most punishing enforcer, Probert put fans in the Joe Louis Arena seats and struck fear in the hearts of the opposition.

"When I played, I didn't have to call (National Hockey League commissioner) Gary Bettman to find out what the punishment was for running a guy from behind in Detroit," former St. Louis Blues tough guy Kelly Chase said. "The punishment was Probert and Kocur."

To some, Probert will simply be remembered for his reign as the dominating enforcer of his era, certainly the most feared fighter during his time in the game, and perhaps in the history of the NHL. Others will choose only to recall the dark side of Probert's existence, the substance-abuse issues that plagued his life and caused him to run afoul of the law.

Those closest to him remember Probert as a loving husband, and a caring father, someone who enjoyed the simple pleasures of life.

"I always looked at him as a very good person who had some demons," Demers said. "I saw a lot of good things about him. He was kind-hearted."

Demers especially remembered Probert's actions after his son Jason was injured in a traffic accident. "When my son got hit by a car in 1987, a big guy like him, here he comes into the dressing room with a huge teddy bear," Demers said. "He goes, 'That's for Jason.' Usually, players don't do that, but that was Probie."

Probert enjoyed his best season as a pro in 1987-88 playing on Yzerman's wing, posting 29-33-62 totals as well as an NHL-leading 398 penalty minutes. He earned a spot in the NHL All-Star Game for his efforts and set

DETROIT HONOURS:

+ Played in NHL All-Star Game, 1988
+ Led NHL in penalty minutes, 1987-88
+ Red Wings all-time leader in penalty minutes
+ Led Red Wings in penalty minutes, 1987-88, 1990-91, 1991-92, 1992-93, 1993-94.

a then club playoff record with 21 post-season points, shattering the mark Red Wings legend Gordie Howe had held since 1955.

"I was fortunate to be able to play on his line," said Probert, who maintained numerous fond memories of his days as Yzerman's teammate. Not surprisingly, many involved fisticuffs.

"One that sticks out and it was a big thing, was when I fought (Tie) Domi, our second fight in New York," Probert said. "He had cut me over the eye in the first fight and did this thing with his hands, like he was wearing the heavyweight championship belt.

"After the second fight, when I beat Domi, I looked over at our bench and there was Yzerman, standing on the bench, giving the heavyweight belt sign with his hands.

"Another time, Stevie was fighting this guy from Buffalo, (Kevin) Maguire, who was the Sabres' tough guy and was on top of Stevie, really giving it to him. Now this is not something I would not normally have done, but no one was going to pick on our captain, so I bent down on one knee and suckered (Maguire).

"I enjoyed my job, especially protecting guys like Stevie. He's a great person."

Deep down, Probert, a father of four, was someone whose main focus was his family and their well-being. He planned his day around making sure he was available to take his children to practice and school events.

Probert gave much of his time to the community, often quietly, away from the glare of the spotlight that so often shone on him during negative times of his life.

Probert made frequent charitable appearances to help fundraise for the Windsor Minor Hockey Association, the organization for which he played as a child. He travelled North America working with the NHL Alumni and twice trekked to Afghanistan to visit with Canadian troops stationed there.

"It's amazing what they do," Probert said of combat soldiers in the Middle East. "Some of them are sleeping on rocks and they're covered in flea bites."

To his credit, Probert never made excuses or blamed others for his difficulties, openly discussing his battle with alcohol and drugs. "My kids know all about my history," Probert said. "Why should I worry about what anyone else thinks?"

He had no airs of celebrity about him and gave the impression he didn't realize how hugely popular he was in the Detroit-Windsor area.

His Detroit career came to an end following an alcohol-induced motorcycle accident in 1994. The Wings opted to let Probert go and he signed as a free agent with the Chicago Blackhawks.

Probert played seven seasons with the Blackhawks and on Feb. 13, 1999, scored the last goal in the history of Maple Leaf Gardens. He also managed to get his life back on track.

Enjoying retirement, Probert had taken his family out on Lake St. Clair for a boating trip when he suffered a fatal heart attack and died at the age of 45.

"It really touched me," Demers said of the news of Probert's death. "As much as he drove me nuts, that was how much I liked him."

Probert may have taken Demers on a roller coaster, but at the end of the ride, he left Demers smiling.

"I'm a Bobby Probert fan," Demers said, a sentiment he shared with thousands of Red Wings supporters.

PROBERT'S RED WINGS STATISTICS:									
	Regular Season					Playoffs			
Season	GP	G	A	P	PIM	GP	G	A	P	PIM
1985-86	44	8	13	21	186	-	-	-	-	-
1986-87	63	13	11	24	221	16	3	4	7	63
1987-88	74	29	33	62	398	16	8	13	21	51
1988-89	25	4	2	6	106	-	-	-	-	-
1989-90	4	3	0	3	21	-	-	-	-	-
1990-91	55	16	23	39	315	6	1	2	3	50
1991-92	63	20	24	44	276	11	1	6	7	28
1992-93	80	14	29	43	292	7	0	3	3	10
1993-94	66	7	10	17	275	7	1	1	2	8
Totals	474	114	145	259	2090	63	14	29	43	210

45 DOMINIK HASEK

Goal

Born: January 29, 1965, Pardubice, Czech Republic
Shot: Left **Height:** 5-11 **Weight:** 180 lbs.
Red Wing From: 2001-02; 2003-04; 2006-07 to 2007-08
Acquired: Traded to Detroit by Buffalo Sabres for Vyacheslav Kozlov and a 2002 NHL first round entry draft pick (later traded to Columbus—later traded to Atlanta—Atlanta selected Jim Slater).
Departed: Announced retirement from hockey June, 12, 2002.
Reacquired: Detroit picked up the option on his contract, July 1, 2003.
Departed: Signed as a free agent by Ottawa Senators, July 6, 2004.
Reacquired: Signed as a free agent by Detroit, July 31, 2006.
Departed: Announced retirement from hockey June 9, 2008.

THE YOUNGSTER MARVELLED AT THE WAY No. 9 PERFORMED on the ice, was awed by how he completely dominated play, right from his teenage years and for decades to come.

Jiri Fischer could have easily been talking about Maurice Richard, Bobby Hull or Gordie Howe, the trio of No. 9s many grew up idolizing, but his No. 9 performed closer to home.

That's because Fischer's hero was—and is—Dominik Hasek, his Czech countryman and former Detroit Red Wings teammate.

"When I was a little kid, even before I started playing hockey, I remember watching him playing for Pardubice (in the Czech League)," Fischer said. "He was only 17 and was wearing No. 9 on his jersey, but he was already the No. 1 goalie in Czechoslovakia."

In the Czech Republic, Hasek is held in the highest regard.

"He is our Michael Jordan," Fischer explained. "Our Muhammad Ali.

"I don't think anyone in sport from our country has accomplished as much. He's put our little country on the map."

The moment the Wings acquired the two-time Hart Trophy winner and six-time Vezina Trophy winner in the summer of 2001, they instantly became Stanley Cup favourites.

"An opportunity presented itself where we could acquire the best goaltender in the National Hockey League," Wings GM Ken Holland said. "It was a deal that we just could not pass up."

Hasek was of those goalies capable of winning a game by himself and of playing mind games with opposing shooters over the course of a game or a playoff series.

"When you've got a goalie that gets into people's heads and you're actually thinking about that rather than just going about playing hockey, it makes a difference," Tampa Bay Lightning left winger Brenden Morrow said. "He could get into people's heads. I saw him giving them more confidence."

The man they called the Dominator brought a different dynamic when he situated himself between the posts.

"In the playoffs, in the final round or in Game 6 or 7, you don't really think too much about defence," suggested

---

DETROIT HONOURS:

+ Stanley Cup champion, 2001-02, 2007-08
+ Led NHL in wins, 2001-02
+ Led Stanley Cup playoffs in wins and shutouts, 2001-02
+ Played in NHL All-Star Game, 2002
+ Shared William Jennings Trophy with Chris Osgood, 2007-08
+ Played in 2002 Winter Olympics with Czech Republic.

coach Ken Hitchcock, who bossed the Dallas Stars against Hasek's Buffalo Sabres in the 1999 Cup final.

With his unorthodox flopping style, incredible reflexes and his Gumby-like flexibility, Hasek defied reason and frustrated his critics. But his passion for the game, his competitiveness and his work ethic were never questioned.

"Dominik Hasek's work habits were legendary," Detroit goalie coach Jim Bedard said. "He never gave up, just battled, battled, battled. That's why he made great saves, because he knew he could make the third save if he had to.

"Good was never good enough for him, He had to be the best."

Twice the Wings lured him out of retirement to return to stopping pucks, and while he struggled with injury in his later years, Hasek still was a top performer. In 2006-07, he finished second in the NHL in goals-against (2.05) and shutouts (eight), and the following campaign at the age of 42, he helped the Wings win another Stanley Cup in what would be his farewell NHL season.

"So many critics didn't think he was capable of doing it again, playing at that level on a consistent basis," former Detroit left winger Kirk Maltby said. "And everyone— I'm sure, even a few guys here—questioned if he could stay healthy."

Questioning Hasek's ability, or the way he could affect the outcome of a game, was never an issue that was debated.

"When the game was on the line," former Detroit coach Mike Babcock said, "he was outstanding."

centre Sergei Fedorov, Hasek's Detroit teammate when the Wings won the Cup in 2001-02. "You focus on doing your thing. It clears your mind from worrying about something."

The other team was left with the worry, seeking to decipher a way to get the puck past Hasek.

"You had to be prepared to outwork him and that took a pretty high level of commitment," said St. Louis Blues

HASEK'S RED WINGS STATISTICS:											
	Regular Season					Playoffs					
Season	GPI	MIN	GA	SO	W-L-T	GAA	GPI	MIN	GA	SO	GAA	W-L
2001-02	65	3872	140	5	41-12-11	2.17	23	1455	45	6	1.86	16-7
2003-04	14	816	30	2	8-3-2	2.20	-	-	-	-	-	-
2006-07	56	3341	114	8	38-11-6	2.05	18	1140	34	2	1.79	10-8
2007-08	41	2350	84	5	27-10-3	2.14	4	205	10	0	2.91	2-2
Totals	176	10379	368	20	114-36-22	2.12	45	2800	89	8	1.90	28-17

46 NIKLAS KRONWALL

Defence

Born: January 12, 1981, Stockholm, Sweden
Shoots: Left Height: 6-0 Weight: 190 lbs.
Red Wing From: 2003-04 to present
Acquired: Selected 29th overall in June 24, 2000 NHL entry draft.

IMAGINE NHL GOALIES COMING OUT IN FAVOUR OF enlarging the nets to increase scoring.

Consider the likelihood of Lloyd Carr ending his retirement to coach the Michigan State football team.

Or perhaps a Swede will step up and endorse a Don Cherry video as an example of the way real men play hockey.

Well, don't hold your breath waiting for the first two impossibilities to arrive, but as far as No. 3 is concerned, please allow us to introduce you to Niklas Kronwall.

Kronwall worships at the altar of Don Cherry, the star of Hockey Night In Canada's Coach's Corner, and the same man who's made his living mocking the men from MODO and Malmö.

"I've seen a couple of those Rock 'em, Sock 'em tapes (Cherry makes) and I really enjoyed them," Kronwall said, his glimmering smile backing up the shocking words passing through his lips.

The Wings defenceman from Stockholm loves to hit. Some might say that he lives to hit and he wouldn't dispute that notion.

"I would say that I'm a guy who enjoys the physical play," Kronwall said. "When you can jump up and really step into a guy, it feels good. It's fun.

"Sometimes, it's almost better than scoring a goal."

When the Wings selected Kronwall 29th overall in the 2000 NHL entry draft, they were aware that he possessed the fluid skating motion and precision puck skills that seem to be a prerequisite with every European hockey star. Soon they discovered that their latest Swedish prodigy came equipped with an added dimension.

"During rookie camp, he was running everybody," Detroit GM Ken Holland recalled. "We were afraid he might get killed in main camp, because he isn't a big guy."

If the words of Kronwall's teammates are to be taken at face value, Holland was worrying about the wrong guy.

"You know, back in Sweden, he nearly killed a couple of guys," claimed Detroit centre Henrik Zetterberg, who played against Kronwall in the Swedish Elite League.

"You shouldn't believe everything Henrik tells you," Kronwall suggested, downplaying his legend.

In 2004-05, Kronwall was the first European to be voted the top defenceman in the American Hockey League, and that spring was named to the all-tournament team at the world championship. The next year, he helped Sweden win Olympic gold in Turin. In the gold-medal game against Finland, the Swedes won 3-2, getting all three goals from Red Wings—Zetterberg, Kronwall and Nicklas Lidstrom.

A key to Kronwall's punishing legacy—to be hit by him is to be Kronwalled—is that he studies his art in the same manner that a scorer works on their release.

"His body positioning is excellent," suggested Chicago Blackhawks pro scout Barry Smith, a former Detroit associate coach. "Defensively, he displays a real knack for gaining body position on an opponent."

DETROIT HONOURS:

• Stanley Cup champion, 2007-08
• Won Olympic gold medal with Sweden, 2006
• Won world championships with Sweden, 2006
• Played for Sweden in 2010 Vancouver Winter Olympic Games.

Regardless, Kronwall's bombsights are always locked and loaded and it's just a matter of time until he delivers his payload. "He's quiet out there," former teammate Darren McCarty said. "You don't hear him coming and BOOM, the next thing you know he's laying somebody out."

"I know if I was playing for the other team, I'd be looking out for him," Zetterberg added.

Babcock admires the way Kronwall can strike fear into an opponent. "He's kind of like a predator," Babcock said. "He's trying to hunt you down. It makes (the other team) nervous out there."

Kronwall smiles at such notions. "It's always fun when you can bump into somebody," he said, hoping he'll run into one specific honour before his career is done, one that few Swedes can dream about.

When hammer time arrives, Kronwall's fervent wish is that the producers of the next volume of Rock 'em, Sock 'em are rolling tape.

"Maybe someday, I'll get to be in one of those tapes," Kronwall said. "If I'm lucky enough."

KRONWALL'S RED WINGS STATISTICS:									
	REGULAR SEASON				PLAYOFFS				
Season	GP	G	A	P	PIM	GP	G	A	P	PIM
2003-04	20	1	4	5	16	-	-	-	-	-
2005-06	27	1	8	9	28	6	0	3	3	2
2006-07	68	1	21	22	54	22	0	15	15	18
2007-08	65	7	28	35	44	23	2	7	9	33
2008-09	80	6	45	51	50	12	0	5	5	12
2009-10	48	7	15	22	32	12	0	5	5	12
2010-11	77	11	26	37	36	11	2	4	6	4
2011-12	82	15	21	36	38	5	0	2	2	4
2012-13	48	5	24	29	44	14	0	2	2	4
2013-14	79	8	41	49	44	5	1	1	2	0
2014-15	80	9	35	44	40	6	0	2	2	4
Totals	674	71	268	339	426	104	5	41	46	81

Technique, more than strength, is the key to his power. "It's all about timing," Kronwall said. "It doesn't matter if the guy is bigger than you or stronger than you, it's all about timing. If you catch him at the right moment, he's going to go down."

Kronwall isn't merely a bruiser, though. Like most Europeans, he plays the game equally impressively with the puck in his possession.

"Kronner's one of our best players," former Wings coach Mike Babcock said. "He has an offensive upside."

47 DALE MCCOURT

Centre

Born: January 26, 1957, Falconbridge, Ontario
Shot: Right Height: 5-11 Weight: 185 lbs.
Red Wing From: 1976-77 to 1981-82
Acquired: Selected first overall in June 14, 1977 NHL amateur draft.
Departed: Traded to Buffalo Sabres with Mike Foligno and Brent Peterson for Derek Smith, Bob Sauve, Jim Schoenfeld and Danny Gare, December 2, 1981.

THE DETROIT RED WINGS WANTED DALE MCCOURT so much that they used the first pick of the 1977 NHL amateur to acquire him.

McCourt wanted so much to remain a Red Wing that he took the NHL to the highest court in the United States to make it so.

After a stellar junior career that saw McCourt earn MVP honours in the 1976 Memorial Cup and Canadian Major Junior Hockey League player-of-the-year recognition in 1976-77, the Wings quickly called his name on draft day.

"You build a team from within and I feel Dale can fill a serious void at centre ice in the coming seasons," Detroit GM Ted Lindsay told the *Windsor Star*, comparing McCourt to another legendary NHL centre.

"The best way I can think of to describe Dale would be to say that he's a lot like Stan Mikita," Lindsay said. "He does a lot of things like Stan—kills penalties, controls the power play, and plays a regular shift.

"It would be unfair to put undue pressure on Dale and call him the saviour of the Red Wings, but he's definitely a step in the right direction."

Certainly, McCourt's credentials were impeccable. He left junior hockey after collecting an OHL-record 477 points and set Canadian records that still stand at the 1977 world junior championships when he accumulated 10 goals and 18 points.

"I think that's probably the tournament that propelled me to first place (in the draft)," McCourt said of the world juniors, where he won praise from an unlikely source.

"He is a perfect skater who has practically all a perfect hockey player should be equipped with," noted the Communist Czech paper *Rude Pravo*, rarely a supporter of the Canadian brand of hockey.

A nephew of former Toronto Maple Leafs captain George Armstrong, which was why McCourt donned Armstrong's No. 10, McCourt was an instant hit with Detroit, leading the team with 33-39-72 totals in 1977-78 as the club made the playoffs for the first time since the 1969-70 season. But the joy would be short-lived.

During the off-season, the Wings signed free agent goalie Rogie Vachon away from Los Angeles. The move would require Detroit to surrender compensation to the Kings and on Aug. 17, 1978, arbitrator Judge Ed Houston ruled that the Wings must send McCourt to Los Angeles.

McCourt balked at the ruling, filing suit two weeks later against the NHL, the Wings, the Kings and the NHLPA. On Aug. 30, 1978, U.S. District Court Judge Robert DeMascio ruled that the NHL rule governing free agents was a restraint of trade and McCourt was allowed to remain a Red Wing while the dispute stretched all the way to the U.S. Supreme Court.

Even though McCourt's numbers during his sophomore season were comparable to his rookie stats, Wings coach

DETROIT HONOURS:

+ First player ever selected first overall in the NHL draft by Red Wings
+ Led team in scoring 1977-78, 1979-80, 1980-81
+ Played for Canada in 1979 and 1981 World Championships.

Bobby Kromm sensed a different player was taking the ice for Detroit.

"McCourt has not played well for us," Kromm noted during the 1978-79 season. "The lawsuit may have something to do with it. He has a lot on his mind."

On May 22, 1979, the 6th U.S. Circuit Court of Appeals ruled that McCourt must go the Kings to uphold the NHL reserve clause, but they overturned their ruling on July 26, 1979, permitting McCourt to stay with the Wings.

Kings owner Jerry Buss offered McCourt a six-year, $3 million contract that would have made him the NHL's highest-paid player, but he rejected it. "He's the most determined young man I've ever met," Buss said.

Instead, the Wings dealt centre Andre St. Laurent and a pair of first-round draft picks to L.A. in order to retain McCourt, but the damage had been done.

"I lost my desire to play the game," McCourt told the St. Catharines Standard, admitting the business side of hockey destroyed his passion for performing.

"I was playing on talent alone and people knew it."

He still put up numbers—back-to-back 30-goal seasons and a career-high 86 points in 1980-81—but McCourt wasn't fooling anyone. "They could see I wasn't going, I wasn't driving," he said.

Midway through the 1980-81 season, McCourt was traded to Buffalo as part of a blockbuster seven-player deal between the Wings and Sabres.

This time, he didn't kick up a fuss. "That was a different thing," he explained. "Had it been a trade (to L.A.), I would have gone."

McCourt played with Buffalo until 1983, then spent one season in Toronto before taking his game to Europe.

He wonders what his Detroit production might have been like minus all the off-ice turmoil. "People expected a lot out of me and I expected a lot out of myself, and when it didn't happen, obviously I was disappointed," McCourt said.

He rediscovered his love for the game playing seven seasons for Ambri-Piotta in the Swiss League, and later turning to coaching, including a stint as an assistant coach with Italy at the 1994 Winter Olympic Games in Lillehammer, Norway.

McCourt and his family returned to North America in 2000 and today he works as a long-haul truck driver.

"It's not a bad job," McCourt said. "You can make good money driving."

He was elected to the Sudbury Sports Hall of Fame in 2011.

MCCOURT'S RED WINGS STATISTICS:

| Season | REGULAR SEASON | | | | | PLAYOFFS | | | | |
	GP	G	A	P	PIM	GP	G	A	P	PIM
1977-78	76	33	39	72	10	7	4	2	6	2
1978-79	79	28	43	71	14	-	-	-	-	-
1979-80	80	30	51	81	12	-	-	-	-	-
1980-81	80	30	56	86	50	-	-	-	-	-
1981-82	26	13	14	27	6	-	-	-	-	-
Totals	341	134	203	337	92	7	4	2	6	2

48 DARREN MCCARTY

Right Wing

Born: April 1, 1972, Burnaby, British Columbia
Shot: Right **Height:** 6-1 **Weight:** 210 lbs.
Red Wing From: 1993-94 to 2003-04; 2007-08 to 2008-09
Acquired: Selected 46th overall in June 20, 1992 NHL entry draft.
Departed: Signed as a free agent by Calgary Flames, August 2, 2005.
Reacquired: Signed as a free agent by Detroit, February 25, 2008.
Departed: Announced retirement from hockey, December 7, 2009.

IT WAS THE GOAL OF A LIFETIME, THE TYPE OF SIGNATURE score which would look at home at the top of any sniper's resumé.

Darren McCarty didn't merely register the Stanley Cup-winning goal for the Detroit Red Wings in 1997, ending the club's 42-year title drought, he undressed Philadelphia Flyers defenceman Janne Niinimaa, deked goalie Ron Hextall and slid the puck into the unguarded net.

For years, the goal held a prominent place in the promotional intros to Hockey Night In Canada each Saturday. It won an ESPY Award as NHL play of the year. But the goal maintains also-ran status on McCarty's highlight reel.

"Around here, more people want to talk to me about the fight," said McCarty of his March 26, 1997 bout with Claude Lemieux of the Colorado Avalanche. "When people come up to me, they say 'What you did to Lemieux, that was awesome, man. And, oh yeah, nice goal, too.'"

Most Detroit fans are of the belief that the revenge taken on Lemieux enabled the Wings to evolve into a championship-worthy squad.

"I always say not so much because of the fight, but because we won the game," said McCarty, admitting that more people remember the beating he put on Lemieux than the overtime goal he scored to win the contest the same night.

In McCarty's world, the fight meant as much as the goal, because he was standing up for teammate Kris Draper, whose face was left bloodied and fractured following a check from behind into the boards delivered by Lemieux in the playoffs the season prior.

"To me, team accomplishments always overshadow individual awards," McCarty said. "It will always be a memorable game, a memorable night, obviously for me and for the Red Wings."

When it came to McCarty, few rose to popularity among Red Wings fans quicker than his rapid ascension after joining the team in 1993. Even his arch-nemesis couldn't find fault in McCarty's game.

"I always actually admired the way he played, admired the way he stuck up for his teammates," Lemieux said. "I admired everything he brought to the game."

McCarty's everyman status certainly played a role in his popularity. McCarty wasn't a true heavyweight, but he took on all comers. He wasn't a goal-scorer, yet displayed a knack for scoring timely goals. Most of all, he was supposed to be too poor of a skater to ever make it as an NHLer.

"He's a much better skater than people give him credit for," said Ottawa Senators GM Bryan Murray, who drafted McCarty when he was GM of the Wings. "He was a tough, grinding type of player who liked to drive to the net and make things happen.

DETROIT HONOURS:

  ♦ Stanley Cup champion 1996-97, 1997-98, 2001-02, 2007-08
  ♦ Scored Stanley Cup-winning goal, 1997
  ♦ NHL Foundation Player Award winner, 2002-03.

"He had really good hands for a big man. We knew he was going to end up scoring quite a few goals in the league."

He owned the town, embracing Detroit with the same passion with which the city embraced him. There was an aura of accessibility about McCarty. He was out there amidst the people and welcomed the attention.

"He's been a fan favourite ever since he came up, he's had so much success with the Red Wings," Draper said.

McCarty befriended Kid Rock and that's his fingers you hear snapping in the background during the song "Picture," a collaborative effort between Kid Rock and Sheryl Crow. "My first No. 1 hit," McCarty proclaimed.

As huge as he was in Hockeytown, and as big as a pop culture icon he grew to be, McCarty never seemed to forget his roots.

After his first title in Detroit, during his day with the Cup, McCarty gathered his family clan together and took Lord Stanley's mug to the Windsor, Ont. cemetery where Darren's grandfather Robert is buried.

"My grandfather had been one of my biggest supporters as I worked my way up the hockey ladder and I wanted to share this with him," McCarty explained.

"That's the thing about the Stanley Cup. It's not just a trophy. It's an icon. My name is on that Cup. It will be there for eternity. Nobody can ever change that.

"I've made my mark on the history of the game."

He beat the odds to make the big leagues, and that alone made McCarty special in the eyes of many in the blue-collar area he called home.

"I'm a grinder, worker kind of guy," McCarty said. "If people are waiting for me to take the puck and go end to end, they'll be waiting for a long time."

McCarty won four Stanley Cups in Detroit, something only 10 Red Wings players have ever done, but the

memories he cherishes from those triumphs aren't the ones you'd expect.

Take his first recollection of 1997, for instance.

He thinks of the bus trip from Detroit to Traverse City, Michigan, in the fall of 1997 for the opening of training camp.

As they rolled on down the highway, the Wings watched Hockey Night In Canada's video footage of their 2-1 win over Philadelphia in Game 4 of the Stanley Cup final, the game that saw McCarty score that famous Cup-winner.

"We watched the entire CBC feed of the game," McCarty recalled. "It was the first time we'd watched it together as a team.

"It was a great feeling, a great sensation. When I think back to all of the things that have happened after we became Stanley Cup champions, watching the game together is one of the moments I'll remember most."

MCCARTY'S RED WINGS STATISTICS:

Season	Regular Season					Playoffs				
	GP	G	A	P	PIM	GP	G	A	P	PIM
1993-94	67	9	17	26	181	7	2	2	4	8
1994-95	31	5	8	13	88	18	3	2	5	14
1995-96	63	15	14	29	158	19	3	2	5	20
1996-97	68	19	30	49	126	20	3	4	7	34
1997-98	71	15	22	37	157	22	3	8	11	34
1998-99	69	14	26	40	108	10	1	1	2	23
1999-00	24	6	6	12	48	9	0	1	1	12
2000-01	72	12	10	22	123	6	1	0	1	2
2001-02	62	5	7	12	98	23	4	4	8	34
2002-03	73	13	9	22	138	4	0	0	0	6
2003-04	43	6	5	11	50	12	0	1	1	7
2007-08	3	0	1	1	2	17	1	1	2	19
2008-09	13	1	0	1	25	-	-	-	-	-
Totals	659	120	155	275	1302	167	21	26	47	213

49 JOHAN FRANZEN

Right Wing

Born: Dec. 23, 1979, Landsbro, Sweden
Shoots: Left **Height:** 6-2 **Weight:** 223 lbs.
Red Wing From: 2005-06 to present
Acquired: Selected 97th overall in June 27, 2004 NHL entry draft.

It was former Detroit captain Steve Yzerman who hung the nickname "The Mule" on Johan Franzen, figuring the hulking forward was willing to carry the load in terms of work ethic each night.

In retrospect, perhaps Allstate would have worked better as a handle for Franzen, since over his years in Detroit, he's proven to be one of the good hands people, especially during the most important games of the season, the Stanley Cup playoffs.

Franzen acknowledged that the playoff style of hockey, with its tighter checking and limited free space, suits his game.

"You get to let it all out," Franzen said, embracing the physical nature of post-season play. "You don't think twice about it because you know you're going to get hit.

"The playoffs, you know it's going to happen. You know what to expect and I like that."

Former Detroit coach Mike Babcock, the only bench boss Franzen knew during the first decade of his NHL career, isn't surprised that Franzen excels on hockey's biggest stage.

"He's got hands and he's got size," Babcock said. "Mule is one of those guys. When he's on top of his game he's as good as anyone in the game. He's one of those guys that seem more excited at playoff time.

"Mule is an important part of our team."

Franzen's scoring touch blossomed late in the 2007-08 season. He scored 15 goals in 14 games to end the regular season and added 13 more in 16 playoff contests. Franzen set a club record with five game-winners during the month of March, shattering the standard previously shared by Gordie Howe and Henrik Zetterberg, doing so in a 1-0 win over the Nashville Predators during which the Wings honoured Howe to mark his 80th birthday.

"I'm sorry I spoiled his birthday," Franzen said.

Franzen's playoff heroics are many. He scored in double-overtime to win a first-round series against the Calgary Flames in 2007, one of two OT winners to his credit. He's fired three hat tricks during Stanley Cup play, including a

---

DETROIT HONOURS:

+ Stanley Cup champion 2007-08
+ Holds NHL record for most goals in a four-game Stanley Cup series (four, 2008 second round vs. Colorado Avalanche)
+ Club record for most goals in one playoff series (four, 2008)
+ Club record for most game-winning goals in a month (March 2008)
+ Club record for most game-winning goals in one playoff year (five, 2008)
+ Shares club record with Henrik Zetterberg for goals in one playoff year (13, 2007-08)
+ Shares club record for consecutive playoff games with a goal (five, Gordie Howe, Ted Lindsay) and a point (12, Gordie Howe)
+ Scored four times May 6, 2010 vs. San Jose Sharks to share club playoff record for goals in a game with Ted Lindsay and Carl Liscombe. His six points in that game were also a club playoff mark
+ Franzen, Sergei Fedorov and Syd Howe are only players in Red Wings history to score at least five goals in a game
+ Won world championship with Sweden, 2006
+ Played for Sweden in 2010 Vancouver Winter Olympic Games.

JOHAN FRANZEN

club record-tying four-goal performance against the San Jose Sharks in 2010.

"I like when the game's on the line," Franzen said. "It calms me down a little bit.

"You see other players rushing their shots, they just want to get a shot off so bad.

"If you hold on to it a little bit and make a play, it's more likely you will score."

What makes Franzen's NHL success so surprising is that he took forever to make the big time back home in his native Sweden.

"Franzen wasn't in the Swedish top leagues until he was about 23," Wings GM Ken Holland said.

Detroit European scout Hakan Andersson liked Franzen. "At our mid-season meetings in 2004, he had him on his list," Holland recalled. "I started grilling him about a 23-year-old and Hakan stuck to his guns, so we drafted him."

The Wings were patient with Franzen and it paid off. With Linkoping, he led Swedish Elitserin with a plus-24 rating in 2003-04. The following season, a punishing hit from Franzen broke the wrist of MODO's Peter Forsberg.

He debuted with Detroit in 2005-06, becoming a scorer and a physical presence for the Wings.

It's the latter as much as the former that Franzen's teammates appreciate.

"Stubbornness I'd say," former Wings captain Nicklas Lidstrom listed as Franzen's best quality. "He's very good at using his body. He's good at using his size.

"It's tough to take the puck away from him."

As the Mule Train rolls, so often do the Wings.

"He can play any physical game you want," Babcock said. "He can do it offensively, but he's big and strong enough to hang on to pucks. That's what makes him real important.

"Mule is a huge man. He plays all over, plays 60 minutes and gives you every ounce of what he's got to give. We need the Mule because he's a big, physical, strong guy and the better he plays the better a team we are."

In the clutch, it's clear that Detroit's Mule is a true thoroughbred. More than one-fifth of his goals (44 out of 187, 23.5 per cent) have been game-winners.

"He's big, he's got a good reach and all that talent," former NHLer Andrew Brunette said of Franzen. "When he gets rolling, he's hard to stop."

FRANZEN'S RED WINGS STATISTICS:									
	REGULAR SEASON					PLAYOFFS			
Season	GP	G	A	P	PIM	GP	G	A	P	PIM
2005-06	80	12	4	16	36	6	1	2	3	4
2006-07	69	10	20	30	37	18	3	4	7	10
2007-08	72	27	11	38	51	16	13	5	18	14
2008-09	71	34	25	59	44	23	12	11	23	12
2009-10	27	10	11	21	22	12	6	12	18	16
2010-11	76	28	27	55	58	8	2	1	3	6
2011-12	77	29	27	56	40	5	1	0	1	8
2012-13	41	14	17	31	41	14	4	2	6	8
2013-14	54	16	25	41	40	5	0	2	2	2
2014-15	33	7	15	22	30	-	-	-	-	-
Totals	600	187	182	369	399	107	42	39	81	80

50 MODERE (MUD) BRUNETEAU
Right Wing

Born: November 28, 1914, St. Boniface, Manitoba
Died: April 15, 1992
Shot: Right Height: 5-11 Weight: 185 lbs.
Red Wing From: 1935-36 to 1945-46
Acquired: Signed as a free agent October 25, 1934.
Departed: Named player-coach of Omaha (USHL), August 15, 1946.

THE MAN WHO SCORED THE GOAL THAT ENDED HOCKEY'S longest game, sending thousands home to their beds in the wee hours of March 25, 1936, actually began his Detroit Red Wings career sleeping in a bathtub.

In the fall of 1934, when Modere (Mud) Bruneteau and his brother Ed travelled to Detroit from Winnipeg with goaltender Turk Broda to try out for the Wings, they opted to rent a room at the local YMCA to cut down on costs. But when they found that the room only slept two, they opted to flip a coin to see who'd get the beds.

Mud lost the toss, and ended up tucking himself into the bathtub for the night.

A little over two years later, he'd tuck home one of the most famous goals in Stanley Cup history.

At approximately 2:25 a.m. the morning of March 25, 1936, Bruneteau took a pass from Hec Kilrea and whipped a shot past Montreal Maroons goalie Lorne Chabot for a 1-0 victory, ending what remains the longest overtime game in Stanley Cup history after 176:30 of play.

"It looked like another of the endless unfinished plays—when suddenly, in shot the slim form of a player, who through this long, weary tide of battle that ebbed and flowed had been almost unnoticed," Elmer Ferguson wrote in the *Montreal Herald*. "He swung his stick at the bobbling puck, the little black disc straightened away, shot over the foot of Lorne Chabot, bit deeply into the twine of the Montreal Maroon cage.

"And so Modere Bruneteau leaped to fame as the player who ended the longest game on professional hockey record."

Suddenly and forever, "that damned Bruneteau," as Maroons forward Gus Marker called him, would be a household name.

"I always knew that boy Bruneteau had the stuff," Detroit coach Jack Adams proclaimed.

After the game, an excited Red Wings fan stuffed $50 into Bruneteau's hand. Wings owner James Norris wired the result to *Ripley's Believe It Or Not*. But perhaps the most unbelievable moment came amidst the exhaustion within the Detroit dressing room.

Chabot had retrieved the puck and had it sent to the Wings room to be presented to Bruneteau. "I guess the kid will always remember that goal he scored and would like to have it as a memento," Chabot told the *Montreal Gazette*.

"Gee whiz, gee whiz, that's swell," an overwhelmed Mud told reporters as he twirled the prize in his hands.

Many of the 9,000 at the Montreal Forum fell into slumber as the game dragged on, and so did members of Bruneteau's family, listening to the radio call of the contest.

DETROIT HONOURS:

- Stanley Cup champion 1935-36, 1936-37, 1942-43
- Team captain 1943-44
- Scored goal that ended NHL's longest Stanley Cup overtime game March 25, 1936 after 176:30 of play
- First player in NHL history to win Stanley Cup in each of his first two seasons.

That fateful night when he scored hockey's most memorable overtime goal was also the night of Bruneteau's Stanley Cup debut. In fact, when the Wings went on to win the Cup that spring and again in 1936-37, Bruneteau became the first player in NHL history to win the Cup in each of his first two seasons.

While there's no questioning the lore of that historic tally, it tends to overshadow what was a solid 11-season career as a Red Wing turned in by Bruneteau.

Three times he topped 20 goals, and in 1943-44 only four NHLers scored more times than the 35 potted by Bruneteau. He was a three-time Stanley Cup champion and tallied another playoff OT goal in 1945.

Bruneteau took over as coach of Detroit's USHL farm club in Omaha in 1946 and among those he groomed for service with the Wings were two future Hall of Famers, goalie Terry Sawchuk and defenceman Marcel Pronovost.

His name may have been Mud, but with one shot, his place in hockey history was etched forever in stone.

"We couldn't keep listening," Mud's brother Ed explained to the *Los Angeles Times*. "It was history, but it was too tough to take.

"I didn't find out who won until the next morning."

Bruneteau was handed his nickname by a high-school teacher who struggled to pronounce his given name. After high school, Bruneteau worked as a clerk at the Norris Grain Company offices in Winnipeg, often taking breaks to study the team photo of the 1933-34 Red Wings that hung in the office of secretary C.E. Babbitt. He boasted of how, someday soon, he'd be part of the roster.

Turning pro in 1934, Bruneteau played with Detroit's farm club in the International League, the Detroit Olympics, during the 1934-35 season, and spent most of the 1935-36 campaign with them as well. The Wings recalled him just a week prior to the start of the playoffs, a move that would pay huge dividends.

	REGULAR SEASON					PLAYOFFS				
Season	GP	G	A	P	PIM	GP	G	A	P	PIM
1935-36	24	2	0	2	2	7	2	2	4	2
1936-37	42	9	7	16	18	10	2	0	2	6
1937-38	24	3	6	9	16	-	-	-	-	-
1938-39	20	3	7	10	0	6	0	0	0	0
1939-40	48	10	14	24	10	5	3	2	5	0
1940-41	45	11	17	28	12	9	2	1	3	2
1941-42	48	14	19	33	8	12	5	1	6	6
1942-43	50	23	22	45	2	9	5	4	9	0
1943-44	39	35	18	53	4	5	1	2	3	2
1944-45	43	23	24	47	6	14	3	2	5	2
1945-46	28	6	4	10	2	-	-	-	-	-
Totals	411	139	138	277	80	77	23	14	37	22

BRUNETEAU'S RED WINGS STATISTICS:

ACKNOWLEDGEMENTS

SPECIAL THANKS ARE OWED TO THE RED WINGS players and management who shared their time with me for this book and who made the memories that exist within these pages.

A tip of the cap is also offered to the staff at Biblioasis for the cooperation, determination and talent that helped make this book happen.

Thanks are also due to the fans of the Red Wings, without whom there would be no game to chronicle. And most of all, thank you to the first person to take these selections to task, because the point of any book of lists is to open up a healthy debate.

CURRENTLY THE SPORTS COLUMNIST for the *Windsor Star*, Bob Duff has covered the NHL since 1988 and is a contributor to *The Hockey News* and HockeyBuzz.com. Duff's book credits include *Marcel Pronovost: A Life in Hockey*, *The China Wall: The Timeless Legend of Johnny Bower*, *Hockey Dynasties*, *Without Fear*, *Nine: Salute to Mr. Hockey*, *On the Wing: A History of the Windsor Spitfires*, and *The Hockey Hall of Fame MVP Trophies and Winners*. Duff lives in Cottam, Ontario, with his wife Cherl and daughter Cecilia.